STUDIES IN LUCIAN'S
DE SYRIA DEA

HARVARD SEMITIC MUSEUM
HARVARD SEMITIC MONOGRAPHS

Edited by
Frank Moore Cross

Number 15
STUDIES IN LUCIAN'S *DE SYRIA DEA*
by
R. A. Oden, Jr.

SCHOLARS PRESS
Missoula, Montana

STUDIES IN LUCIAN'S *DE SYRIA DEA*

by

R. A. Oden, Jr.

Published by

SCHOLARS PRESS

for

Harvard Semitic Museum

Distributed by

SCHOLARS PRESS
University of Montana
Missoula, Montana 59812

STUDIES IN LUCIAN'S *DE SYRIA DEA*
by
R. A. Oden, Jr.

Library of Congress Cataloging in Publication Data

Oden, R. A., 1946-
Studies in Lucian's De Syria Dea

(Harvard Semitic monographs ; no. 15)
Bibliography: p.
1. Lucianus Samosatensis. De dea Syria.
2. Hierapolis, Asia Minor — Religion. 3. Cultus —
Hierapolis, Asia Minor. I. Title. II. Series.
BL1060.L783033 887'.01 76-54988
ISBN 0-89130-123-2

Printed in the United States of America
1 2 3 4 5

Edwards Brothers, Inc.
Ann Arbor, Michigan 48104

TABLE OF CONTENTS

PREFACE vii

LIST OF ABBREVIATIONS ix

Chapter I. LUCIAN AND THE *DE SYRIA DEA* 1

Introduction 1
The Problems of Authorship and Trustworthiness 4
The Evidence Reevaluated 14
The Stories of the Flood and of Kombabos 24
Summary 41

Chapter II. ATARGATIS 47

Hera/Atargatis and Zeus/Hadad 47
The Identity of Atargatis 58
The Three Major Goddesses of the Canaanite Pantheon 73
Atargatis and the Three Major Canaanite Goddesses 98
Conclusion 105

Chapter III. ΣΗΜΉΙΟΝ 109

The Problem 109
Is Σημήιον a Divine Name? 115
Σημήιον = "Symbol," "Image" 132
The Hierapolis "Symbol" and ʾAšerah in the Old Testament 149

Chapter IV. CONCLUSIONS 157

FIGURES 159

BIBLIOGRAPHY 163

PREFACE

This monograph is a slight reworking of my 1975 Harvard University dissertation. That dissertation was directed by the Hancock Professor of Hebrew and other Oriental Languages, Frank Moore Cross. As a student of the ancient Near East at Pembroke College, Cambridge and at Harvard, my obligations to many are great; but it is Professor Cross to whom I owe the most. Those who have worked with Professor Cross know him as a scholar of great knowledge and greater insight and as a teacher who encourages independent thought. I know that this monograph contains many of his insights; I hope it includes little that might embarrass him. Both the dissertation and the present monograph were typed by Carol Cross. Her remarkable ability to shape chaos into order is something at which I marvel and for which I am deeply grateful. Finally, I thank Dartmouth College for a grant which made possible the present publication.

There is now a translation of *The Syrian Goddess*, together with a brief introduction, by Dr. Harold Attridge and myself, in the Society of Biblical Literature's Texts and Translations series, edited by Hans D. Betz.

R. A. Oden, Jr.
Dartmouth College

ABBREVIATIONS

AJA — *American Journal of Archaeology*

AJSL — *American Journal of Semitic Languages and Literatures*

ANEP — *The Ancient Near East in Pictures*, ed. James B. Pritchard, 2d ed. with supplement (Princeton: Princeton University Press, 1969)

ANET — *Ancient Near Eastern Texts*, ed. James B. Pritchard, 3d ed. with supplement (Princeton: Princeton University Press, 1969)

ARI — *Archaeology and the Religion of Israel*, by W. F. Albright, 4th ed. (Baltimore: Johns Hopkins University Press, 1956)

BA — *The Biblical Archaeologist*

BASOR — *Bulletin of the American Schools of Oriental Research*

CAD — *Chicago Assyrian Dictionary* (Chicago: The Oriental Institute, 1956-)

CBQ — *Catholic Biblical Quarterly*

CIL — *Corpus Inscriptionum Latinarum* (Berlin, 1869-)

CIS — *Corpus Inscriptionum Semiticarum* (Paris, 1881-)

CMHE — *Canaanite Myth and Hebrew Epic:* Essays in the History of the Religion of Israel, by Frank Moore Cross (Cambridge, Mass.: Harvard University Press, 1973)

CTCA — *Corpus des tablettes en cunéiformes alphabétiques*, by Andrée Herdner (Paris: Imprimerie Nationale, 1963)

DISO — *Dictionnaire des inscriptions sémitiques de l'ouest*, by Ch. Jean and J. Hoftijzer (Leiden: E. J. Brill, 1965)

D.S.D. — *De Syria Dea*, cited from *Luciani Samosatensis Opera*, ed. Caroli Iacobitz, vol. 3 (Leipzig: Teubner, 1912)

EH — *Le sanctuaire punique d'El-Hofra à Constantine*, by A. Berthier and R. Charlier (Paris: Arts et Metiers Graphiques, 1952-1955)

Eph. — *Ephemeris für semitische Epigraphik*, by M. Lidzbarski (Giessen: Alfred Töpelmann, 1900-1915)

FSAC — *From the Stone Age to Christianity*, by W. F. Albright. 2d ed. (Baltimore: Johns Hopkins University Press, 1946)

HTR — *Harvard Theological Review*

ICC — International Critical Commentary

IEJ — *Israel Exploration Journal*

JAOS — *Journal of the American Oriental Society*

JBL	*Journal of Biblical Literature*
JNES	*Journal of Near Eastern Studies*
JPOS	*Journal of the Palestine Oriental Society*
KAI	*Kanaanäische und aramäische Inschriften*, by H. Donner and W. Röllig (Wiesbaden: Harrassowitz, 1964-1968)
LS	Henry George Liddell and Robert Scott, *A Greek-English Lexicon*, rev. by H. S. Jones and R. McKenzie (Oxford: Oxford University Press, 1940)
LSSG	*Lukians Schrift über die syrische Göttin*, by Carl Clemen (Leipzig: J. C. Hinrichs, 1938)
MUSJ	*Mélanges de l'université Saint-Joseph*
NE	*Handbuch der nordsemitischen Epigraphik*, by M. Lidzbarski (Weimar: Emil Felber, 1898)
NSI	*A Textbook of North-Semitic Inscriptions*, by G. A. Cooke (Oxford: Oxford University Press, 1903)
PPG	*Phönizisch-punische Grammatik*, by J. Friedrich and W. Röllig, 2d ed. (Rome: Pontifical Biblical Institute, 1970)
PW	*Paulys Realencyclopädie der classischen Altertumswissenschaft*, ed. Georg Wissowa (Stuttgart: J. B. Metzler, 1894-)
PWSup	Supplement to *Pauly-Wissowa*
RB	*Revue biblique*
Stadelmann	*Syrisch-Palästinensische Gottheiten in Ägypten*, by Ranier Stadelmann (Leiden: E. J. Brill, 1967)
Ugaritica V	"Les nouveaux textes mythologiques et liturgiques de Ras Shamra," ed. Ch. Viroleaud, ch. 3 of *Ugaritica V*, ed. J. Nougayrol, *et al.* (Paris: Imprimerie Nationale, 1968)
VT	*Vetus Testamentum*
WM	*Wörterbuch der Mythologie*, ed. H. W. Haussig, vol. 1 (Stuttgart: Ernst Klett, 1965)
WP	*The World of the Phoenicians*, by S. Moscati (New York: Praeger, 1968)
YGC	*Yahweh and the Gods of Canaan*, by W. F. Albright (Garden City: Doubleday, 1968)
ZAW	*Zeitschrift für die alttestamentliche Wissenschaft*
ZDMG	*Zeitschrift der deutschen morgenländischen Gesellschaft*

Chapter I

LUCIAN AND THE *DE SYRIA DEA*

"Les orientalistes et les philologues classiques ne peuvent encore se tendre la main par-dessus la Méditerranée."[1]

Introduction

Among the works transmitted under the name of Lucian of Samosata is that entitled Περὶ τῆς Συρίης θεοῦ.[2] In the digressive style of a travelogue, the author of this work describes, in the Ionic dialect, the rites of several sites along the eastern coast of the Mediterranean Sea. He then proceeds to his central concern, a lengthy account of the temple and cult of the north Syrian city of Hierapolis (modern Manbij), which lies about fifty miles northeast of Aleppo, near the Euphrates River.[3] The "Sacred City" drew many visitors, both pilgrims

---

1. Franz Cumont, *Les religions orientales dans le paganisme romain*, 4th ed. (Paris: Paul Geuthner, 1929), p. 16.

2. Hereafter abbreviated *D.S.D.* *(= De Syria Dea)*. All references to the *D.S.D.* are cited from the edition of Caroli Iacobitz [Karl Jacobitz], *Luciani Samosatensis Opera*, vol. 3 (Leipzig: Teubner, 1912). I follow modern convention in referring to the work as *De Syria Dea*, rather than *De Syra Dea*.

3. For the identification of modern Manbij with ancient Hierapolis see D. G. Hogarth, "Hierapolis Syriae," *Annual of the British School at Athens* 14 (1907-1908) 183, and Godefroy Goossens, *Hiérapolis de Syrie:* essai de monographie historique, Université de Louvain, Recueil de Travaux d'Histoire et de Philologie, 3d series, 12th fascicle (Louvain: Université de Louvain, 1943), p. 3. Though this identification is certain, the names by which various authors, ancient and modern, call the site can lead to some initial confusion. Thus the city is called Hierapolis, Hieropolis, Bambyce, Mabog, and other names as we will see below. With respect to the correctness of Hierapolis or Hieropolis, Goossens argued that the latter is the more correct and primitive form, as first given to the city by Seleucus I Nicator (*Hiérapolis de Syrie*, p. 7). One does find

and sceptics, in antiquity; and, in modern times, was visited by Henry Maundrell at the end of the seventeenth century,[4] by Francis Rawdon Chesney a century and a half later,[5] and by many others in more recent days.

---

the spelling Ἱεροπολίτων on 3rd century B.C. coins from the city (see Warwick Wroth, *Catalogue of the Greek Coins of Galatia, Cappadocia, and Syria* [London: British Museum, 1899], p. 143); but Louis Robert demonstrates convincingly that the correct form for the name of the various "sacred cities" in Anatolia and the Near East is Ἱεράπολις, of which the ethnic form is Ἱεροπολίται (cf. Νεάπολις but Νεοπολίται), and expresses regret at the continued confusion of the city's name with the ethnic form which still obtains in the work of many scholars ("La déesse de Hiérapolis Castabala à l'époque gréco-romaine," in André Dupont-Sommer and Louis Robert, *La déesse de Hiérapolis Castabala (Cilicie)* [Paris: Adrien Maisonneuve, 1964], pp. 18-20). Henry Seyrig had anticipated Robert's argument by fifteen years: "Le nom est bien Hiérapolis, et non Hiéropolis. Il est étrange de voir presque tous les numismates, et des historiens notables à leu suite, parler de Hiéropolis, sous pretexte que les monnaies portent l'ethnique sous la forme Hiéropolitains" ("Antiquités syriennes," *Syria* 26 [1949] 19, n.1). The distinction made by Seyrig and Robert eliminates the need felt by James George Frazer to translate Hieropolis "City of the Sanctuary" but Hierapolis "the Sacred City" (*The Golden Bough:* A Study in Magic and Religion, vol. 4, Adonis Attis Osiris, 2d ed. [London: Macmillan, 1907], pp. 134-135, and p. 135, n.1). The city's native name will be discussed at length below in the section dealing with the flood narrative.

4. Henry Maundrell, *A Journey from Aleppo to Jerusalem at Easter, A.D. 1697*, 6th ed. (Oxford, 1740), pp. 153-154. Maundrell calls the city "Bambych" and notes that "this Place has no remnant of its Ancient Greatness, but its Walls" (p. 154).

5. Francis Rawdon Chesney, *The Expedition for the Survey of the Rivers Euphrates and Tigris*, Carried on by Order of the British Government in the Years 1835, 1836 and 1837 (London: Longman, Brown, Green, and Longmans, 1850), pp. 420-421. The city is variously called "Magog," "Munbedj," or "Bambuche" by Chesney, who identifies the temple of the city's goddess as consisting of "some fragments of massive architecture, not unlike the Egyptians" (p. 421).

The *De Syria Dea* falls neatly into four distinct sections, with cleverly executed transitions between the sections. After an introduction to the entire work (para. 1), the author leads his audience hurriedly through several cities which lie "in Syria" (ἐν Συρίῃ),[6] as does Hierapolis itself (para. 2-9). In

6. The problems of the imprecise and frequently indiscriminate use of Syria or Assyria, Syrian or Assyrian, in Greek and Latin literature are discussed in deatil in Th. Nöldeke, "'Ασσύριος, Σύριος, Σύρος," *Hermes* 5 (1871) 443-468. This imprecision obtains throughout the *D.S.D.*, as in the works of other classical authors. Indeed, Nöldeke concludes that "der einzige selbständige griechische Schriftsteller, der gleich den Orientalen Assyrien von Babylonien wie von Syrien genau unterscheidet, ist Ktesias" ("'Ασσύριος," 457). Some Greek grammarians even explained "Assyrian" as an alpha privative of "Syrian" (Nöldeke, "'Ασσύριος," 443, n.1). Plutarch calls the same province near the Euphrates Σύρια (*Crassus* 29) and 'Ασσύρια (*Crassus* 22). In the *D.S.D.* the author says Hierapolis lies "in Syria" (ἐν Συρίῃ, para. 1), but calls the inhabitants "Assyrians" ('Ασσύριοι, para. 23); and he, writing as one born in Assyria ('Ασσύριος 'εών, para. 1), labels the goddess of the Syrian city Hierapolis "the Assyrian Hera" ("Ηρης τῆς 'Ασσυρίης, para. 1). Lucian witnesses this same imprecision in *De Saltione* 58, on which see Wolf Wilhelm Graf Baudissin, *Adonis und Esmun:* Eine Untersuchung zur Geschichte des Glaubens an Auferstehungsgötter und an Heilgötter (Leipzig: J. C. Hinrichs, 1911), p. 84. And two and a half centuries after Lucian, Macrobius writes, in discussing the statue of the bearded Apollo at Hierapolis (cf. *D.S.D* , para. 35), *Hieropolitani praeterea, qui sunt gentis Assyriorum* (*Saturnalia* 1.17.66). For further discussion of this confusion, see Wm. Robertson Smith, "Ctesias and the Semiramis Legend," *English Historical Review* 2 (1887) 312-313; A. M. Harmon, *Lucian*, Loeb Classical Library, vol. 4 (Cambridge, Mass.: Harvard University Press, 1925), p. 339, n.2; Goossens, *Hiérapolis de Syrie*, p. 18; and Paul-Louis van Berg, *Répertoire des sources grecques et latines* (sauf le *De Dea Syria*), Corpus Cultus Deae Syriae, 1. Les sources littéraires, première partie (Leiden: E. J. Brill, 1972), p. 9, n.2. Already in the seventeenth century John Selden had noted this, observing that the area known as Assyria to foreigners *(vocabulum barbarum)* is called Syria by the Greeks (*De Dis Syris*, Syntagmata II, 2d ed. [Leipzig, 1662], p. 4).

this first section, the author speaks of Tyre, Sidon, Byblos and the surrounding area, about all of which he claims either eyewitness or accurate second-hand knowledge. In the second section (para. 10-27), he presents a more detailed description of the founders both of the cult of Hierapolis and of the temple there. The author reports five different foundation legends: (1) the flood hero Deucalion established the cult in memory of the inundation and his salvation from it (para. 12-13); (2) Semiramis of Babylon built the temple for her mother Derceto (para. 14); (3) the Lydian Attis founded the shrine in honor of the goddess Rhea (para. 15); (4) according to the Greeks, the establishment of the cult is to be credited to Dionysos (para. 16);[7] and (5) whoever originally began the cult of Hierapolis, the present temple is the work of Stratonike, the wife of the Assyrian king (para. 17-27). Attached to this fifth and final foundation legend is an elaborate tale of Stratonike's love for Kombabos, a steward of the king, in the course of which Kombabos unmans himself to prove the innocence of his relationship with Stratonike. The third section consists of a description of the temple at Hierapolis, as it stood in the author's day, including descriptions of the sacred area around the temple as well as of the temple's interior, particularly the representations of the deities (para. 28-41). As is true throughout the *D.S.D.*, all of these deities are given Greek names; thus, the author speaks of the divine pair Hera and Zeus, of a bearded, enthroned Apollo, and of Atlas and Hermes, among others. Paragraphs 42-60 constitute the fourth section of the *D.S.D.*, an account of the cultic rites practiced by the inhabitants of Hierapolis and by those making pilgrimages to the city.

The Problems of Authorship and Trustworthiness

Along with eighty-one other works,[8] the *D.S.D.* is attributed

---

7. This is the legend accepted, predictably, by the author. See the discussion below of the fashion in which Greek deities and Greek myths are made to dominate the cult of Hierapolis as the cult is described in the *D.S.D.*

8. Fewer than half of these eighty-two works have escaped the charge of inauthenticity, especially in the nineteenth century when a favorite dissertation topic was to deny a work or works to a classical author under whose name the work or works had been listed previously. Today, most scholars question the

to the second-century satirist and rhetorician Lucian of Samosata. Aside from the brief account in *The Suda*, there are only a few references to the life of Lucian, most from the pens of Christian polemicists by whom Lucian was unjustly labeled a foe of Christianity;[9] thus, any account of his life is necessarily tentative.[10] Lucian was born in the second decade of the second century in Samosata, the capital of the Syrian province of Commagene; and he calls himself a native Syrian (*De Historia Conscribenda* 24; *Bis Accusatus* 14). He says that as a "youth" (μειρᾴκιον), he still spoke a "foreign language" (βάρβαρον φωνήν,

---

authenticity of at most eight of these eighty-two works (*Charidemus, De Astrologia, Demosthenis Encomium, De Syria Dea, Halcyon, Macrobii, Nero,* and *Philopatris).* See Arthur Joost, "Beobachtungen über den Partikelgebrauch Lucians. Ein Beitrag zur Frage nach der Echtheit und Reihenfolge einiger seiner Schriften," in *Festschrift zum fünfzigjährigen Doctorijubiläum Ludwig Frielaender* (Leipzig: S. Hirzel, 1895), pp. 163-164, and *passim.*

9. Christianity was little more than one minor cult among many rivals in Lucian's lifetime, so direct references to Christianity are few in Lucian's works. Many have seen behind his account of the ship which sails into the whale's mouth in the *Verae Historiae* a jab at the Jonah story; but this is unnecessary and unlikely. In the *De Morte Peregrini*, Lucian pillories Peregrinus for joining the sect briefly; however, Lucian's barb is aimed not at Christianity, but at Peregrinus, who became a Christian, claims Lucian, in the hope of gaining money and glory, the same motives behind all the acts of Lucian's Peregrinus.

10. See the following works for summaries of Lucian's life: Maurice Croiset, *Essai sur la vie et les oeuvres de Lucien* (Paris: Hachette, 1882), ch. 1; E. S. Bouchier, *Syria as a Roman Province* (Oxford: Blackwell, 1916), p. 216; R. Helm, "Lukianos," in *PW*, vol. 13, cols. 1725-1728; Goossens, *Hiérapolis de Syrie*, pp. 17-18; Francis G. Allinson, *Lucian:* Satirist and Artist (Boston: Marshall Jones, 1926), ch. 3; Hans Dieter Betz, *Lukian von Samosata und das Neue Testament*, Texte und Untersuchungen zur Geschichte der altchristlichen Literatur, 76 (Berlin: Akademie-Verlag, 1961), pp. 3-5; Jacques Schwartz, *Biographie de Lucien de Samosate*, Collection Latomus, 83 (Bruxelles-Berchem: Latomus, 1965); and especially the balanced and excellent account of Barry Baldwin, *Studies in Lucian* (Toronto: Hakkert, 1973), pp. 1-16.

Bis Accusatus 27), though this could also be interpreted to mean merely a "bad Greek accent."[11] In any case, his native language was not Greek. From his works, Lucian is seen to have wandered about Ionia as a lad, and later to have visited Rome, Gaul, many parts of Greece proper, and Egypt. Although his reputation has fluctuated widely,[12] many, including the present writer, view Lucian as a satirist of the first rank. Certainly the *Verae Historiae* and the *De Morte Peregrini* contain passages both of subtle wit and of truly outrageous humor.

As is true of the general assessment of Lucian and of his place in literary history, the *De Syria Dea* has received widely divergent marks. Both its value as a trustworthy account of the cult of Hierapolis and its place among the works of Lucian have been hotly debated issues during the past century and a half.[13] Some scholars are willing to grant that the *D.S.D.* may be a potentially valuable source of information about the gods worshipped at Hierapolis; but even these do so with little confidence. Thus, Godefroy Goossens, in his book *Hiérapolis de Syrie*, describes the work as "une petit traité de Lucien de Samosate sur le culte local, exposé incomplet, déficient à tout point de vue, rédigé par l'auteur le plus mal qualifié pour décrire une religion."[14] Similarly, Cumont, while admitting

---

11. The latter is the interpretation of Baldwin (*Studies in Lucian*, p. 15). But Herodotus uses φωνή to mean "language," e.g. in 4.117, with reference to the "Scythian language"; and in view of Lucian's familiarity with Herodotus, this is surely a possible interpretation here. Plutarch reflects the same usage in *Crassus* 31 (ἑλλάδι φωνή).

12. Among those with a low opinion of Lucian is Gilbert Highet, who writes of Lucian, "as a foreigner, he wished to be more Greek than the Greeks themselves. Therefore, he modeled his satirical dialogues and comedies on the work of Greek authors of the long-departed classical age, filling his prose with obsolescent idioms and citations borrowed from the most approved sources" (*The Anatomy of Satire* [Princeton: Princeton University Press, 1962], p. 43).

13. For an excellent bibliography of Lucianic studies, see Betz, *Lukian und das Neue Testament*, pp. 218-251.

14. P. ix. However, Goossens does make extensive use of the *D.S.D.*, and later admits that "la *'Déesse Syrienne'* pourrait être une source fidèle, quoque superficielle" (p. 21).

that the *D.S.D.* is a "précieux traité," which "relate ce qu'a vu en passant un voyageur intelligent, amusé et ironique,"[15] ultimately labels the work "très superficiel."[16] Almost alone, in a voice unheard amongst the shriller cries, Baudissin states emphatically, though without supporting evidence, that the value of the *D.S.D.* is "unbestreitbar...denn der Autor hat ohne Frage den Kult nicht nur des syrischen Hierapolis, den er an erster Stelle beschreibt, sondern auch den von Byblos, den er damit kombiniert, an Ort und Stelle beobachtet und aus dem Munde der Eingeweihten eine gewisse Kenntnis von der Bedeutung der Riten und den zugrunde liegenden Mythen erlangt."[17]

The question of the value for religious history of the *D.S.D.*, however, is usually ignored, and thus has not fired a controversy as hot as that which surrounds the question of Lucianic authorship. For many centuries, the genuineness of the *D.S.D.* was unquestioned; in the seventeenth century, for example, the English loyalist author Thomas Nash refers to the *"De Siria Dea"* as a work of Lucian without further comment.[18] But the nineteenth century witnessed a number of attacks on the work's authenticity, so that by the middle of that century the Lucianic authorship of the *D.S.D.* had to be defended, rather than assumed. One who did defend the Lucianic authorship with vigor and with a voice whose authority grew as the last century drew to a close was Jakob Burckhardt, in his *Die Zeit Constantin's des Groszen*, which first appeared in 1853.[19] Against those who denied the *D.S.D.* to Lucian because they could find there none of Lucian's characteristic cynicism, Burckhardt argued that the work "die Stellung des frivolen, griechisch

---

15. *Les religions orientales*, 4th ed., p. 12. The context insures that Cumont intends "précieux traité" as a positive evaluation.

16. *Les religions orientales*, 4th ed., p. 107.

17. Wolf Wilhelm Graf Baudissin, "Die Quellen für eine Darstellung der Religion der Phönizier und der Aramäer," *Archiv für Religionswissenschaft* 16 (1913) 414.

18. As cited in Allinson, *Lucian*, p. 157.

19. (Leipzig: Seemann). In 1949 there appeared an English translation of the 4th ed. of Burckhardt's book, translated by Moses Hadas (New York: Pantheon); but I cite the first edition of the work in German, since it was this edition that swayed Nöldeke and others.

gebildeten Ehrers zu seinem heimischen Cultus so merkwürdig bezeichnet"; indeed, continued Burckhardt, "nirgends hat er [Lucian] den Hohn so weit getrieben als hier, wo er sich naiv stellt und den Styl und den ionischen Dialekt des ehrlichen alten Herodot nachahmt um die ganz gloriöse Lächerlichkeit jenes Götzendienstes recht unmittelbar wirken zu lassen."[20] Further, the author's intimate acquaintance with the cult of Hierapolis led Burckhardt to flatly assert, "ein Athener hätte dieser Bücher nicht schreiben können."[21] So compelling were the arguments from one of Burckhardt's stature, that Th. Nöldeke, who had labeled the *D.S.D.* a work of "Pseudo-Lucian" in 1871,[22] seventeen years later accepted the Lucianic authorship of the work on the basis of Burckhardt's arguments: "Dass *De dea syra* wirklich von Lucian verfasst ist, kann...nicht mehr verzweifelt werden."[23] Nor was this view limited to German scholars. In an article published in 1886 called "Pseudo-Ionism in the Second Century A.D.," F. G. Allinson pointed to "the suppressed satire running through the piece," and, going beyond mere assertion, exemplified this "covert satire" which clearly pointed, in Allinson's judgment, to Lucian as the author of the *D.S.D.*[24]

---

20. *Die Zeit*, p. 182.

21. *Die Zeit*, p. 182; Burckhardt goes on to list examples of Lucian's humor and satire in pp. 183-184.

22. "'Ασσύριος," 464.

23. "Baethgen's *Beiträge zur semitischen Religionsgeschichte*," *ZDMG* 42 (1888) 473, n.4. Nöldeke never again changed his mind, for in a letter to Cumont he writes, "Ich habe jeden Zweifel [toward the authenticity of the *D.S.D.*] schon lange aufgegeben" (Cumont, *Les religions orientales*, 4th ed., p. 12, n. 23). Nöldeke long contemplated a commentary on the work: "Da ich schon seit Jahren für einen sachlichen Commentar zu der Schrift *'De dea syra'* sammle" (Th. Nöldeke, "Karkemisch, Circesium und andre Euphratübergänge," *Nachrichten von der Königl. Gesellschaft der Wissenschaften und der G. A. Universität zu Göttingen* 1886 7, n.*). Nöldeke repeated his design in a letter to Cumont (Cumont, *Les religions orientales*, 4th ed., p. 12, n.23); the commentary never did appear, but the promise of it from Nöldeke apparently prevented others from working on the *D.S.D.*

24. *American Journal of Philology* 7 (1886) 206-207. Allinson repeated his belief in the Lucianic authorship of the *D.S.D.* in *Lucian*, p. 37 and p. 37, n.12.

Further, in his *Essai sur la vie et les oeuvres de Lucien* (1882), M. Croiset sounded a note to be heard repeatedly later, in describing the *D.S.D.* as "une habile et plaisante contrefaçon d'Herodote" which was a work of Lucian.[25]

With men like Burckhardt and Nöldeke behind the Lucianic authorship of the *D.S.D.*, the majority of Lucianic scholars of the present century have joined the ranks of the believers, though, unfortunately, most simply state as much without evidence or argument. Thus Baudissin, in 1913, noted "da der schalkhafte und ungläubige Humor, der überall zwischen den Zeilen dieser Schrift herauszuspüren ist, durchaus der Art Lucians entspricht."[26] About the same time, Cumont, in *Les religions orientales dans le paganisme romain*, stated his firm belief in the Lucianic authorship of the *D.S.D.*,[27] as did E. S. Bouchier,[28] and as did Strong and Garstang.[29] In a *Festschrift* in honor of Baudissin, which appeared at the end of World War I, Carl Clemen expressed agreement with his teacher's approval of the genuineness of the *D.S.D.*,[30] an opinion which Clemen later repeated in his *Lukians Schrift über die syrische Göttin*; in the latter work, Clemen does doubt the prevailing opinion that the *D.S.D.* is "eine gelungene Satire auf den diesem natürlich wohlbekannten Gottesdienst," but still feels there are occasional

---

25. P. 63.

26. "Die Quellen," 415. Baudissin expressed the same view in equally strong terms two years previously in *Adonis und Esmun*, p. 55 and p. 73.

27. 4th ed., p. 12, n.23. This book first appeared in 1906. There is an English translation from the second ed. of 1911; but the 4th ed. (1929) of the work in French is much expanded from that which is the basis of the English translation.

28. *Syria as a Roman Province*, p. 218. However, Bouchier sees the work not as a satire but as "straightforward exposition of the ludicrous or discreditable rites" and as such "far more damaging than any satire" (p. 218).

29. John Garstang and Herbert A. Strong, *The Syrian Goddess* (London: Constable, 1913), p. 31.

30. "Miszellen zu Lukians Schrift über die syrische Göttin," in *Abhandlungen zur semitischen Religionskunde und Sprachwissenschaft:* Wolf Willhelm Grafen von Baudissin, ed. Wilh. Frankenberg and Friedr. Küchler, Beihefte zur *Zeitschrift für die alttestamentliche Wissenschaft* 33 (1918), p. 83.

suggestions within the work which do point to Lucian as the author.[31] The Yale classicist A. M. Harmon retains the *D.S.D.* in his edition and translation of Lucian for the Loeb Classical Library, arguing that it is the very artistry of this work which has prompted doubts about its authorship - the *D.S.D.* is too cleverly executed for some to see the subtle satire.[32] In a note on the text of the *D.S.D.*, Harmon promises a further article which will bring to light "conclusive" evidence for the Lucianic authorship;[33] but this promise, like that of Nöldeke to publish a commentary on the *D.S.D.*, was not fulfilled.

Thus, by the second decade of this century W. F. Albright could write with accuracy that the *D.S.D.* is "now admitted to be a genuine production of his [Lucian's] youth."[34] And the years since Albright's statement was made have yielded further support for this position. The seventh edition of Wilhelm von Christ's *Geschichte der griechischen Literatur*, which appeared in 1924, labels the *D.S.D.* "eine gelungene Satire," whose Lucianic authorship is no longer to be doubted.[35] Twenty years later, Goossens and H. Stocks agree with what was by then the consensus opinion among both orientalists and classicists in accepting the *D.S.D.* as genuine;[36] Goossens further speculates that Lucian wrote the work as a bet to prove that he could parody Herodotus.[37] In his monumental *Lucien ecrivain* (1958), J. Bompaire notes that, while the *D.S.D.* seems to exhibit little of the scepticism of Lucian in that the author appears to accept

---

31. Der Alte Orient, 37, part 3/4 (Leipzig: J. C. Hinrichs, 1938), p. 5; hereafter, Clemen's important study will be abbreviated *LSSG*. Clemen's disapproval of the view that the work is an uproarious satire is directed at the opinion in Christ-Schmid, cited below.

32. *Lucian*, vol. 4, p. 337.

33. "An Emendation in Lucian's *Syrian Goddess*," *Classical Philology* 19 (1924) 72, n.1.

34. "Some Cruces in the Langdon Epic," *JAOS* 39 (1919) 84.

35. Ed. Wilhelm Schmid and Otto Stählin (Munich: Oskar Beck), p. 721.

36. *Hiêrapolis de Syrie*, p. 17; and H. Stocks, "Studien zu Lucians 'De Syria Dea'," *Berytus* 5 (1937) 1-40. Stocks argues especially that the *D.S.D.* must have been written by one familiar with Aramaic (16).

37. *Hiêrapolis de Syrie*, p. 17.

all that is told him at Hierapolis, the attitude of the work is to be explained "par la présence d'un humour diffus, d'une 'parodie voilée,' qui empêcheraient de prendre au sérieux ces racontars."[38] Finally, in an excellent study which has just been published, Barry Baldwin regards the Ionic dialect of the *D.S.D.* as insufficient evidence of its unauthenticity, since Lucian could well use the pseudo-Ionic revival of the second century as a butt for his satire, and thus sides with those who restore the work to Lucian.[39]

Thus speak the majority, indeed the overwhelming majority, of Lucianic scholars. But there are still those who deny the *D.S.D.* to Lucian; and their arguments must be heard, especially since so many in the majority camp simply assert that the *D.S.D.* is a work of Lucian, without producing evidence for the assertion. One, or both, of two grounds are usually adduced by those denying the work to Lucian: (1) the work is written in Ionic,[40] the use of which Lucian repudiates in *De Historia Conscribenda* 16, 18 and 40; and (2) the author of the *D.S.D.* does not seem as cynical as Lucian, whom Clemen well styles the Heinrich Heine of his day.[41] The first objection has been answered effectively by many supporters of the Lucianic authorship: the *D.S.D.* is written in Ionic because the revival of the dialect in the second century was another in a series of such artificial practices which Lucian parodies in his other works, and because the *D.S.D.* is probably a parody of Herodotus and hence utilizes the language

---

38. Bibliothèque des Ecoles Françaises d'Athènes et de Rome, 190 (Paris: E. De Boccard), p. 647.

39. *Studies in Lucian*, p. 33, p. 33, n.60, and p. 106.

40. Examples of the Ionic dialect of the *D.S.D.* meet one in every paragraph. Thus one finds δέκομαι for δέχομαι; κάρτα; ἱρόν for ἱερόν; ἐπωνυμίη for ἐπωνυμία; ἀπηγέομαι for ἀφηγέομαι; ὁκόθεν for ὁπόθεν; θωῦμα for θαῦμα; συντυχίη for συντυχία; ὁρτή for ἑορτή; ἐπικνέομαι for ἐφικνέομαι; ἀγγήιον for ἀγγεῖον; σημήιον for σημεῖον; etc. The conclusion of Smyth is that the dialect of the *D.S.D.* "save for occasional lapses in the direction of Attic and Homeric Ionic, agrees with that of Herodotus" (Herbert Weir Smyth, *The Sounds and Inflections of the Greek Dialects: Ionic* [Oxford: Oxford University Press, 1894], p. 118). See also Allinson, "Pseudo-Ionism," 208-217.

41. *LSSG*, p. 5.

of Herodotus.[42] The supporters of the genuineness of the Lucianic authorship of the *D.S.D.* might also have noted that Lucian's *De Historia Conscribenda* specifically condemns the use of Ionic in writing history, a genre to which the *D.S.D.* does not properly belong if it is a parody of Herodotean history.

But the second objection - that the presumed satire of the *D.S.D.* is only reading into this work the clear satire of Lucian's (other) works - is more serious and it is this objection which is taken up by most who believe the *D.S.D.* is not by Lucian. In the "Lukianos" article in *Pauly-Wissowa*, R. Helm denies the *D.S.D.* to Lucian "wegen des ernsten Tones," which reveals "keine Spur" of any ridiculing humor; thus, the Kombabos story, writes Helm, is related in total earnestness; and the Deucalion legend is "veil zu gross und ganz zwecklos für eine Parodie." "In Lucianos' Leben," concludes Helm, "ist kein Raum für eine derartige Phase gläubiger Gesinnung, wie sie diese Schrift voraussetzt."[43] These objections are repeated by Marcel Caster in his *Lucien et la pensée religieuse de son temps* (1937).[44] Caster points to "le gôut du merveilleux et la crédulité, qui s'expriment dans la *Déesse Syrienne*," whose author stands in awe, "sans broncher," and marvels at the redness of the Adonis River or the powers of the bearded Apollo. Nor can Caster believe that Lucian could have recounted the practice of child sacrifice "avec impassibilité." In short, Caster, like Helm, finds the author's credulous stance incompatible with that exhibited in the (certainly genuine) works of Lucian.[45] Henri Seyrig too finds "tout l'esprit du traité...étranger à celui de Lucien."[46] Most recently, Hans Dieter Betz has voiced disagreement with the attribution of the *D.S.D.* to Lucian. Betz calls its author "der fromme Verfasser," and finds the humor too "verborgen" for one to claim that Lucian's wit lies concealed

---

42. Burckhardt, *Die Zeit*, p. 182; Croiset, *Essaie sur la vie*, p. 63; Allinson, "Pseudo-Ionism," 207 and *Lucian*, p. 120; Daniel A. Penick, "Notes on Lucian's *Syrian Goddess*," in *Studies in Honor of Basil L. Gildersleeve* (Baltimore: Johns Hopkins University Press, 1902), p. 393; and Baldwin, *Studies in Lucian*, p. 33.

43. *PW*, vol. 13, col. 1761.

44. (Paris: Société d'édition "Les belles lettres").

45. *Lucien et la pensée religieuse de son temps*, p. 362.

46. "Antiquités syriennes," *Syria* 37 (1960) 238, n. 1.

beneath the surface of the *D.S.D.*[47]

The only other objection raised by the minority against the authenticity of the *D.S.D.* is that of linguistic usage, especially the use of particles in the work. In part, this objection is answered by the specifically Herodotean cast of the *D.S.D.* Still, Arthur Joost feels the criterion of "Sprachgebrauch...ist das sicherste Kriterium," while yet conceding the "grossen Modulationsfähigkeit" of Lucian.[48] But this criterion as applied to the *D.S.D.* fails to yield any satisfactory conclusion. Thus, the use of πλήν in the *D.S.D.* agrees with some works denied to Lucian, but also with some whose Lucianic authorship has remained unquestioned:[49] or, the combination ναὶ μὴν καὶ occurs only in the *D.S.D.* and the *Astrologia*, which many deny to Lucian,[50] but these are also the only lengthy works among those attributed to Lucian which are composed in Ionic. As a counter of Joost's argument, one ought to note the study of Penick, for the latter finds striking agreement between Herodotus, the *D.S.D.* and some of (the remainder of) Lucian's works with respect to the usage of particles, and hence concludes that the *D.S.D.* is a work of Lucian and one in conscious parody of Herodotus.[51] Ultimately, one is in sympathy with Baldwin's pessimistic assessment of this method: "Linguistic statistics on one side can generally be countered by rival sets."[52] Thus, the question of the visibility of the satire in the *D.S.D.* remains the strongest objection to its authenticity.

One last work of Lucianic scholarship needs to be reviewed before turning to a new assessment of the *D.S.D.* This is the edition of Strong and Garstang,[53] an edition which, unfortunately, has had great influence, simply because it is the only

---

47. *Lukian und das Neue Testament*, p. 24 and p. 24, n.4. As will become clear below, I disagree with Betz here; but his study is among the best on Lucian and is a marvel of industriousness and accuracy.

48. "Beobachtungen über den Partikelgebrauch Lucians," 165.

49. Arthur Joost, "Beobachtungen über den Partikelgebrauch Lucians," 168.

50. Arthur Joost, "Beobachtungen über den Partikelgebrauch Lucians," 174.

51. "Notes on Lucian's *Syrian Goddess*," pp. 387-393.

52. *Studies in Lucian*, p. 4.

53. *The Syrian Goddess*, 1913.

translation of the work into modern English.[54] Aside from errors in translation,[55] this edition errs in overlooking the many parallels to the cult and myths of Hierapolis from the traditions of the neighboring Semitic lands and instead claiming that this cult is paralleled best and alone by Hittite practices.[56] This position has been effectively refuted by Goossens;[57] and the ensuing chapters of the present work are themselves directed partially against the influence of Strong and Garstang's work. Already in 1918, Clemen noted in the Strong and Garstang commentary the almost total absence of reference to or knowledge of previous work on the *D.S.D.*; Clemen is here surely correct, whatever the accuracy of his attribution of this omission to the "Kriegspsychose" of the years prior to World War I, and to the fact that Strong, at the time at least, knew little German.[58]

The Evidence Reevaluated

This review of some of the problems surrounding the trustworthiness and the authorship of the *D.S.D.* has yielded one sure result: a reassessment of the work is necessary. To the question of the value of the sources at one's disposal for the reconstruction of the oriental religions at the time of the Roman Empire, Cumont's answer, first articulated almost seventy years ago in *Les religions orientales dans le paganisme romain*, still carries some force: "Il faut le reconnaître, ces sources

---

54. Harmon's translation in the Classical Library is done in pre-Elizabethan English, to capture something of the archaizing style of the *D.S.D*. This translation is extremely well done by a master of both Greek and English literature, but is also extremely time consuming to read.

55. Henri Seyrig calls the work a "traduction extraordinairement inexacte" ("Antiquités syriennes," *Syria* 37 [1960] 240, n.4). In paragraph 36, for example, an entire sentence has been lost by homoeoteleuton.

56. See especially Strong and Garstang, *The Syrian Goddess*, pp. 11-12.

57. *Hiérapolis de Syrie*, p. 45. Goossens demonstrates that those elements in the cult of Hierapolis which Strong and Garstang found most characteristic of Hittite practice are in fact elements with parallels from all over the ancient Near East.

58. "Miszellen," pp. 83-84, especially p. 83, n.3.

sont insuffisantes et ont été encore insuffisamment exploitées."[59] But the emphasis today ought to be less upon the deficiencies inherent in these sources and more upon their inadequate utilization, for some of the sources regarded as hopelessly deficient in Cumont's day have been shown to be most valuable when used carefully. For example, in the same book Cumont writes, "l'ouvrage de Philon de Byblos, interprétation évhémériste d'une prétendue cosmogonie phénicienne, est un alliage de très mauvais aloi."[60] About this same material transmitted by Philo Biblios, Baethgen wrote, "seine Nachrichten sind völlig werthlos,"[61] and even Baudissin, who regarded the *D.S.D.* as valuable for a reconstruction of the Hierapolis cult, wrote, "durch seine euemeristische Auslegung und synkretistischen Zutaten hat Philo sein wertvolles Material so sehr entstellt, dass eine Rekonstruktion seiner Vorlagen nahazu überall ausgeschlossen zu sein scheint."[62] Yet through the research of Eissfeldt, Albright, and others,[63] the material now contained in Eusebius' *Praeparatio Evangelica* has been shown to be of inestimable value in filling out the still sketchy picture of Canaanite religion.[64]

---

59. P. 9.

60. *Les religions orientales*, p. 107.

61. Friedrich Baethgen, *Beiträge zur semitischen Religionsgeschichte:* der Gott Israel's und die Götter der Heiden (Berlin: H. Reuther, 1888), pp. 276-277.

62. "Die Quellen," 411; in *Adonis und Esmun*, Baudissin similarly wrote that though Philo's material was potentially valuable, Philo "hat es durch tendenziöse Deutung und willkürliche Vermischung fast unkenntlich gemacht" (p. 8).

63. See Otto Eissfeldt, *Ras Schamra und Sanchunjaton*, Beiträge zur Religionsgeschichte des Altertums, vol. 4 (Halle: Max Niemeyer, 1939), pp. 67-71 and 75-95, and *Sanchunjaton von Berut und Ilumilku von Ugarit*, Beiträge zur Religionsgeschichte des Altertums, vol. 5 (Halle: Max Niemeyer, 1952); William Foxwell Albright, *Yahweh and the Gods of Canaan* (Garden City, New York: Doubleday, 1968), pp. 223-226, 244-247, and 259-263, with the references cited there; and, most recently, Lynn Roy Clapham, "Sancuniathon: The First Two Cycles" (unpublished Ph.D. dissertation, Harvard University, 1969).

64. As Delbert Hillers notes, "it is now evident that much of what later writers like Lucian and Philo of Byblos (also second century) report of Syrian religion is based on

Furthermore, it is not just the general confusion surrounding the *D.S.D.* which demands a fresh look at the work. Most of the judgments made about the work, and still repeated with little variation today, were made before the vast increase in our knowledge of the ancient Near East brought about by this century's series of archaeological discoveries. Much of the epigraphic material which has fundamentally altered our views of Canaanite religion was unknown to Nöldeke, Baethgen, and Baudissin, none of whom lived to see the single greatest corpus of this material, the texts from Ugarit. And as these texts have prompted a reevaluation of Philo Byblios' traditions, so too they demand a reassessment of the *D.S.D.* It is such a reassessment, based upon material which the scholars of the nineteenth century could not have used, which will constitute the further chapters of this study.

But first, the question of authorship. As noted above, the strongest objection of those who deny the *D.S.D.* to Lucian is that the supposed satirical elements in the work are very vague at best and mostly the creation of readers under the influence of the (certainly genuine) works of Lucian. If the satirical elements were at best vague, then this objection would be weighty, for it is possible to read many straightforward accounts as satires or parodies; a great deal of Herodotus, for example, can be thus understood. But if there are numerous passages in the *D.S.D.* which are understood best or only as satire, then one is justified in reading the rest of the work with an eye to less obvious examples of satire. Since this is the case, since the *D.S.D.* contains a dozen or more examples of satire so glaring that to ignore them is to give a forced reading to the text, the work is undeniably a satire and as such a prime candidate for inclusion among the works of Lucian of Samosata.

To anyone not himself an initiate, much of the cult of Hierapolis must have seemed ludicrous and barbaric. Given this character, the temptation to ridicule the cult would have been strong, and was plainly too strong for the author of the *D.S.D.*[65]

---

reliable old sources" ("The Goddess with the Tambourine: Reflections on an Object from Taanach," *Concordia Theological Monthly* 41 [1970] 615-616).

65. See Cumont, *Les religions orientales*, pp. 11-12, for the general tendency of Juvenal, Apuleius, Lucian, and others

"L'esprit de lucre des Syriens était proverbial," notes Cumont;[66] and thus the love of money and the great profit reaped from the cult of Hierapolis are prime targets for the satiric barbs of the author of the *D.S.D.* The author's first words about the city, after his introduction in paragraph 1 and his survey of other Syrian sites in paragraphs 2-9, are that the city consists of numerous "costly works" (ἔργα πολυτελέα, para. 10). "The temple," continues the author, "I know to be among them [the Phoenician and Syrian temples] the first in wealth" (ναὶ μὴν καὶ ὄλβου πέρι ἐν τοῖσιν ἐγὼ οἶδα πρῶτόν ἐστι). Many of the city's treasures are stored up "by stealth" (λάθρῃ). When the king is listing for Kombabos the responsibilities which the latter will have in accompanying Stratonike on her mission to Hierapolis, he lists these responsibilities in what must have seemed to an outsider the order appropriate for an oriental despot: χρήματα καὶ γυναῖκα καὶ ἔργον ἱρόν (para. 19) - with the care of "money" first in the king's mind, followed by the safety of his "wife" and only then, as an afterthought, the completion of the "holy work" which was the original motive for the entire mission. In describing the statue of Hera in paragraph 32, the author makes pointed reference to the fact that it is the "precious stones" (λίθοι κάρτα πολυτελέες), rather than any reverence due the goddess, which attracts visitors from all over the Near East to Hierapolis. Not even the animals of the Holy City are free from this greed which the Greeks considered so typical of Syrians, for the "holy cock" (ἀλεκτρυὼν ἱρός) demands a fee before performing his service (para. 48).

Though the author of the *D.S.D.* makes particularly clear the satirical intent of his comments on the great profit reaped from the cult, other examples of satire are no less transparent. On the two pillars before the entrance to the temple, which he labels φαλλοί, the author reports an inscription which reads, "I, Dionysos, erected these φαλλοί for my stepmother Hera" (τούσδε φαλλοὺς Διόνυσος Ἥρῃ μητρυιῇ ἀνέθηκα, para. 16); this inscription, the author wryly adds, proves the case for him

---

to submit to this temptation whenever describing an oriental cult.

66. *Les religions orientales*, p. 99; see also p. 96 for the widespread belief in the insatiable greed of the priests of Atargatis.

that the columns are φαλλοί belonging to the cult of Dionysos ('Εμοὶ μέν νυν καὶ τάδε ἀρκεέι). But, as Harmon notes, "the inscription is much too pointed to be genuine; it is a hoax."[67] The Kombabos story abounds with examples of the author's wit. After Kombabos unmans himself, he calmly carries out an elaborate scheme of storing up and sealing his pudenda, presumably bleeding all the time, and only then dresses the wound (para. 20). Stratonike's attempt to seduce Kombabos finds her drinking herself under the table rather than her intended victim (para. 22); and, when she does discover the proof of Kombabos' inability to comply with her wish, she promises yet "to abide with him always" (πάντα οἱ συνεοῦσα), a statement that contains a pun on social and sexual intercourse (para. 22). The king, after falsely convicting Kombabos of adultery and leading him off to be executed, finally learns what Kombabos had done to himself; this prompts him to say, "I did not need this proof of your innocence" (οὐ γάρ μοι ταύτης ἀπολογίης ἔδεεν), though it is clearly only this proof which satisfies the king (para. 25). As partial expiation for the wrong done him, Kombabos is granted free access to the king's chamber, even, says the king, "if I am having intercourse with my wife" (ἤν γυναικὶ ἅμα εὐνάζωμαι, para. 25) - hardly a desired reward for one in Kombabos' condition.

Puns, such as that on συνεοῦσα noted above, are not confined to the Kombabos story. Though many have missed it (for example, Caster, who denies the *D.S.D.* to Lucian),[68] Baudissin notes the pun in paragraph 7, where κεφαλὴν βυβλίνην means both "Byblian head" and "papyrus head."[69] The "holy cock" (ἀλεκτρυὼν ἱρός) in paragraph 48 is perhaps seen as a punning reference to the Hierapolis "eunuchs" (γάλλοι) since Latin *gallus* means "cock."[70] The author's repeated use of a phrase like σύμπαν

---

67. *Lucian*, vol. 4, p. 360, n.1. That the inscription as quoted by the author is in Ionic (note the form μητρυιῇ) may add evidence to its character as a hoax, though it was normal practice in ancient literature to adopt the testimony of others into the dialect of the work at hand.

68. *Lucien et la pensée religieuse*, p. 361.

69. *Adonis und Esmun*, p. 186; the entire tale, writes Baudissin, is to be seen "als ein ironisches Wortspiel" (p. 186). Cf. Harmon, *Lucian*, vol. 4, p. 345, n.4.

70. Though the author probably also intended the word as

θωῦμα (para. 7) surely carries both the meaning "totally miraculous" and also "quite a deception"; this is clearest when he refers to the coloring of the River Adonis as a θωῦμα (para. 8), even after relating the commonplace explanation of the phenomenon as due to the annual spring rains.[71]

Similar rhetorical tricks are in evidence elsewhere in the *D.S.D.* Of the claim that the gods have appeared to the inhabitants of Hierapolis, the author says, "there are godlike statues, so the gods do indeed appear bodily to them [the inhabitants]" (ξόανα θεοπρεπέα, καὶ θεοὶ δὲ κάρτα αὐτοῖσιν ἐμφανέες, para. 10). Frequently, the audience's expectations are upset, a literary device whose application was widespread in classical literature. Paragraph 1 of the *D.S.D.*, for example, announces the four-fold plan of the work, beginning with the rites and assemblies and concluding with tales about the founders of the cult; but the work actually proceeds from stories about the founders of the cult to an account of the city's rites and assemblies.[72] Paragraph 17, again, promises a description of the temple followed by an account of the temple's builder; but

---

a double entendre to make the point that even Hierapolis fowls were greedy. Others have seen here an error by the author in confusing Aramaic *śekwî* ("cock") with *sakyâ* ("watchman"). In Job 38:26, the Vulgate translates Hebrew *śekwî* as *gallus*, an understanding also witnessed in Talmudic texts (see Samuel Rolles Driver and George Buchanan Gray, *A Critical and Exegetical Commentary on the Book of Job*, ICC [Edinburgh: T. &. T. Clark, 1921], part 2, p. 311, and Marvin H. Pope, *Job*, Anchor Bible, 3d ed. [Garden City: Doubleday, 1973], p. 302). But Lucian knew Aramaic, and, if he is the author, would only make such a punning error intentionally. Even if Lucian is not the author, the author of the *D.S.D.* describes himself as an "Assyrian" (para. 1) and so again would be unlikely to make this error.

71. For θαῦμα meaning both "wonder" and "trick," see *LS*, sub voce (p. 785). Clemen correctly labels this Adonis River story an example of the author's humor (*LSSG*, p. 35), though Caster again takes it seriously (*Lucien et la pensée religieuse*, p. 361).

72. This reversal has been noted also by René Dussaud ("Peut-on identifier l'Apollon barbu de Hiérapolis de Syrie?" *Revue de l'histoire des religions* 126 [1943] 128-129).

this order is reversed in what follows, so that it is paragraph 30 before the author actually does describe the temple. Or, the author introduces the Aphrodite temple above Byblos, arousing the curiosity of his readers who are, as Harmon notes, familiar with the temple's reputation and thus "all agog to hear about it,"[73] but then concludes his discussion of this temple with nothing more than this tantalizing introduction. The same anticlimactic build-up occurs in paragraph 5, where the author mentions another "shrine" (ἱρόν) but leaves his audience frustrated to learn anything about it. Also to be included in any list of the *D.S.D.*'s rhetorical humor is the understatement of the author's account of the early "Stylites" of Hierapolis, whose wakefulness atop their tall columns the author attributes to their fear of falling off (δοκέει δέ μοι, μέγα ες ἀγρυπνίην συμβάλλεται καὶ τῆς πτώσιος ἡ ὀρρωδίη, para. 29). Thus too the account of child sacrifice as practiced at Hierapolis; the author says those sacrificing their children shout, as they commit the barbarous act, "these are not children but cattle" (ἅμα δὲ αὐτέοισιν ἐπικερτομέοντες λέγουσιν ὅτι οὐ παῖδες, ἀλλα βόες ἐισί, para. 58), reversing the substitution formula that obtained in the Punic world and doubtless too at Hierapolis.[74]

To move beyond cataloging transparent examples of humor in the *D.S.D.*, one notes that the work is best read along with Herodotus. The verbal and thematic parallels between the *D.S.D.* and the *Historia* of Herodotus are many and striking. The author of each frequently gives two or more accounts of the same event,

---

73. *Lucian*, vol. 4, p. 348, n.1.

74. The Punic formula I refer to is "*molchomer* [= *mlk ʾmr*] breath for breath, blood for blood, life for life," on which see William Foxwell Albright, *Yahweh and the Gods of Canaan*, p. 235; hereafter, this work will be abbreviated *YGC*. It is in fact most unlikely that children were thrown ἐκ τῶν προπυλαίων as the author says, since the height of the porch would result in little damage to any victims dropped from it (Stocks, "Studien," 24). Lucian, if he is the author of the *D.S.D.*, heard that child sacrifice was practiced at Hierapolis, and invented the ridiculous method of their death to satirize the cult. The mention of child sacrifice here makes likely the presence of an ʾĒl/Kronos cult at Hierapolis, on which see the comments in chapter III below.

choosing that which seems best; compare "they do not agree (οὐκ ὁμολογέουσιν) that this temple is Europa's" (*D.S.D.*, para. 4) with "concerning Io, the Phoenicians do not agree" (οὐκ ὁμολογέουσι, Herodotus 1.5). Examples of this similarity of technique are many.[75] Both authors often impute the source of a war or the building of a shrine to illicit or unrequited love. Compare especially the Kombabos story in the *D.S.D.* with Herodotus 1.8-9; in both cases a king forces a trusted servant (Kombabos, Gyges) to do that which the servant knows will result in an unhappy turn of events. Both associate the displeasure of a goddess with sickness (*D.S.D.*, para. 19, and Herodotus 1.20-22); and both are impressed with the antiquity of things Egyptian.

But the similarities between the *D.S.D.* and Herodotus are not a token of the admiration felt by the author of the former for the great historian. Rather, the author of the *D.S.D.* is exaggerating and thus parodying the methods, eccentricities and language of Herodotus. That this is the case has been noted previously by Croiset,[76] Penick,[77] Burckhardt,[78] and Bompaire,[79] and is given its happiest formulation by Allinson: "*The Syrian Goddess*, flaunting her oriental nakedness through the diaphanous Ionic dress, has touches of humour that suggest a deliberate satire on the naïveté of Herodotus and on the current fad of Ionicizing."[80] The details of this parody are far more impressive than are the assertions of successive witnesses in favor of thus viewing the *D.S.D.* Thus, Herodotus' weakness for great numbers of troops or vast sums of money or enormous dimensions of a city or temple (an excellent example is the description of Babylon in 1.178ff., especially in 1.192) is parodied by the author of the *D.S.D.* in the great height he ascribes to the columns before the temple (para. 28),[81] or the dimensions he

---

75. Compare, for example, *D.S.D.*, para. 8 (ταῦτα μὲν οἱ πολλοὶ λέγουσιν) with Herodotus 1.24 (ταῦτα μέν νυν Κορίνθοι τε καὶ Λέσβοι λέγουσι), 1.64, 1.70, 1.171, etc.

76. *Essai sur le vie*, p. 63 and p. 204.

77. "Notes on Lucian's *Syrian Goddess*," p. 393.

78. *Die Zeit*, p. 182.

79. *Lucian ecrivain*, pp. 648-650.

80. *Lucian*, p. 120.

81. Thus too Harmon (*Lucian*, vol. 4, p. 379, n.3) who notes that "it is in unimportant details like this that Lucian gives rein to his inclination to parody." See also Burckhardt

gives for the temple itself (para. 28). Herodotus' *Historia* is replete with statements of awe at the marvelous works of various barbarians; and it is difficult to see similar statements by the author of the *D.S.D.* with respect to patent deceptions as other than parodies of Herodotus.[82] Compare, for example, Herodotus 1.194 (τὸ δὲ ἁπάντων θῶμα μέγιστον) with *D.S.D.*, para. 36 (ἐρέω δὲ τὸ μάλιστα θωυμάζειν ἄξιον).[83] Similarly, between several divergent accounts, Herodotus chooses that which he considers most credible (for example, πιθανώτατος in 1.214); the author of the *D.S.D.* mocks this characteristic of Herodotus in repeating similar phrases (for example, πολλὸν πιστοτέρην), but in applying the phrase to that account which is always the most unlikely and usually the most in accord with native Greek practice (for example, para. 15 and 28). The reticence concerning those customs about which the audience has been made to feel most eager to learn more in the *D.S.D.* (for example, para. 5 and 9) also parodies Herodotus' habit of dropping the discussion of religious customs in mid-stream (for example, 2.65, 2.86, or 2.170). Finally, there are examples of a specific account in Herodotus finding its satirical parallel in the *D.S.D.*; compare Herodotus' description of the floating shrine of Apollo (2.156) with paragraph 46 of the *D.S.D.*, where the author's rationalizing explanation of the same phenomenon at Hierapolis only heightens the satire.

It is not sufficient, however, merely to note that the *D. S.D.* has a satiric strain or that this strain is further in parody of Herodotus. Any attempt to search through the work for hints of its authorship or for elements valuable in reconstructing the myths and cult of Hierapolis must also note that the *D.S.D.*, like other works of Greek visitors to the Near East, forces Syrian customs and deities, however foreign, into the

---

(*Die Zeit*, p. 185, n.2) who dismisses the attempt to emend τριηκοσίων to τριήκοντα, since the text as it stands is an example of Lucian's characteristic "Uebertreibung." Stocks too notes the author's pointed "Übertreibung" both here ("Studien," 2) and in para. 46 where the lake at Hierapolis is said to be over one thousand feet deep ("Studien," 6).

82. Allinson ("Pseudo-Ionism," 207) makes a similar observation, buttressed with examples.

83. Other similar statements from Herodotus can be found in 2.35 and 2.175.

Greek mold. Lest this escape his audience, the author announces his bias toward things Greek in paragraph 16: "Those things seem satisfactory to me which they say about the shrine in accord for the most part with the Greeks" (ἁνδάνει δέ μοι τὰ λέγουσι τοῦ ἱροῦ πέρι τοῖσιν Ἕλλησιν τὰ πολλὰ ὁμολογέοντες). Or, in paragraph 28, he rejects the explanations offered by both "the people" (οἱ πολλοί) and by another, unnamed group for the origin and significance of the columns which are ascended, and writes, "to me these [explanations] seem unlikely, and I think they so act also for Dionysos" (ἐμοὶ μέν νυν καὶ τάδε ἀπίθανα. δοκέω γε μὲν Διονύσῳ σφέας καὶ τάδε ποιέειν). Harmon's choice of "outlandissche" to translate βάρβαρος[84] is a happy one if he means thereby to indicate that the author of the *D.S.D.* in the use of this adjective, as throughout, reflects the Greek habit of equating foreign with ridiculous and hence giving a Greek dressing to foreign deities and customs.[85] Thus, all of the deities of Hierapolis are given Greek names; and we hear of Dionysos,[86] a bearded Apollo, Hermes, Atlas, and Zeus and Hera, each with only a single characteristic in common with or only a faint rumor of a similarity with an oriental deity. That these names are a product of the author's Greek training and not their native titles is clear from the names cited by other visitors to Hierapolis and also from hints in the *D.S.D.* itself. For example, after labeling the two main deities of the cult Hera and Zeus, the author admits of the latter that the inhabitants "call him by another name" (ἑτέρῳ οὐνόματι κληίζουσιν, para. 31).

There are, then, two clear tendencies of the author to be

---

84. For example, in para. 11 (*Lucian*, vol. 4, p. 351).

85. For the widespread syncretism of the Hellenistic world and the practice of giving Greek dress to oriental gods and cults, see Boucher, *Syria as a Roman Province*, p. 5; W. F. Albright, "Islam and the Religions of the Ancient Orient," *JAOS* 60 (1940) 290; H. J. Rose, *Religion in Greece and Rome* (New York: Harper, 1959), pp. 108-109; M. Avi-Yonah, "Syrian Gods at Ptolemais-Accho," *IEJ* 9 (1959) 12; and Clapham, "Sancuniathon," 12 and 19.

86. R. Ganszyniec has demonstrated well the imprecision and inaccuracy of the Dionysos identification here ("Zu [Lucian] *De dea Syria*," *Archiv für Religionswissenschaft* 21 [1916] 499-501).

noted at scattered points in the *D.S.D.*: (1) that the author rarely overlooks an opportunity to satirize this bizarre oriental cult with its equally bizarre myths; and (2) that he imposes Greek deities and Greek myths upon their native Syrian counterparts.[87] Both tendencies are typical of Greek visitors to Syria and the Near East in general; and both need to be noted before seeking the ancient Semitic background of the Hierapolis cult in the *D.S.D.* The tendencies are apparent not only in occasional comments in the work but also and especially in the author's telling of the flood story and of the tale of Kombabos. We turn now to a discussion of these two instructive legends.

The Stories of the Flood and of Kombabos

The Flood

The flood legend is related in paragraph 12 of the *D.S.D.* The author begins his tale of Deucalion "the Scythian" (τὸν Σκύθεα) with the twice repeated assurance that the tale is that told among the Greeks as the author himself has heard it (Δευκαλίωνος δὲ πέρι λόγον ἐν Ἕλλησιν ἤκουσα, τὸν Ἕλληνες ἐπ' αὐτῷ λέγουσιν). The repetition already raises the suspicion that the author protests too much and cannot mean what he says.[88] The story is as follows. The present generation is not the first, but a second generation which multiplied from Deucalion (ἐκ Δευκαλίωνος ἐς πληθὺν ἀπίκετο). A great calamity befell the former generation, because of their great arrogance, lawlessness, oath-breaking, and refusal to receive strangers. The manner of the calamity was the earth's giving forth great amounts of water (ἡ γῆ πολλὸν ὕδωρ ἐκδιδοῖ), together with rains, until the entire world became water. Of all men, only

---

87. This tendency has been noted by Baethgen: Lucian "den mit den griechischen Mythen überstimmenden Bericht vorzog" (*Beiträge*, p. 71).

88. So pointed is this repetition of the Greek nature of the ensuing tale that it weakens Betz's claim "dass der Veffasser nicht mehr in der Lage war, die verschiedenen Versionen zu unterscheiden" (*Lukian und das Neue Testament*, p. 165); a similar misinterpretation of the flood story is offered by Helm ("Lukianos," *PW*, vol. 13, col. 1761). On the contrary, the author knew well the sources of the various flood stories; and he knew that his story was definitely not Greek in origin.

Deucalion survived, on account of his prudence (εὐβουλίης) and piety (εὐσεβέος), for he, together with his children and wives (παῖδάς τε καὶ γυναῖκας ἑωυτοῦ) plus all sorts of animals in pairs (ἐς ζεύγεα), went into a great ark (λάρνακα μεγάλην) on which they sailed as long as the flood ruled (ἔστε τὸ ὕδωρ ἐπεκράτεε).

Thus is related the story. It begins and ends with assurances of its Greek pedigree; but an analysis of the flood tale's various elements so thoroughly refutes these assurances that the author can have made them only in a spirit of satire. The name Deucalion is shared by both the *D.S.D.* and the accounts of the flood preserved in classical authors; we hear of Deucalion in Pindar (*Olympian Odes* 9.42-46), Plutarch (*Moralia* 5.12.13), Apollodorus (*Bibliotheca* 1.7.2), and Ovid (*Metamorphoses* 1.259-417), as well as in the *D.S.D.* But the *D.S.D.* also preserves a name which is not found in the classical accounts, for Deucalion "the Scythian" is without parallel and the emendation to Σισύθεα, involving only the common error of κ for ισ, was suggested first by Buttmann and is almost universally accepted today.[89] As such, the name is a variant of Xisuthros, Berossos' name for the flood hero; and both are forms of the Sumerian name of the flood hero, translated into Akkadian as Utnapishtim.[90] At the outset, then, a name for the hero is found in the *D.S.D.* absent from the above mentioned accounts in classical sources, which also omit any references to Deucalion's piety, a theme found in

---

89. See Harmon, *Lucian*, vol. 4, p. 350, n.1 (though Harmon believes the error is as likely Lucian's as it is the error of later transmission) and Goossens, *Hiérapolis de Syria*, p. 49, n.2. Of Deucalion Stocks writes, "der Name 'Deucalion' ist natürlich der Sage ebenso fremd wie die Namen Zeus, Hera, Apollon dem hierapolitanischen Kult" ("Studien," 8), a statement which echoes the formulation of Stephen Herbert Langdon (*Semitic Mythology*, The Mythology of All Races [ed. John Arnott MacCulloch and George Foot Moore], vol. 5 [Boston: Marshall Jones, 1931], pp. 37-38).

90. On the name Utnapishtim see W. F. Albright, "The Evolution of the West-Semitic Divinity ʿAn-ʿAnat-ʿAttâ," *AJSL* 41 (1925) 79, and "Islam and the Religions of the Ancient Orient," 289; and Emil G. Kraeling, "Xisouthros, Deucalion and the Flood Tradition," *JAOS* 67 (1947) 178.

the *D.S.D.* and throughout the Semitic versions.[91] Of the physical causes of the flood, the author of the *D.S.D.* writes αὐτίκα ἡ γῆ πολλὸν ὕδωρ ἐκδιδοῖ, touching again a motif present in Semitic flood traditions but absent from those accounts in Greek and Latin literature.[92] The motif finds its closest parallel in Genesis 7:11.[93] Ovid says only that Jove decided "to send down rain from every part of the sky" (*ex omni nimbos demittere caelo*, *Metamorphoses* 1.261), and Apollodorus that "Zeus poured an exceedingly heavy shower from the sky" (Ζεὺς δὲ πολὺν ὑετὸν ἀπ' οὐρανοῦ χέας, *Bibliotheca* 1.7.2). Moreover, we read in the *D.S.D.* that "the flood ruled" (τὸ ὕδωρ ἐπεκράτεε); and this finds a verbal echo in the Greek text of Genesis 7:18, 19 (ἐπεκράτει τὸ ὕδωρ), but nowhere else. On the question of the survivors of the flood, thc *D.S.D.* again sides with the Semitic traditions. In all of these, more than the flood hero and his wife alone are brought aboard the ship,[94] though it is not clear in the Atraḫasīs epic just how many more are saved.[95] In Pindar,[96] Apollodorus, and Ovid, only Deucalion and his wife Pyrrha escape the deluge. Further, the *D.S.D.* account is again

---

91. For the presence of this theme in the Semitic versions, see Alexander Heidel, *The Gilgamesh Epic and Old Testament Parallels* (Chicago: Phoenix, 1963), p. 228. Pp. 224-259 of this book provide a good general account of the various flood traditions.

92. This has been noted by Clemen ("Miszellen," p. 96 and *LSSG*, p. 36), as well as by Kraeling (Xisouthros," 181).

93. On the antiquity and original poetry of Genesis 7:11, see John S. Kselman, "A Note on Gen. 7:11," *CBQ* 35 (1973) 491-493.

94. See Heidel, *The Gilgamesh Epic*, pp. 237-238.

95. In Atraḫasīs 3.2.40 (p. 92 in W. G. Lambert and A. R. Millard, *Atra-ḫasis: The Babylonian Story of the Flood* [Oxford: Oxford University Press, 1969]), we read that the hero "invited his people" *(nišīšu iqri)* aboard the ship, but this probably means just "his family" *(kimtašu)* as we learn in the following lines.

96. Presumably only Deucalion and Pyrrha are saved because they alone are mentioned here (*Olympian Odes* 9.42-46), though Pindar's reference here is only as a metaphor and thus brief, so that one could not build a case on this evidence alone.

here closer to that in Genesis than to any other flood tradition; compare Genesis 7:7 or 8:10 with the statement in the *D.S.D.* with regard to the survivors of the flood, especially if the latter's παῖδάς τε καὶ γυναῖκας ἑωυτοῦ is to be understood to refer to the hero's wife and to his daughters-in-law, a possible understanding of γυναῖκας ἑωυτοῦ.[97] As with the people aboard the ark, so too with the animals, the *D.S.D.* agrees with Semitic tradition. Compare Genesis 6:19-20, the P account of the animals who boarded the ark, with the *D.S.D.*'s πάντα ἐς ζεύγεα.[98] The Gilgamesh epic's telling of the deluge story also mentions animals; but in Ovid's account, for example, the absence of fauna aboard the ark is accented when, after the flood waters' recession, Ovid notes that other forms of animal life arose spontaneously from the mud (*cetera diversis tellus animalia formis sponte sua peperit*, *Metamorphoses* 1.416-417).

In ascribing the reasons for the flood's occurrence to the former generation's arrogance, lawlessness, oath-breaking, and refusal to receive strangers, the account in the *D.S.D.* again betrays its close relationship to the account in Genesis 6-9. Apollodorus and Ovid relate no motive for the disaster, beyond the statement that it was Zeus/Jove's doing. In Atraḫasīs, the *rigmu* made by Mami's creatures deprives Enlil of sleep, and so the flood is chosen as a way to silence this noise after lesser plagues have proved ineffective.[99] Though a reason for the

---

97. Thus too Clemen ("Miszellen," p. 96, and *LSSG*, p. 36). It would seem most natural for a Greek-speaking author to use γυναῖκας ἑωυτοῦ in reference to the wives of his extended family.

98. This has been noted by Clemen ("Miszellen," p. 96, and *LSSG*, 36) as well as by Kraeling ("Xisouthros," 181).

99. In a recently published article, Anne Draffkorn Kilmer argues that man's noisiness is not the real offense here; rather, it is the overpopulation responsible for this clamor to which the flood is the final response ("The Mesopotamian Concept of Overpopulation and its Solution as Reflected in the Mythology," *Orientalia* NS 41 [1972] 160-177). In a second article entitled "How Was Queen Ereshkigal Tricked? A New Interpretation of the Descent of Ishtar" (*Ugarit-Forschungen* 3 [1971] 299-309), Kilmer finds Mesopotamian parallels to the offense noted in para. 12 of the *D.S.D.*, that of the antediluvian generation's inhospitality. Note too that the theme of the formal hospitality

flood is at least articulated in this Akkadian epic, thus contrasting it with the legends of Apollodorus and Ovid, by far the closest parallel to the motive for the flood given in the *D.S.D.* is that of the Old Testament flood story. Both ascribe the flood specifically to man's wickedness. And both accounts contrast the previous generation with the character of the flood hero; compare Δευκαλίων μοῦνος with μόνος Νῶε in the Greek text of Genesis 7:23. Indeed, the more closely one examines the legend in the *D.S.D.* the more striking are its affinities with the account in Genesis. Because of Deucalion/Sisythes, the second generation became a multitude (ἐκ Δευκαλίωνος ἐς πληθὺν ἀπίκετο), which reminds one of the injunction in the biblical account for man to multiply (πληθύνεσθε in the Greek text of Genesis 8:17, 9:1, and 9:7). In the flood tales of Pindar, Apollodorus, and Ovid, the resurgence of life after the flood is a result of stones hurled by Deucalion and Pyrrha turning into men and women respectively; incidentally, this motif used to be compared to Mami's creation in Atraḫasîs, and hence considered a part of at least one Near Eastern flood story, but the correct ordering of the tablets of this epic, first perceived by Jørgen Laessøe, reveals that Mami's creation of man to do the gods' drudgery occurred *before* man's great numerical increase which brought on the flood.[100] Finally, both in the *D.S.D.* and in Genesis, a sign is instituted to commemorate the deluge and its aftermath; compare Genesis 9:12 (σημεῖον in the Greek version) with paragraph 13 of the *D.S.D.*, where we read that the σῆμα of the misfortune and its outcome was the χάσμα of the Hierapolis temple with its accompanying rites.

Scholars have noted before the Semitic character of the flood legend as related in the *D.S.D.*;[101] but many of the

---

required of some Hierapolis residents recurs in *D.S.D.*, para. 55-57.

100. This faulty comparison of Atraḫasîs with the classical accounts is found in Heidel, *The Gilgamesh Epic*, p. 260, in Kraeling, "Xisouthros," 179-180, and indeed everywhere before the mistake in ordering the tablets was perceived by Laessøe in 1956. See Jørgen Laessøe, "The Atraḫasîs Epic: A Babylonian History of Mankind," *Bibliotheca orientalis* 13 (1956) 89-102, especially 98-100.

101. Harmon (*Lucian*, vol. 4, p. 352, n.1), Clemen ("Miszellen," p. 96, and *LSSG*, p. 36), and Kraeling ("Xisouthros," 181-182) all have noted this.

parallels between the oriental flood legends and that in the *D.S.D.* have gone unnoted. This is especially the case with the similarities between the latter and the account in Genesis. Given this established character of the flood story in the *D.S.D.*, the author's claim that his story is the same as that told by the Greeks is absurd. And thus is confirmed our suspicion that his thrice repeated claim of the Greek origin of the tale he relates is all too pointed. The author knew his tale was thoroughly Semitic; and, in calling it Greek, he demonstrates again his adoption of the traditional Greek attitude toward the myths of the Near East.

It is of equal significance to note that the presence at Hierapolis of an ancient link with the flood tradition, as stated in the *D.S.D.*, is trustworthy despite the author's Greek coloring of the tradition. That Hierapolis was long considered the site of a χάσμα venerated as a sacred spring and linked with the deluge is substantiated by the city's native name. The author of the *D.S.D.* himself knows that Hierapolis bore another name, for he reports at the outset of the *De Syria Dea*, "I think that this name did not originally belong to the city when it was founded, but that it had another earlier" (δοκέει δέ μοι, τόδε τὸ οὔνομα οὐκ ἅμα τῇ πόλει οἰκεομένῃ ἐγένετο, ἀλλὰ τὸ μὲν ἀρχαῖον ἄλλο ἦν, para. 1). While he does not give his readers the more ancient name and avoids non-Greek words throughout, other ancient authors are less scrupulous. Pliny speaks of "Bambyce which is called by another name Hierapolis, Mabog by the Syrians" *(Bambycen quae alio nomine Hierapolis vocatur, Syris vero Mabog)*.[102] Plutarch tells of Antony's gift of "the Holy City which they earlier called Bambyce" (Ἱερὰν πόλιν ἣν Βαμβύκην πρότερον ἐκάλουν).[103] Aelian not only gives both the ancient and the more recent name, but lists Seleucus as the one responsible for the latter; Aelian tells of the holy fish "in ancient Bambyce, now called Hierapolis, thus named by Seleucus" (κατὰ τὴν πάλαι Βαμβύκην, καλεῖται δε νῦν Ἱεράπολις, Σελεύκου ὀνομάσαντος τοῦτο αὐτήν).[104]

---

102. *Naturalis Historia* 5.81.

103. *Antonius* 37.1.

104. *De Natura Animalium* 12.2. Modern scholarship is inclined to accept Aelian's attribution of the name Hierapolis to one of the Seleucids, probably Seleucus I Nicator; see Nöldeke, "Karkemisch," 6-7.

Further witnesses to the Semitic name of Hierapolis are many and widespread both in date and provenance. Assyrian sources speak of a place variously called ^{māt}*na-an-pi-gi*, ^{āl}*nam-pi-gi*, and ^{āl}*nap-pi-gi*;[105] and all have been justly equated with other Semitic names for the city.[106] Allowing for the phenomenon in Akkadian called Barth's law (that preformative *m>n* in a root containing a labial), we can reconstruct the Assyrian name as **Manpigu*.[107] Pliny, as we have seen, gives

---

105. The Assyrian names are now conveniently assembled in Simo Parpola, *New-Assyrian Toponyms*, Alter Orient und Altes Testament, vol. 6 (Neukirchen-Vluyn: Neukirchener Verlag, 1970), p. 257. Essad Nassouhi has published a hand copy of the inscription containing *Nanpigi* ("Inscription de Tiglatphalasar III provenant d'Assur, avec mention de Membidj," *Mitteilungen der Altorientalischen Gesellschaft* [Leipzig] 3,1/2 [1927] 16); and *Nampigi* can be seen in cuneiform copies in C. H. W. Johns, *An Assyrian Doomsday Book*, Assyriologische Bibliothek (ed. Friedrich Delitzsch and Paul Haupt), vol. 17 (Leipzig: J. C. Hinrichs, 1901), tablet 7, col. 3, l.12, and in Robert Francis Harper, *Assyrian and Babylonian Letters*, Belonging to the *K.* Collection of the British Museum, part 3 (London: University of Chicago Press, 1896), no. 323, l.6. The last syllable of the name in all of these texts is represented by the standard *GI* sign (no. 60 in Wolfram von Soden and Wolfgang Röllig, *Das akkadische Syllabar*, Analecta Orientalia, 42, 2d ed. [Rome: Pontifical Biblical Institute, 1967]), which has the phonetic value *ki* only exceedingly rarely (see *Das akkadische Syllabar*, p. 12); hence the Assyrian forms must be based directly upon a spelling in which the *k* of the root *nbk* (see below) has already become *g*.

106. See Fritz Hommel, *Grundriss der Geographie und Geschichte des altens Orients*, Handbuch der klassischen Altertumswissenschaft, vol. 3, part 1, 1st half (Munich: Beck, 1904), col. 733; René Dussaud, *Topographie historique de la Syrie antique et médiévale*, Bibliothèque archéologique et historique, vol. 4 (Paris: Paul Geuthner, 1927), p. 462, n.3., and p. 468; and Nassouhi, "Inscription de Tiglatphalasar," 16.

107. So too W. F. Albright, "The Evolution of the West-Semitic Divinity ʿAn-ʿAnat-ʿAttâ," 79, n.1, and *ARI*, p. 72, n.7. For preformative *m>n*, see Wolfram von Soden, *Grundriss der akkadischen Grammatik*, Analecta Orientalia, 33 (Rome: Pontifical Biblical Institute, 1952), para. 31, b (p. 31).

the Syriac form as *Mabog*. In Syriac texts, the city's name is spelled consonantally as *mbwg*,[108] which can represent a variety of pronunciations. Albright vocalizes the word *"Mabug"*[109] or *"Mabbug"/"Mabbog"*;[110] Nöldeke had earlier claimed *"Mabbog"* as the original Syriac form,[111] in which he was followed by a number of other scholars.[112] The doubling of the *b* is surely correct, though we will argue with respect to the second vowel that *mbwg* is equally well understood as *Mabbûg*, based on an assimilation to a *maqtūl* formation. A Nabataean text contains the name *mnbgyt'*,[113] a form best seen as a feminine gentilic ending[114] onto a form of the city's name as *Manbig*[115] or *Manbug*. The usual Greek spelling of the city's name is Βαμβυκ;[116] but other texts witness the forms Μαμβογ,[117] Βονβογ,[118] and

---

108. For example, in the *Apology* ascribed to Melito of Sardis (which will be discussed at length in ch. III below), *mbwg* occurs in ll. 14 and 17, p. 25 in the edition of William Cureton (*Spicilegium Syriacum*, Containing Remains of Bardesan, Meliton, Ambrose and Mara Bar Serapion [London: Rivington, 1855]), and in Jacob of Sarug's homily on the "Fall of the Idols" *mbwg* occurs in l.59 in the edition of M. l'Abbé Martin ("Discours de Jacques de Saroug sur la chutes des idoles," *ZDMG* 29 [1875]). See R. Payne Smith, *Thesaurus Syriacus* (Oxford: Clarendon Press, 1879), col. 2000 for further attestations to *mbwg*, some of which indicate the doubling of the *b*.

109. "The Evolution of the West-Semitic Divinity ʿAn-ʿAnat-ʿAttâ," 79, n.l.

110. *ARI*, p. 72, n.7.

111. "Karkemisch," 5.

112. For example, E. Honigmann, "Hierapolis," in *PWSup.*, vol. 4, col. 733.

113. *CIS*, vol. 2, no. 422.

114. So Mark Lidzbarski, *Eph.*, vol. 1, p. 195 ("eine Nisbe fem.").

115. Albright writes, "the later Aramaean (Nabataean) spelling is *Mnbg*, i.e. *Manb(p)ig*" ("The Evolution of the West-Semitic Divinity ʿAn-ʿAnat-ʿAttâ," 79, n.l).

116. Thus, as we have seen, in Plutarch and Aelian (both Βαμβύκην, acc.). The form recurs often, for example in a third-century A.D. scholium cited in van Berg, *Répertoire*, p. 19.

117. In an inscription from Perrin, ancient Perre; no. 22 in V. W. Yorke, "Inscriptions from Eastern Asia Minor," *Journal of Hellenic Studies* 18 (1898) 316.

Βοββυκ.[119] With the exception of those spellings with a κ for Syriac *g*, these forms are all derivable from an Aramaic spelling, since, as Nöldeke writes, "in der Assimilierung und Nichtassimilierung eines *n* (welches vor *b* natürlich *m* gesprochen wird) schwanken die aramäischen Dialecte gar sehr,"[120] and the change of a form *Μαμβυκ to Βαμβυκ represents too a regular phenomenon.[121] The Latin spellings *Bambycen* (accusative)[122] and *Bambycii* (genitive)[123] follow the Greek. In more recent times, the usual Arabic spelling of the city's name is *Manbij*.[124]

In seeking to explain the etymology of the city called today *Manbij*, one is confronted with an embarrassing richness of Semitic roots of similar sound and meaning. Thus the Syriac verbal roots *nbg*, *nbʿ*, and *npq* all mean "to break forth," "to come out," all used often of the action of water from a spring. Indeed, of *nbg*, which he defines as *"erupit, provenit,"* Payne Smith writes, *"syn. cum* ܢܒܥ *, et forte altera forma verbi* ܢܦܩ*."*[125] From *nbg* comes the noun *nebgâ*, "spring"; and from *nbʿ* come the nouns *nebʿâ* and *mabbûʿ*, both meaning again "spring." Represented in the Hebrew Bible are the verb *nbʿ*, "to bubble, flow," from which comes *mabbûʿ*, "spring," and the noun *nēbek*, "source." Ugaritic witnesses nearly synonymous nouns *nipku*, *mabbikā/mabbūkā*

---

118. In an inscription dated to A.D. 367 from northern Syria; no. 179 in William Kelly Prentice, *Greek and Latin Inscriptions*, Publications of an American Archaeological Expedition to Syria in 1899-1900, part 3 (New York: Century, 1908), p. 171.

119. Pseudo-Eratosthenes, *Catasterismi* 38 (cited in van Berg, *Répertoire*, p. 23, n.2).

120. "Karkemisch," 5, n.*. It is difficult to disassociate the Greek spellings with κ, which preserve the *k* of the root *nbk*, from a Canaanite form of the city's name.

121. Nöldeke, "Karkemisch," 7, and Dussaud, *Topographie historique*, p. 474.

122. Pliny, *Naturalis Historia* 5.81, as we have seen.

123. Avienus, *Aratea* 11.542 and 646 (cited in van Berg, *Répertoire*, p. 21).

124. Nöldeke, "Karkemisch," 6; Hommel, *Grundriss der Geographie*, p. 44, n.2; and Dussaud, *Topographie historique*, p. 474. The spellings *Mumbij* and *Mambij* also occur in modern Arabic sources.

125. *Thesaurus Syriacus*, col. 2264.

(dual), and *ʾapiqā* (dual). A bi-colon from the Keret epic establishes "spring" as the meaning of *nipku*, parallel to *maqāru* (Hebrew *māqôr*, "spring," "fountain"): *ba-nipki šāʾibāti / wa-ba-maqāri mumalliʾāti* ("from the spring the ones drawing water / And from the fountain the ones filling").[126] The *p* of *nipku*, Hebrew *nēbek*, is explained by Andrée Herdner as "resulte d'une assimilation partielle de *b* à une sourde subsequent."[127] The correctness of this explanation seems substantiated by the preservation of the *b* in *mabbikā/mabbūkā*, where the *b* is separated from the *k* by a vowel.[128] *Mabbikā/Mabbūkā* and *ʾapiqā* occur in parallelism throughout the Ugaritic myths in the bi-colon descriptive of ʾĒl's dwelling: *ʿim ʾili mabbikê/mabbūkê naharêmi / qirba ʾapiqê tihāmatêmi* ("To ʾĒl at the springs of the two rivers / In the midst of the channels of the double deep").[129]

Nearly all of these Syriac, Hebrew, and Ugaritic words have been utilized in etymological discussions of the native name for Hierapolis. Given that the words are synonymous and nearly homophonous, and that the pronunciation and meaning of toponyms are often a murky issue for both ancients and moderns, it is impossible to label various etymological explanations as surely correct or clearly wrong; and, as we will see, the

---

126. *CTCA* 14.216-217. For a discussion of Hebrew *nbk*, especially as corrected from the MT in Job 28:11 and Proverbs 8:24, see G. M. Landes, "The Fountain at Jazer," *BASOR* 144 (1956) 30-37.

127. "Note lexicographique: RŠ *lpš*," *Syria* 23 (1942-1943) 136.

128. It is also to be noted, however, that *p* and *b* alternate in a number of West-Semitic words. Thus Hebrew *npš* ("soul") is *nbš* in several Aramaic inscriptions (*KAI*, no. 214, 1.17; no. 215, 1.15; and Sefire, 1.A.37); and Hebrew *npt* ("honey") is Ugaritic *nbt* (e.g., in *CTCA* 14.2.72).

129. The bi-colon occurs, for example, in *CTCA* 2.3.4 (broken); 3.5.14-14; 4.4.21-22; 6.1.32-35; 17.6.47. See Richard J. Clifford, *The Cosmic Mountain in Canaan and the Old Testament*, Harvard Semitic Monographs, vol. 4 (Cambridge, Mass.: Harvard University Press, 1972), pp. 50-51, for a discussion of the nature of ʾĒl's dwelling, which is neither a "sterile steppe" nor a "miry bog" and hence is not to be located in the underworld.

evidence demands that we posit at least two divergent forms. Nöldeke offers as the original form either *Mabbog* or *Mambog*, with a vacillation in the assimilation or not of the *n* (>*m*); "ist der Name '*Mambog*' 'Sprudel' so einfach, aus den natürlichen Verhältnissen erklärbar, dass es schwer denkbar ist, derselbe wäre nicht der ursprüngliche, sondern erst nachträglich aufgekommen."[130] Albright too finds the root *nbk*>*nbg* here, but explains the name as a *maqtil* formation. Thus he writes of Greek Bambyce, "it was originally *Mabbigu*, 'Fountain,' from Syriac *nbg*, 'to gush forth,' a partial assimilation of Heb.-Can. *nbk* with the same meaning."[131] Paton suggests yet another explanation: "Mabog, the native name of Hierapolis, is apparently מַבּוּעַ, 'spring.'"[132]

The major distinction between these suggestions is the choice of a *maqtul*, a *maqtūl*, or a *maqtil* formation[133] as the primitive form of the name; and this distinction in turn depends

---

130. "Karkemisch," 7; see 6, n.* for the vacillation in assimilating the *n* and for *n*>*m* before *b*. When Nöldeke says that the "ursprüngliche Form" was *Mabbog/Mambog*, he implies that the name's most primitive form is that already in Aramaic, which witnesses the root *nbg* and which has a short *o* among its repertoire of vowels, unlike earlier Semitic. See also Theodor Nöldeke, *Kurzegefasste syrische Grammatik*, 2d ed. (Leipzig: Tauchnitz, 1898), para. 48 (p. 33). We will argue to the contrary that *mbwg* represents the Aramaic spelling of a Canaanite form *mabbūk*; the preservation of the *k* in the Greek spellings of the city's name has been noted above.

131. *ARI*, p. 72, n.7. The first to compare Ugaritic *mbk* with Hierapolis' native name was, as far as I know, J. A. Montgomery ("Notes on the Mythological Epic Texts from Ras Shamra," *JAOS* 53 [1933] 111).

132. Lewis Bayles Paton, "Atargatis," in James Hastings, ed., *Encyclopaedia of Religion and Ethics* (New York: Scribner, 1913-1927), vol. 2 (1913), p. 167.

133. On Semitic *maqtil* see Carl Brockelmann, *Grundriss der vergleichenden Grammatik der semitischen Sprachen*, vol. 1: Laut- und Formenlehre (Berlin: Reuther & Reichard, 1908), para. 200 (p. 380); the formation is used for "Abstr. und Ortsnom." On *maqtūl* see para. 203 (p. 382) in the same work; a formation in Hebrew and Aramaic "als Konkr. wie *mabbūa̯ʿ*."

on the split evident in the forms of the name in different languages. Assyrian *Nappigi/Nanpigi* and Arabic *Manbij* support a *maqtil* formation, while Syriac *mbwg*, Greek Βαμβυκ, and Latin *Bambyc-* all can lend weight to a *maqtul* or *maqtūl* formation. Albright, alone, takes note of the divergent evidence and views *Mabbug* as derived from *Mabbigu* "with change of the short *i* to short *u* or *o* after the labial."[134] Albright thus explains *mbwg* as subsequent to and dependent on a more primitive form *Mabbigu*. There is, however, an alternate explanation for the vocalization and origin of Syriac *mbwg*, Greek Βαμβυκ, which neatly accounts for the split in the evidence between these two forms and those in Akkadian, Nabataean, and Arabic. The spelling *mbwg* can readily represent a pronunciation *Mabbûg*, a *maqtūl* formation from the root *nbg* (<*nbk*), representing an assimilation to the vocalization of *mabbûʿ*, "spring," or *mabbûl*, "heavenly ocean." Of the latter Albright himself argued "*mabbûl* probably meant 'heavenly ocean' originally...the vocalism is perhaps due to the analogy of *mabbûʿ*, 'fountain.' The word is thus perfectly good West-Semitic, presumably going back to great antiquity."[135] The word's antiquity is established by its presence in Psalm 29, whose origin as a Canaanite hymn has been repeatedly demonstrated.[136] We would thus argue that both **Manbig* (a *maqtil* formation meaning "place of the spring") and **Manbūg* are legitimate and independent forms of the city's Aramaic name, the latter recalling the city's association with the deluge tradition (*mabbûl*) rather than witnessing a later derivation directly from *Manbig* whose *i* became *u* because of the labial. Nor are we dependent alone on such philological data for confirming the antiquity and tenacity of the belief that Hierapolis possessed a special link with the subterranean waters. Lucian reports a ceremony in which water was poured down the χάσμα in the temple (*D.S.D.*, para. 13, 35, and 48), a ceremony most

---

134. *ARI*, p. 72, n.7.

135. William F. Albright, "The Babylonian Matter in the Predeuteronomic Primeval History (JE) in Gen 1-11," *JBL* 58 (1939) 98.

136. See Frank M. Cross, Jr., "Notes on a Canaanite Psalm in the Old Testament," *BASOR* 117 (1950) 19-21, and the references cited there. Cross translates *lammabbûl* in Psalm 29:10 "on the Flooddragon" (*CMHE*, p. 147, n.4), calling attention to a nuance of *mabbûl* surely present in Canaanite.

naturally interpreted as a pacification or memorialization of the subterranean sources responsible for the deluge.[137] This cultic act and the myth behind it find confirmation in Jacob of Sarug's homily on the "Fall of the Idols," in which we hear of Mabbug's error in worshipping "the sources of water" *(ʾygʾ dmyʾ)*.[138] Much later, Maundrell observed that Hierapolis was notable among Syrian cities for its "multitude of Subterraneous aqueducts," by one of which Maundrell's company pitched its camp.[139] Hierapolis' intimate association with the *mabbûl* tradition is, then, difficult to deny; and the association confirms the trustworthy character of the author's report in paragraph 12 of the *De Syria Dea*, even if the report is given a strained and stretched Greek dress.

The Kombabos Tale

The tale of Kombabos and his master's wife Stratonike (para. 17-27), with its predictably unhappy outcome for Kombabos, is equally instructive of the character of the *De Syria Dea*. While the length of this section of the work and indeed the story's very presence in the *D.S.D.* are doubtless due to the numerous opportunities the tale presents to one wishing to satirize the oriental court in general and the Hierapolis legend in particular, none of which opportunities the author was able to resist as we have seen, the tale as related yet preserves traces of authentic and ancient Semitic tradition. These traces are clearest in the Mesopotamian origin of the name Κομβάβος and in the legend's organizing motif of the love of a fertility and war goddess for an attractive young man.

That Κομβάβος is a Greek reflex of *Ḫuwawa/Ḫumbaba*, the name of the monster who guards the cedar forest in the Gilgamesh epic, has been observed by many.[140] But the significance of

---

137. Cf. Albright: "some connection was thought to exist between...[the water-bringing ceremony in the *D.S.D.*] and the subterranean source of fertility-bringing fresh water in the Great Deep" (*ARI*, p. 72, n.7).

138. Ll.61-62 in the edition of Martin, "Discours de Jacques de Saroug." On *ʾygʾ* see Payne Smith, *Thesaurus Syriacus*, col. 1545 *("magna aquae copia in fluvio")*. Martin translates the phrase *ʾygʾ dmyʾ* "source sacrée" (145).

139. *A Journey from Aleppo*, p. 154.

140. See P. Jensen, *Assyrisch-babylonische Mythen und*

this equation has been variously assessed. E. Benveniste, whose article "La legende de Kombabos" is the longest treatment of our tale,[141] concludes that while the two names are the same, "la comparaison se borne au nom; les personnages sont aussi dissemblables que possible."[142] At first glance it is difficult to take issue with Benveniste, for the monster of the Gilgamesh epic and the handsome young steward Kombabos do seem to share a name only. However, P. Jensen noted, at the turn of this century, that there is also a similarity in function. *Ḫumbaba*, who guards the cedar forest which is "das Allerheiligste der *Irnini-Ištar*," is "wohl der Schirmer auch der *Irnini-Ištar*, und Κομβαβος der Wächter der Στρατονίκη, vermutlich als einer ursprünglichen *Ištar*-Astarte, wie schon ihr Name nahelegt."[143]

That Kombabos and *Ḫumbaba* share not only a name but also an association with a goddess of love and war is clear not only from the name in the *D.S.D.* of the goddess' surrogate Stratonike but also from further hints in this section of the *De Syria Dea*. Stratonike is the immediate cause for Kombabos' misfortune; but the author reports that the people of Hierapolis knew that Kombabos' fate was in fact due to the goddess whom the author calls Hera. The tale's plot begins with Hera's appearance in a dream to Stratonike in which Hera bids Stratonike to build for her a temple in Hierapolis (para. 19). Though on the earthly stage on which the story unfolds it is Stratonike who loves and brings misfortune to Kombabos, "those in Hierapolis say that Hera was the willing cause of these matters" (καὶ λέγουσιν οἱ ἐν τῇ ἱρῇ

Epen, Keilinschriftliche Bibliothek (ed. Eberhard Schrader), vol. 6, part 1 (Berlin: Reuther & Reichard, 1900), pp. 437-438, and Harmon, *Lucian*, vol. 4, p. 366, n.1.

141. The article appeared in *Mélanges syriens*, offerts à monsieur René Dussaud, secrètaire perpétual de l'Akadémie des Inscriptions et Belles-lettres, par ses amis et ses élèves, vol. 1 (Paris: Paul Geuthner, 1939), pp. 249-258. The ancient stories parallel to the Kombabos story in the *D.S.D.*, which parallel stories Benveniste recounts in pp. 252-255, are instructive of the satiric purpose of the *D.S.D.*, for none of these parallel tales contains the comic touches of the author of the *D.S.D.*

142. "La legende de Kombabos," p. 250.

143. *Assyrisch-babylonische Mythen und Epen*, pp. 437-438. For the link between the names Stratonike and ʻAštart, see the discussion in chapter II below.

πόλι τὴν Ἥρην τουτέων αἰτίην ἐθέλουσαν, para. 21). More directly, the author reports of the eunuchs at Hierapolis that "others give a divine interpretation to this matter, saying that Ḥera, being in love with Kombabos, suggested the act of emasculation to many men" (ἄλλοι δὲ ἱρολογέουσιν ἐπὶ τῷ πρήγματι λέγοντες ὡς ἡ Ἥρη φιλέουσα Κομβάβον πολλοῖσι τὴν τομὴν ἐπὶ νόον ἔβαλεν, para. 26).

With this last statement, the ancient mythic basis of the Kombabos legend is clear. Immediately following the *Ḫumbaba* episode, the epic of Gilgamesh turns, in tablet six, to that in which Gilgamesh is first the object of Ištar's love and then, when he rejects her passion, the victim of her hatred. The motif is in fact common to the worship of Ištar or ʿAštart and ʿAnat[144] from Egypt to Mesopotamia, and is just what we should expect of the author's Hera, who is, as we will see, the goddess Atargatis, a composite of ʿAštart, ʿAnat, and ʾAšerah. That the motif is found also in the Ugaritic Aqhat epic has been suggested by Albright. Aqhat, writes Albright,

> aroused the passionate desire of the goddess Anath, because of his strength and beauty. Like Bitis and Joseph in Egypt, like Eshmun and Kombabos in Syria, like Gilgamesh in Babylonia, the chaste hero spurns the advances of the goddess of love and war. A more characteristic specimen of Near-Eastern mythology would be hard to find.[145]

The suggestion has been taken up and carried much further in a recent article by Hillers;[146] and his discussion of this basic motif and its presence in the Aqhat epic makes clearer its place in the Kombabos tale. Hillers cites a number of texts in which the goddess of love and war is "the one who takes away men's bows, that is, who changes men into women."[147] In the

---

144. On ʿAštart and ʿAnat as goddesses of both love and war, see chapter II below.

145. W. F. Albright, "The 'Natural Force' of Moses in the Light of Ugaritic," *BASOR* 97 (1944) 34.

146. Delbert R. Hillers, "The Bow of Aqhat: The Meaning of a Mythological Theme," in *Orient and Occident:* Essays Presented to Cyrus H. Gordon on the Occasion of his Sixty-fifth Birthday, ed. Harry A. Hoffner (Neukirchen-Vluyn: Neukirchener Verlag, 1973), pp. 71-80.

147. "The Bow of Aqhat," p. 74. Hillers might also have cited *CTCA* 23, in which ʾĒl's arsenal of hunting equipment becomes a punning reference to his virility.

Era epic, for example, we read of "'the male prostitutes and sodomites, whom Ishtar, in order to make people reverent, had turned from men into women.'"[148] Hillers concludes that the Aqhat epic exhibits "the Virgin Anath, deceiving, violent, emasculating, the one who turns a man into a woman."[149]

The author's telling of the Kombabos legend, then, allows the ancient Near Eastern framework of this motif to be visible at several points, even if he uses this framework to his own satiric end. As such, the story is both typical of his method throughout and demonstrative of the basic trustworthiness of his observations. The Kombabos story, however elaborated, preserves the tradition that it was the goddess of Hierapolis who

---

148. Era 4.55-56, as translated by Hillers ("The Bow of Aqhat," p. 74). It should be noted, however, that not all would agree with Hillers' translation of *kurgarrû* and *assinnu* here. Thus the *CAD* entry under the latter reads "the *assinnu* seems to have functioned mainly in the cult of Ištar, to have sung specific songs and dressed in distinctive garments. There is no specific evidence that he was a eunuch or a homosexual; the Era passage may mean simply that Istar turned his interest from the masculine role to the feminine role" (*A*, part 2, pp. 341-342). And under *kurgarrû* in *CAD* we read that "there is no evidence that they [the *kurgarrû* and the *assinnu*] were eunuchs or homosexuals. However, in the Descent of Ištar the reference to the *kurgarrû* as neither male nor female may indicate that they were transvestites performing in female apparel" (*K*, pp. 558-559). William L. Moran translates *ass*[*innu*] in a text from Mari "'the cult-[player]'" ("New Evidence from Mari on the History of Prophecy," *Biblica* 50 [1969] 30; see n.2). Others are less tentative. H. W. F. Saggs sees the *kurgarrû* and *assinnu* as "probably eunuchs, who took part as actors, possibly in cultic performances" (*The Greatness that was Babylon* [New York: Mentor, 1962], p. 322). D. Winton Thomas asserts that "the Ishtar cult knew pederastic priests (*assinnu, kurgarû*)" ("*Kelebh* 'Dog': Its Origin and Some Usages of it in the Old Testament," *VT* 10 [1960] 426). And Kilmer finds "'sexless creatures'" too vague a translation and prefers to see them "as some kind of transvestites, or male prostitutes, or even 'hermaphrodites'" ("How was Queen Ereshkigal Tricked?," 300).

149. "The Bow of Aqhat," p. 80.

was responsible for Kombabos' emasculation. The story further suggests that the origin of the cult of eunuchs at Hierapolis is to be sought in the cult of a Near Eastern goddess of love and war. For the presence of such personnel in this cult there is ample evidence.[150] The goddess called Hera by the author of the *D.S.D.* is a goddess whose name and attributes embrace those of ʻAštart and ʻAnat; and that the mythic traditions of Hierapolis should preserve one in which this goddess seeks emasculating vengeance on a young hero is both expected from the Near Eastern character of the city's traditions and explicitly spelled out in the *De Syria Dea*.

---

150. For male and female cult prostitutes and eunuch priests in the cults of Ištar and ʻAštart throughout the ancient Near Eastern world see the following: Baethgen, *Beiträge*, p. 220; Frazer, *The Golden Bough*, vol. 4, 2d ed., pp. 14-15; Arthur Darby Nock, "Eunuchs in Ancient Religion," in *Arthur Darby Nock*: Essays on Religion and the Ancient World, ed. Z. Stewart (Cambridge, Mass.: Harvard University Press, 1972), vol. 1, p. 7; Beatrice A. Brooks, "Fertility Cult Functionaries in the Old Testament," *JBL* 60 (1941) 246-250; D. Winton Thomas, "*Kelebh* 'Dog'," 425; Roland de Vaux, *Ancient Israel*: Its Life and Institutions (New York: McGraw-Hill, 1961), p. 384; Donald Harden, *The Phoenicians* (London: Thames and Hudson, 1962), p. 103; Rainer Stadelmann, *Syrisch-Palästinensische Gottheiten in Ägypten*, Probleme der Ägyptologie (ed. Wolfgang Helck), 5 (Leiden: E. J. Brill, 1967), p. 99 (hereafter, this work is referred to as Stadelmann); Sabatino Moscati, *The World of the Phoenicians* (New York: Praeger, 1968), p. 205 (hereafter, this work is abbreviated *WP*); Donner and Röllig, *KAI*, vol. 2, p. 17, p. 55, and p. 62 (the last on a second-century B.C. Rhodes inscription which mentions *mtrḥ ʻštrny* = "'Bräutigam der ʻAštart'"); Samuel Terrien, "The Omphalos Myth and Hebrew Religion," *VT* 20 (1970) 326-327; Hans Walter Wolff, *Hosea*: A Commentary of the Book of the Prophet Hosea, ed. Paul D. Hanson, Hermeneia (Philadelphia: Fortress, 1974), pp. 14-16; and especially the comments by W. F. Albright in "Some Cruces in the Langdon Epic," 83-87, in *ARI*, p. 160, and in *FSAC*, p. 178 and n.46. The presence of such cultic personnel in the cults of a Near Eastern fertility goddess, which is surely one of the aspects of Atargatis, makes unnecessary the argument that the eunuchs at Hierapolis witness a cult of Attis.

Summary

The legends of Kombabos and the flood related in the *De Syria Dea* demonstrate the work's accurate preservation of the ancient material in the myths associated with Hierapolis. Yet these legends, along with other passages noted previously, reveal as well the stamp of an author in the Greek tradition whose description of Hierapolis is motivated above all by his irrepressible desire to demonstrate the ridiculous elements in the city's cult. This already removes much of the doubt about the work's Lucianic authorship, since the strongest argument against the work's genuineness is that the work lacks that cynicism exhibited in those works which are undeniably Lucianic. The case for the Lucianic authorship would be yet stronger if it could be shown that the objects of satire in the *D.S.D.* are the same as those pilloried by Lucian elsewhere; and it is to a demonstration of this that we can now proceed.

It was noted above that in the *D.S.D.* the most consistently satirized element in the Hierapolis cult was the material profit which the cult brought to the inhabitants of the city and which was consistent with the author's view of the oriental character. Precisely the same can be said about the (other) works of Lucian. To Lucian, greed is the overriding motive for the variously absurd actions of men and gods.[151] Thus, Peregrinus becomes a Christian in the hope that his conversion will bring him some honor and much profit (*De Morte Peregrini* 13 and 16). The *Saturnalia* is an especially pointed diatribe against avarice; Lucian's mouthpiece here, Kronos, complains that the festival has become primarily an opportunity for the greedy (*Saturnalia* 8). The theme of the income to be derived from elaborately falsified oracles, which is reflected in the description of the bearded Apollo in *D.S.D.*, paragraph 36, occurs again in Lucian's *Alexander*.[152]

A second major satiric strain in the *D.S.D.* is directed against what the author sees as new and inauthentic tales told

---

151. See the description of Lucian's works in Joseph William Hewitt, "A Second Century Voltaire," *The Classical Journal* 20 (1924) 132-142, and in Baldwin, *Studies in Lucian*, pp. 106-109.

152. Such counterfeit, speaking statues did apparently actually exist, if we interpret correctly the mechanism discovered at Corinth; see Allinson, *Lucian*, p. 93, n.36.

about the gods whose authentic actions are properly represented by the Greeks. This too recurs in the works of Lucian, most clearly in the *Deorum Concilium* where Momus criticizes the expansion of the pantheon beyond the Olympian Twelve (plus those of Kronos' generation) to include various half-breeds and oriental gods unable to speak Greek. Momus proposes that the pantheon be pared down and all statues replaced by those of legitimate gods. The necessity for Momus' proposal is demonstrated in the *D.S.D.*, where, for example, a fully clothed oriental deity, complete with a beard, is called Apollo. As Hewitt accurately says, Lucian's satire is repeatedly aimed at "the motley array of gods from everywhere that are horning their way into Olympos."[153]

In addition to such broad thematic parallels between the *De Syria Dea* and the (other) works of Lucian, there are also numerous examples of similar dramatic technique and of shared objects of scorn. Thus the story told of Peregrinus after his death is reminiscent of the bearded Apollo's levitation in the *D.S.D.*[154] The obviously falsified inscription on the base of the columns described in the *D.S.D.* finds a parallel in the *Verae Historiae* where the footprints of Heracles and Dionysos are authenticated by an inscription reading, "Thus far reached Heracles and Dionysos" (Ἄχρι τούτων Ἡρακλῆς καὶ Διόνυσος ἀφίκοντο, *Verae Historiae* 1.7; compare also 1.37 and 2.4). Like the reticence exhibited by the author of the *D.S.D.* toward practices about which he had purposely created great curiosity in his readers' minds is the conclusion of the *Verae Historiae*. The work ends with the deliberately provocative promise that the story will be concluded, and, presumably, the voyagers returned home safely, in the next installment - which installment never arrives. The technique of unfulfilled promises, even though it is one widespread in Greek literature, suggests a common authorship for the *De Syria Dea* and the *Verae Historiae*, and the effect in each work is as if Charles Dickens had left his panting audience ignorant of the ultimate fate of David Copperfield.

In view of the evidence for reading the *D.S.D.* as a work motivated by a satirical purpose throughout, the work is surely

---

153. "A Second Century Voltaire," 134.

154. This is argued too by Allinson ("Pseudo-Ionism," 207).

a candidate for inclusion among the works of Lucian; and in view of the satiric techniques and themes shared by the *D.S.D.* and the (certainly genuine) works of Lucian, the case for the Lucianic authorship of the *De Syria Dea* becomes increasingly difficult to deny. Furthermore, the manuscript traditions are unanimous in ascribing the work to Lucian.[155] The cumulative force of this evidence is, then, sufficient for one to regard the *D.S.D.* as a work of Lucian, or, at the very least, to demand solid proof for the work's ungenuineness from those who would deny the *D.S.D.* to Lucian. Since this solid proof has not been forthcoming, the *D.S.D.* will be regarded as a work of Lucian in the present study.

But if the *D.S.D.* is a satirical work of Lucian, is its value for reconstructing the cult of Hierapolis thereby damaged or even denied? In presenting the case for the Lucianic authorship of the work have we inadvertently shown it to be worthless as a source of information about the deities worshipped in north Syria in the second century A.D.? These questions are to be answered negatively, for satire as satire must be firmly based on fact to be effective. This is true of the *D.S.D.* as it is true of Lucian's other works. The *De Morte Peregrini*, for example, has lost much of the power it must have had for audiences of Lucian's day simply because Lucian's account of this charlatan's suicide (self-immolation before a large crowd on a day and at a place publicized in advance) sound too ludicrous to be true. However, we know from the testimony of a host of Lucian's contemporaries that Peregrinus' death did occur as related in the *De Morte Peregrini*.[156] So too the *D.S.D.* abounds with accounts of the worship at Hierapolis whose authenticity we would suspect were it not for the corroborating testimony of ancient witnesses. Lucian's description of the bearded, clothed deity whom the inhabitants call Apollo reads oddly because the statue bears no resemblance to the normal representations of Apollo; yet we know from Macrobius' *Saturnalia* that Lucian's

---

155. On the manuscript traditions of the Lucianic corpus, see Hewitt, "A Second Century Voltaire," 138; Martin Wittek, "Liste des manuscrits de Lucien," *Scriptorium* 6 (1952) 309-323; and Helm, "Lukianos," in *PW*, vol. 13, col. 1775.

156. For this testimony, see Allinson, *Lucian*, p. 109 and p. 109, n.43.

description of the statue is accurate,[157] even if his fanciful account of the statue's extraordinary powers is plainly satirical. Despite the pun on κεφαλῆν βυβλίνην in paragraph 7, "there may be something," writes Harmon, "in the tale of its drift, for the Nile current sets over to the Phoenician shore, and it is Nile mud that silts up Phoenician harbours."[158] The account of the holy fish, decorated with gold, in paragraph 45 of the *D.S.D.* sounds absurd; but the factual basis of the satire here is established by similar accounts in Aelian and Pliny. In his *De Natura Animalium* 12.2, Aelian writes that in Bambyce "there are holy fish; they swim in troops and have leaders" (ἰχθύες εἰσὶν ἱεροί, καὶ κατ' ἴλας νήχονται καὶ ἔχουσιν ἡγεμόνας); and Pliny notes, "in the lake of Venus at the Syrian Hierapolis, [fish] obey the voices of those in charge of the temple; they come when called, adorned with gold" *(Hieropoli Syriae in lacu Veneris aedituorum vocibus parent, vocati veniunt exornati auro)*.[159] There is something of the fabulous in all three accounts; but the combined testimony does establish that golden fish were important parts of the cult of Atargatis at Hierapolis. The custom related in paragraph 6 of women having public intercourse with foreigners finds parallels in Herodotus, Athanasius, Lactantius, and others.[160] The greed of the inhabitants of Syria and the profitable use to which they put their temple and cult are butts of Lucian's satire; yet Plutarch's Crassus spends his time in Syria counting "the treasures of the goddess in Hierapolis" (τὰ χρήματα τῆς ἐν Ἱεραπόλει θεοῦ),[161] so this too rests on fact. Lucian appears to be speaking nonsense when he

---

157. *Saturnalia* 1.17.66-68. This is not to claim that the two descriptions tally exactly; there are slight differences and Macrobius' statue is more elaborate than Lucian's. But these differences are minor and may well be a result of the two and a half centuries which separate Lucian from Macrobius.

158. *Lucian*, vol. 4, p. 345, n.4.

159. *Historia Naturalis* 32.8[17].

160. See Clemen, "Miszellen," pp. 89-90 for a full list of the witnesses in antiquity to this practice, and for a discussion of the custom's significance.

161. *Crassus* 17. On the great wealth generated by Near Eastern temples see A. Leo Oppenheim, "The Mesopotamian Temple," *BA* 7 (1944) 59-62, and G. Ernest Wright, "The Temple in Palestine-Syria," *BA* 7 (1944) 67.

says the temple faces east (ὁ δὲ νηὸς ὁρέει μὲν ἐς ἠέλιον ἀνιόντα, para. 29), after previously describing it as facing north (τὰ δὲ προπύλαια τοῦ ἱροῦ ἐς ἄνεμον βορέην ἀποκέκλιται, para. 28); but Herodotus, whom Lucian knew well, makes a distinction between "shrine" (νηός) and "temple" (ἱρός)[162] which can salvage Lucian's credibility here; Lucian is then saying that the shrine within faces east while the temple itself is oriented to the north, and this arrangement is paralleled closely by the Baal temple at Palmyra.[163] Of the description in the *De Syria Dea* of the city and shrine in general Stocks writes, "die Angabe Lukians hinsichtlich des Tempelgrundstückes im heutigen Membidj entsprechen dem modernen Befund,"[164] though again Lucian exaggerates the dimensions of the various constructions in the fashion of Herodotus. Coins from Hierapolis similarly prove reliable Lucian's descriptions of the representations of Hera, Zeus and the "image/symbol" (σημήιον) between them;[165] and other coins verify

---

162. See, for example, Herodotus 1.183, where we read of the Babylonian sanctuary that "in the temple" (ἐν ἱροῦ) there is "another shrine below" (ἄλλος κάτω νηός), where the νηός is clearly a smaller part of the ἱρός, just as in the *D.S.D*. The same distinction occurs in Herodotus 2.138, where the inner shrine contains the images, and in 2.155-156. An alternate explanation of this apparent discrepancy is to compare the temple with others in Syria where the προπύλαια faced north, the entrance to the temple east (so Stocks, "Studien," 3 and Arthur Bernard Cook, *Zeus*: A Study in Ancient Religion, vol. 1 [Cambridge: Cambridge University Press, 1914], p. 582).

163. The temple of Bēl at Palmyra is oriented to the west, while the divine images within the temple are in a small niche on the north side of the interior, so one could say that the temple faces west, the shrine looks to the south. See the description of this temple in Jean Starcky and Salahud'din Munajjed, *Palmyra:* "The Bride of the Desert" (Damascus: Directorate-General of Antiquities, 1948), pp. 11-12.

164. "Studien," 1; cf. Goossens, *Hiérapolis de Syrie*, p. 19.

165. See chapter III below for a discussion of these coins. From this and similar confirming data both Goossens (*Hiérapolis de Syrie*, p. 19) and Baudissin ("Die Quellen," 414) are persuaded that Lucian had to have visited Hierapolis personally.

Lucian's description of the Hierapolis priests' dress.[166]

Examples such as the foregoing, and they will be augmented in the course of this study, suffice to permit an important observation of method here. This observation can be epitomized as follows: the *D.S.D.* is a satire and must be treated as such for there to be any validity to conclusions drawn from information contained in the work. As satire, the work rests on a firm factual basis. But, again as satire, the work is replete with fanciful and exaggerated personal explanations about the cult of Hierapolis from an author whose intent is to ridicule this cult. Furthermore, the author is wholly within the tradition of calling by Greek names the native deities and disparaging the inaccurate, for him, myths told about these deities, so that the Semitic names of the deities and the Semitic origins of the cult are always hidden beneath the surface of the *De Syria Dea*.

It is because of this problem of method that so much space has been devoted here to establishing the *D.S.D.* as a work from an author who was within the tradition of Greek visitors to the Near East and whose motive was to ridicule the Hierapolis cult and lore. This author need not be Lucian; and the conclusions reached here about the Near Eastern background of the Hierapolis worship stand independently of the question of the *D.S.D.*'s authorship. But the author does need to be someone with an intimate familiarity with Hierapolis, so intimate that his description of the several layers of tradition at the city is probably based on discussions with natives of Hierapolis in their native language, and yet someone born into, or thoroughly trained in, the Greek tradition. Lucian meets these twin demands; and he does so more naturally than any other ancient of whom we know, or whose birth and training we can conjecture. Viewing the *D.S.D.* as a work of such an author, we have firmer control over the tendencies and prejudices exhibited in the work; hence, we often can make the critical distinction between an accurate factual basis and an exaggerating, satirical interpretation. The remainder of this study will seek out that accurate factual basis and the ancient Near Eastern character of the Hierapolis legends, which character is yet visible through the intentionally murky syncretism of the *De Syria Dea*.

---

166. Stocks, "Studien," 5. The description is in *D.S.D.*, para. 42; and the verifying *ʿbd hdd* coins will be discussed below.

Chapter II

ATARGATIS

Hera/Atargatis and Zeus/Hadad

As is evident already from its title, the greatest single contribution of the *De Syria Dea* to our knowledge of the religion of Hierapolis and its ancient Near Eastern forerunners is the information Lucian relates about the identity and worship of the goddess of the "Holy City." Though occasionally puzzled about which Greek deity is best identified with the Syrian Goddess, Lucian ultimately decides that it is Hera with whom the goddess is to be equated. He knows that there are those who attribute Hierapolis' temple to a goddess known as Δερκετῶ, yet affirms with mock solemnity, "it is impossible for me to believe that the shrine belongs to Derceto" (Δερκετοῦς δὲ τὸ ἱρὸν ἔμμεναι οὐδαμὰ πείθομαι, para. 14). "Another piece of Lore" (ἄλλος λόγος ἱρός) claims that the goddess worshipped at Hierapolis is Rhea (para. 15) but this identification he also dismisses as "clearly false" (ἀληθέα δὲ οὔ, para. 15). Lucian admits the statue of the goddess bears traits of Athena, Aphrodite, Selene, Rhea, Artemis, Nemesis, and the Fates; still, the characteristics of the representation "are on the whole, when seen correctly, Hera" (καὶ τὰ μὲν ξύμπαντα ἀτρεκέϊ λόγῳ Ἥρη ἐστίν, para. 32). Thus, he opens his discussion of the "Holy City" as so named because "it is sacred to the Assyrian Hera" (καὶ ἔστιν ἱρὴ τῆς Ἥρης τῆς Ασσυρίης, para. 1); and he ascribes to the bidding of Hera both the construction of the temple (para. 19) and the origins of the eunuch priests (para. 26-27). There is in Lucian's mind no question about the identity of this Hera's consort; he is plainly Zeus. In the "inner chamber" (θάλαμος) of the temple, the two primary idols are one of Hera and the other of Zeus (ἥ τε Ἥρη καὶ τὸν αὐτοὶ Δία, para. 31); though the idol of Hera seems to combine the attributes of several goddesses, Lucian says of Zeus' idol, "you could not make it out to be anyone else, even if you wished" (καί μιν οὐδὲ ἐθέλων ἄλλως εἰκάσεις, para. 31). The sacrifices of Hierapolis, performed twice daily, are in honor of Zeus and Hera (para. 44); and the two actors in the cultic drama which Lucian titles

"Descents to the Lake" (ἐς τὴν λίμνην καταβάσιες) are again Zeus and Hera (para. 47).

In thus identifying the Syrian Goddess with a Greek deity, Lucian is only following the convention of other Greek visitors to the Near East; and Hera is plainly not the native name of the goddess of Hierapolis, nor is Zeus the native name of her consort. About Zeus, Lucian himself admits as much; Zeus "they call by another name" (ἑτέρῳ οὐνόματι κλήιζουσιν, para. 31). The unanimous and undeniably correct opinion of a century of scholarship is that Lucian's Hera and Zeus are the Syrian Atargatis and Hadad (earlier Haddu).[1] Indeed, speaking a bit hyperbolically, Henry Seyrig says, "tout le monde reconnaît que les deux principaux dieux de Mabog sont Hadad et Atargatis, que Lucien nomme Zeus et Héra."[2]

Nor is this recognition without impressive ancient witnesses. Two centuries before Lucian, Strabo writes of "Bambyce which they also call Edessa[3] and the Holy City, in which they worship the Syrian Goddess Atargatis" (ἡ Βαμβύκη, ἣν καὶ Ἔδεσσαν καὶ Ἱερὰν πόλιν καλοῦσιν, ἐν ᾗ τιμῶσι τὴν Συρίαν θεὸν τὴν Ἀταργάτιν).[4] But the most impressive body of evidence for the identity of the two chief gods of Hierapolis comes from the island of Delos, where in the second century B.C. Hierapolitans built a temple to their native gods.[5] Am. Hauvette-Besnault writes

---

1. See, for example, A. B. Cook, *Zeus*, vol. 1, pp. 582-589; Comte du Mesnil du Buisson, "L'étendard d'Arargatis et Hadad à Doura-Europos ou la déesse Sèmia," *Revue des arts asiatiques* 11 (1937) 76 and "De Shadrafa, dieu de Palmyre, à Baʿal Shamīm, dieu de Hatra, aux IIe et IIIe siècles après J.-C.," *MUSJ* 38 (1962) 157; and Wolfgang Fauth, "Dea Syria," in Konrat Ziegler and Walther Sontheimer, eds., *Der Kleine Pauly:* Lexikon der Antike (Stuttgart: Alfred Druckenmüller, 1964-), vol. 1, col. 1401.

2. "Antiquités syriennes," *Syria* 37 (1960) 241.

3. Though Hierapolis is called by many names, Edessa is of course not among them; for Strabo's error here, see van Berg, *Répertoire*, p. 53, n.3 to selection no. 83.

4. 16.1.27. Strabo's words are reproduced in van Berg, *Répertoire*, no. 83 (p. 52). The work of van Berg is of immense value in its collection of ancient evidence about the Syrian Goddess, evidence which is otherwise fragmentary and scattered.

5. A full account of the cult of Atargatis on Delos can

of the Delos evidence, "tous ces témoignages ne permettent pas de douter qu'Adad et Atargatis ne soient les divinités syriennes d'Hiérapolis, que Lucien (ou l'auteur quel qu'il suit du traité parvenu sous son nom) a décrites dans l'ouvrage intitulé Περὶ τῆς Συρίης θεοῦ."[6] From the Delos temple of Atargatis come dedications to 'Αταργάτει 'Αγνεῖ θεῷ,[7] alone, and also those which honor both Atargatis and Hadad: 'Αδάτωι καὶ Αταργάτει,[8] for example, or 'Αγνῇ 'Αφροδίτῃ 'Αταργάτι καὶ 'Αδάδου.[9] The pair are labeled the θεοῖς πατρίοις[10] of the Syrians living on this Greek island; and, as Morin notes, though inscriptions

---

be found in Paul John Morin, "The Cult of Dea Syria in the Greek World" (Ph.D. dissertation, Ohio State University, 1960; Ann Arbor, Michigan: University Microfilms, Inc., Mic 60-4116), 85-131. Though she may have been worshipped privately on Delos before 127-126 B.C., it is at this date that Atargatis' public worship began (Morin, 91), after the Syrians had obtained permission from Athens to build her a temple (Morin, 97). See also Cumont, *Les religions orientales*, p. 97, n.5, and 99; Stocks, "Studien," 22; and Arthur Darby Nock, "The Roman Army and the Religious Year," *HTR* 45 (1952) 246 and n.235 (= *Arthur Darby Nock:* Essays on Religion and the Ancient World, ed. Zeph Stewart [Cambridge, Mass.: Harvard University Press, 1972], vol. 2, p. 785 and n.235).

6. "Fouilles de Délos: temple des dieux étrangers, divinités syriennes: Aphrodite syrienne, Adad et Atargatis," *Bulletin de correspondance hellênique* 6 (1882) 483.

7. Hauvette-Besnault, "Fouilles de Délos," 498-499 (no. 18). For a description of the "stereotyped phraseology" of the Delos dedications, see Morin, "The Cult of Dea Syria," 90-91; "the bulk of these inscriptions," writes Morin, "commemorates the devotion of the many faithful of low station who could do little more than offer a drachma or two to have their names scratched upon a stone, to insure for themselves and their families the good will of the Syrian Goddess" ("The Cult of Dea Syria," 91).

8. Hauvette-Besnault, "Fouilles de Delos," 495 (no. 12), 496 (no. 13), and 497 (no. 14).

9. Hauvette-Besnault, "Fouilles de Delos," 497 (no. 15). The identification with Aphrodite will be discussed below.

10. Hauvette-Besnault, "Fouilles de Delos," 495 (no. 12), and 496 (no. 13).

honoring Hadad become less frequent, "both names appeared regularly in the dedications of the Hierapolitan period."[11]

The worship of Atargatis with her consort Hadad was not limited to Hierapolis and to the Delos residents from this city, but spread throughout both Syria and, eventually, the entire Mediterranean world.[12] There is a large relief of Hadad and Atargatis from Dura-Europos, now in the Yale University Art Gallery,[13] where the goddess' name appears uniquely as Ἀταραγάτιδι.[14] Nelson Glueck has found much evidence for the worship of this same pair in the Nabataean world; it is not to exaggerate, writes Glueck, "to speak of her [Atargatis] as the reigning monarch of the Temple of Tannur and of Zeus-Hadad as her royal consort."[15] And from Accho, Greek Ptolemais, comes an altar bearing a second-century B.C. inscription which begins with a dedication to [Ἀ]δάδωι καὶ Ἀταργάτει.[16] As Avi-Yonah notes,

---

11. "The Cult of Dea Syria," 119. The "Hierapolitan period" is the late second and early first century B.C.

12. For listings of Atargatis' cult sites, see F. R. Walton, "Atargatis," in Theodor Klauser, ed., *Reallexikon für Antike und Christentum* (Stuttgart: Hiersemann, 1950-), vol. 1, cols. 856-859, and, for the Greek world alone, Morin, "The Cult of Dea Syria," *passim.*

13. P. V. C. Baur, M. I. Rostovtzeff, and Alfred R. Bellinger, eds., *The Excavations of Dura-Europos, Preliminary Report of the Third Season of Work:* November 1929-March 1930 (New Haven: Yale University Press, 1932), pl. 14. The relief is described on pp. 100-101, and also by Nelson Glueck, *Deities and Dolphins* (New York: Farrar, Straus and Giroux, 1965), p. 207. Additional photographs of the relief may be seen in du Mesnil du Buisson, "L'étendard," pl. 27a, in Harald Ingholt, "Parthian Sculptures from Hatra," *Memoirs of the Connecticut Academy* 12 (1954) pl. 4, no. 1, and in Ann Perkins, *The Art of Dura-Europos* (Oxford: Oxford University Press, 1973), pl. 38.

14. P. V. C. Bauer, *et al.*, *Dura-Europos, Preliminary Report of the Third Season*, p. 45: "This form, from a nominative Ἀταραγάτις, is otherwise unknown."

15. *Deities and Dolphins*, p. 288. See pp. 196-203 for the identification of Atargatis' consort here as Zeus-Hadad.

16. Avi-Yonah, "Syrian Gods at Ptolemais-Accho," 2-3, and Fig. 1. The inscription recounts the dedication of "the altar" (τὸν βωμόν) in fulfillment of a "vow" (κατευχήν) to Hadad and Atargatis as the "deities listening to prayers" (θεοῖς ἐπηκόοις).

the altar is especially significant since "the deities to whom the altar was dedicated were of purely oriental character, not even disguised by a syncretistic appellation,"[17] and hence is "evidence for the worship of oriental gods by the Greek settlers in Phoenicia at an early date."[18]

In paragraphs 31-32 of the *D.S.D.*, Lucian gives a detailed description of the representation of the deity whom he calls Hera and a briefer account of Zeus' statue. His descriptions accord well with representations of Hadad and Atargatis, both on coins of Hierapolis and elsewhere, and as portrayed on reliefs from Syria and Rome. Zeus, writes Lucian, "sits upon bulls" (ὁ δε ταύροισιν ἐφέζεται), while "lions bear Hera" (τὴν μὲν Ἥρην λέοντες φέρουσιν). Hera "holds a sceptre in one hand, a spindle in the other, and she bears, upon her head, rays and a tower, and a girdle" (χειρὶ δὲ τῇ μὲν ἑτέρῃ σκῆπτρον ἔχει, τῇ ἑτέρῃ δὲ ἄτρακτον, καὶ ἐπὶ τῇ κεφαλῇ ἀκτῖνάς τε φορέει καὶ πύργον καὶ κεστὸν). Both Lucian's trustworthiness and the Hera-Atargatis, Zeus-Hadad identifications are confirmed by comparing this description with coins and reliefs. Especially instructive is a coin of Hierapolis from the era of Alexander Severus.[19] The goddess, who is fully clothed, sits above and between two lions with a sceptre in her hand, while her consort is enthroned between two bulls. The relief from Dura-Europos mentioned above shows Atargatis' throne "flanked with very large and conspicuous lions";[20] Atargatis wears a chiton and a girdle, and there is a hole in one hand into which fit, presumably, a sceptre or a spindle.[21] Reflecting the general predominance of Atargatis over her consort, Hadad, in the same relief, "is supposed to be flanked with bulls. There is, however, just enough room for

---

17. "Syrian Gods at Ptolemais-Accho," 5.

18. "Syrian Gods at Ptolemais-Accho," 8.

19. That is, from the first quarter of the third century A.D. The coin is pictured especially clearly in Stocks, "Studien," pl. 1, no. 5. We will return to a discussion of this coin, along with a similarly instructive Caracalla coin from Hierapolis, in chapter III.

20. P. V. C. Baur, *et al.*, *Dura-Europos, Preliminary Report of the Third Season*, p. 100.

21. P. V. C. Baur, *et al.*, *Dura-Europos, Preliminary Report of the Third Season*, p. 101.

one inconspicuous and small bull at the left of his throne."[22] From Palmyra, across the Euphrates from Dura-Europos, come similar representations. Atargatis, writes M. Rostovtzeff, "appears often on the coins of Palmyra seated on a lion."[23] A Palmyra tessera shows a goddess, identified as Atargatis by Rostovtzeff, seated between two lions, a calathos on her head and a sceptre in her right hand;[24] and others show Hadad alone between two bulls,[25] and Hadad together with Atargatis, with Hadad holding an axe[26] or a spear.[27] In the Atargatis temple at Palmyra, a relief portrays the goddess with a lion nearby.[28]

In addition to the Hierapolis coins of Severus and Caracalla which show both Atargatis and Hadad, there are several coins from Hierapolis with representations of the goddess alone, or of her animal alone. A coin of Commodus has a lion on the reverse, and above and below the lion is inscribed θεᾶς Συρίας.[29] On two Caracalla coins the goddess is enthroned between two

---

22. P. V. C. Baur, *et al. Dura-Europos, Preliminary Report of the Third Season,* p. 101. Again, cf. the description of this relief in Glueck, *Deities and Dolphins*, p. 207. Much earlier, Baʿl Hadad was represented symbolically with a "horned helmet" (Hörnermütze) in north Syria; see Herbert Donner, "Ein Orthostatenfragment des Königs Barrakab von Sam'al," *Mitteilungen des Instituts für Orientforschung* (Deutsche Akademie der Wissenschaften zu Berlin: Institut für Orientforschung) 3 (1955) 78.

23. "Hadad and Atargatis at Palmyra," *AJA* 37 (1933) 58.

24. "Hadad and Atargatis at Palmyra," pl. 9, no. 1. For a comprehensive collection and study of the Palmyra tesserae, see Harald Ingholt, Henri Seyrig, and Jean Starcky, *Recueil des tessères de Palmyre* (Paris: Paul Geuthner, 1955).

25. Rostovtzeff, "Hadad and Atargatis at Palmyra," pl. 9, no. 4.

26. Rostovtzeff, "Hadad and Atargatis at Palmyra," pl. 9, no. 5.

27. Rostovtzeff, "Hadad and Atargatis at Palmyra," pl. 9, no. 6. Rostovtzeff's entire article is instructive of the iconography of these two deities.

28. *WM*, p. 426.

29. Wroth, *Catalogue of the Greek Coins*, pl. 17, no. 11, and p. 142.

lions, with a tall headdress atop her head;[30] and on a third she is similarly portrayed riding a single lion.[31] This frequent representation of Atargatis with lions is borne out also by Macrobius; at Heliopolis-Baalbek, Macrobius describes a "statue of Atargatis" *(Adargatis simulacrum)*, "underneath which statue are the figures of lions" *(sub eodem simulacro species leonum sunt)*.[32]

Zeus and Hadad

Before turning to the question of why Lucian chose to call Atargatis Hera and to a full discussion of the etymology of Atargatis, let us look briefly at the deity Hadad whom Lucian identifies with Zeus. This identification Lucian shares with nearly all of his contemporaries; and, indeed, the functions and iconography of Canaanite Baʿl Haddu[33] and Greek Zeus are so

---

30. Wroth, *Catalogue of the Greek Coins*, pl. 17, no. 14 and no. 17.

31. Wroth, *Catalogue of the Greek Coins*, pl. 17, no. 15. See also J. P. Six, "Monnaies d'Hiérapolis en Syrie," *The Numismatic Chronicle* N.S. 18 (1878) pl. 6, no. 1 (a lion) and no. 2 (a goddess on a lion), both inscribed *ʿth*. Six dates the coins to 333-311 B.C. (106).

32. *Saturnalia* 1.23.17-20. For the date of Macrobius and his sources, see van Berg, *Répertoire*, pp. 95 and 97.

33. That Haddu is the god called Baʿl *(simpliciter)* in the Ugaritic texts is especially clear in *CTCA* 4.6.38-40: "Fixings [Baʿ]l makes for [his] house(s) / Haddu makes [fix]ings for his palace(s)" *(ʿidabati bahatī[hu baʿ]lu yaʿdubu / haddu ʿadaba [ʿida]bāti hêkalīhu)*. See Herdner, *ad loc.*, for the restoration of the god's name in the first line of the couplet, a restoration made the more plausible by the parallel syllable count (13:13). Cf. also *CTCA* 4.7.38 for the Baʿl-Haddu parallel. This is not to claim thab Baʿl is always Haddu, or that Baʿl was not used as a part of other gods' titles, but only that, in the words of Albright, "from an early period (not later than the fifteenth century B.C.) the ancient Semitic storm-god Hadad (Accadian *Adad*) became 'the lord' *par excellence*" (*ARI*, p. 73). Baʿl Haddu is to be identified with neither *bʿl ḥmn*, as Landsberger and Cross have demonstrated, nor with *bʿl šmm/šmn*, as I hope to demonstrate elsewhere.

similar that the identification seems inevitable.[34] Both are portrayed in literature and in plastic art as war gods whose weapon was the lightning bolt and whose animal was the bull. A standard title of Baʿl Haddu in the Ugaritic myths is "Cloud Rider" *(rākibu ʿurapāti)*,[35] an epithet which accords well with the description of Baʿl found in a recently published text (RS 24.245),[36] in which we see Baʿl enthroned and prepared to hurl his "lightning bolts" *(ʿiṣī baraqi)*. Upon the completion of his house in Text 4, which act signals the kingship of Baʿl, the god announces his triumph in characteristic fashion: "And he utters his voice in the clouds / Letting loose (his) lightning bolts to the earth" *(wa-<ya>ttinu qālahu ba-ʿurapāti / šārihu la-ʿarṣi baraqīma)*.[37] Statues of Baʿl from Ugarit show the god wearing "vêtements caractéristiques des dieux combattants ou lutteurs."[38]

---

34. For a brief summary of Baʿl and his natural identification with Zeus, see Albright, *YGC*, pp. 124-125; and for the tendency in Hellenistic literature and inscriptions in general to equate the two deities, see Frank L. Benz, *Personal Names in the Phoenician and Punic Inscriptions*, Studia Pohl: Dissertationes Scientificae de Rebus Orientis Antique, 8 (Rome: Pontifical Biblical Institute, 1972), p. 302. Commentators on the *D.S.D.* are united in seeing Hadad behind Lucian's Zeus; see, for example, Baethgen, *Beiträge*, p. 72; A. B. Cook, *Zeus*, vol. 1, pp. 582-589; Frazer, *The Golden Bough*, vol. 4, 2d ed., p. 130; Paton, "Atargatis," in Hastings' *Encyclopaedia of Religion and Ethics*, vol. 2, p. 166; Walton, "Atargatis," in *Reallexicon für Antike und Christentum*, vol. 1, col. 858; and D. G. Hogarth, "Hierapolis Syriae," 191.

35. He is thus entitled in *CTCA* 2.4.8; 2.4.29; 3.3.35; 3.4.48; 3.4.50; 4.5.122; etc.

36. *Ugaritica V*, no. 3. The text is fully discussed by Cross in *CMHE*, pp. 147-148.

37. *CTCA* 4.5.70-71; see Herdner, *ad loc.*, for the restoration of *<ya>ttinu*. There is a good discussion of Baʿl's association with the bull and with lightning bolts in Wolff, *Hosea*, p. 39.

38. Claude F. A. Schaeffer, "Nouveaux temoignages du culte de El et de Baal a Ras Shamra-Ugarit et ailleurs en Syrie-Palestine," *Syria* 43 (1966) 8. Schaeffer is describing a recently discovered representation of Baʿl (Schaeffer's pl.

A great deal of additional evidence could be marshalled to demonstrate the similarity of Canaanite Baʿl Haddu to Greek Zeus, and their constant identification in the Hellenistic world; but their similarities and this identification are so clear that little more is necessary here. There is, however, a significant piece of direct evidence for the identification on a first-century B.C. Phoenician-Greek bilingual inscription from Piraeus,[39] where the Phoenician *šmʿbʿl* is rendered by the Greek Διοπείθην; this translation makes the equation directly, even if "the Greek equivalent Διοπείθης i.e. *obeying Zeus* is founded on a misunderstanding of the Phoenician."[40] With Baethgen, then, we can affirm confidently of Lucian's Zeus that "dieser einhemische Name kann nur *Hadad* sein."[41]

Atargatis and Hera

The evidence that Lucian's Hera is Atargatis is as convincing as that which points to Hadad behind Lucian's Zeus. In the "Atargatis" article in Hastings' *Encyclopaedia of Religion and Ethics*, L. B. Paton offers a particularly compelling summary of this evidence, much of which has been noted here previously:

> There is no doubt that his [Lucian's] 'Syrian goddess' is really Atargatis. His title Συρία θεός is one that is constantly applied to this divinity by other writers. Hierapolis is known to have been a chief centre of her cult. The priests of Atargatis at Delos entitle themselves Hierapolitans. In the temple was a pond of sacred fish, such as Pliny describes in the temple of Atargatis at Hierapolis; and Lucian himself narrates that the people said that the temple was built by Semiramis in honour of her mother Dercĕtó, and that they abstained from eating fish and doves, in the same manner as the people of Askalon.[42]

---

3 and fig. 4); but the description is appropriate for Baʿl's iconography at Ugarit in general.

39. *KAI*, no. 60.

40. George Cooke, *NSI*, p. 96.

41. *Beiträge*, p. 72.

42. Vol. 2, p. 166. A similarly strong statement is to be found in Baethgen's *Beiträge*: "Es ist klar, das wir in dieser allumfassenden Gestalt die grosse Göttin der Syrer vor uns haben, welche wir anderweitig als *Atargatis* kennen" (p. 72).

It is equally clear that Hera/Atargatis is the goddess who goes by the name *Dea Syria*, or a variant of this title,[43] in the West, where her consort is again Hadad.[44] Particularly instructive are the Roman reliefs of the *Dea Syria*; these show the goddess enthroned between two lions, with a sceptre, spindle, or mirror in her hands, and with a calathos, sometimes surmounted by a crescent, atop her head.[45] As such, they correspond strikingly to the portrayals of Atargatis in the Near East.

But if it is clear that Atargatis and *Dea Syria*/Συρία θεός are variant names for the goddess whom Lucian calls Hera, it is less immediately transparent why Lucian chose to call the goddess Hera. He would, of course, equate her with a Greek deity and hence give her the name of a Greek goddess, since this is his procedure throughout the *De Syria Dea*. But why Hera? In paragraph 32 Lucian lists a host of goddesses with attributes in common with the goddess of Hierapolis: Athena, Aphrodite, Selene, Rhea, Artemis, Nemesis, and the Fates. And we have seen that Atargatis is called Aphrodite on Delos. Yet Lucian chooses to call her Hera. The primary motive for the choice would seem to be the close association of Atargatis with a

---

43. Among the variants are *Dea Syria*, *Diasuria*, *Dasyria*, and *Iasura*; see O. Höfer, "Syria," in W. H. Roscher, ed., *Ausführliches Lexikon der griechischen und römischen Mythologie* (Leipzig: Teubner, 1884-1937), vol. 4, col. 1630.

44. For the worship of *Dea Syria* at Rome, see Cumont, *Les religions*, p. 98, n.11; Höfer, "Syria," in Roscher's *Ausführliches Lexikon*, vol. 4, cols. 1641-1642; Walton, "Atargatis," in *Reallexicon für Antike und Christentum*, vol. 1, col. 857; and van Berg, *Répertoire*, p. 92, n.2 to no. 116.

45. Drawings of some of these Roman reliefs may be found in Cumont, *Les religions*, p. 96, fig. 6 (inscribed *Dea Syria*), reproduced in Cumont's article, "Syria Dea," in Ch. Daremberg, Edmond Saglio, Edmund Pottier, eds., *Dictionnaire des antiquités grecques et romaines* (Paris: Librairie Hachette, 1877-1919), vol. 4, pt. 2, fig. 6701 (p. 1594); and as the frontispieces in Paul-Louis van Berg, *Répertoire*, and *Étude critique des sources mythographiques grecques et latines* (sauf le *De Dea Syria*), Corpus Cultus Deae Syriae, 1. Les sources littéraires, deuxième partie (Leiden: E. J. Brill, 1972), inscribed, respectively, *deae syriae* and *diae syriae*.

consort whom Lucian, like others, names Zeus. This latter identification was natural and inevitable; and from the Hadad-Zeus identification arose as inevitably the equation of the god's consort with Hera. The pairing of Hera with Zeus, and their "holy marriage" (ἱερὸς γάμος), has a firm foundation in Greek literature.[46] As C. C. McCown writes of a goddess of Gerasa named Hera, "the rite of the ἱερὸς γάμος, widely practiced in Greece, was doubtless sufficiently famous to identify her with any goddess who was the consort of the chief male deity of a region or cult."[47]

In calling Atargatis Hera, Lucian does not stand alone. Plutarch, speaking of "the riches of the goddess in Hierapolis" (τὰ χρήματα τῆς ἐν Ἱεραπόλει θεοῦ), says, "some call her Aphrodite, others Hera" (ἣν οἱ μὲν Ἀφροδίτην, οἱ δὲ Ἥραν.[48] Aelian labels a pair of deities at a site near Hierapolis Hera and Zeus.[49] Plutarch's note that Atargatis was called not only Hera but also Aphrodite and Lucian's association of the Hierapolis Hera with Aphrodite (para. 32) are both to be compared with the fifth-century B.C. Pyrgi inscription.[50] Here, the Phoenician ʿAštart *(ʿštrt)* is rendered in the Etruscan parallel text as *Unia lastres*, where *Unia* is Latin Juno/Greek Hera,[51] while ʿAštart's usual Greek equivalent is Aphrodite.

There are, then, parallels to Lucian's name of Atargatis as Hera; and the ready identification of Hadad with Zeus has supplied one motive for the Hera-Atargatis equation. But more is to be inferred from the Hera-Atargatis identification than merely that she is a fit consort for Zeus-Hadad. The further inference is that Atargatis, the goddess of Hierapolis, is to be distinguished from the other Greek goddesses Lucian names

---

46. It is related, for example, in the *Iliad* 14.292-351; in Diodorus Siculus 5.72.4; in Pausanias 2.17.4; and in Aelian, *De Natura Animalium* 12.30.

47. "The Goddesses of Gerasa," *Annual of the American Schools of Oriental Research* 13 (1931-1932) 157.

48. *Crassus* 17.

49. *De Natura Animalium* 12.30; van Berg rightly says of Aelian's Hera here, "C.-à-d. Atargatis" (*Répertoire*, p. 45, n.2 to no. 66).

50. *KAI*, no. 277.

51. Joseph A. Fitzmyer, S.J., "The Phoenician Inscription from Pyrgi," *JAOS* 86 (1966) 288; and *KAI*, vol. 2, p. 331.

(Athena, Aphrodite, Selene, Rhea, Artemis, Nemesis, and the Fates) and hence from these Greek goddesses' usual Semitic equivalents. Atargatis combines the functions and attributes of several of these goddesses; and it is because of this that Lucian passes over Aphrodite or Athena, for example, yet admits the Hierapolis goddess' similarity with these goddesses. Lucian ultimately labels the goddess Hera only because the goddess is the mate of "Zeus" here, and because any other identification would give a misleadingly one-sided view of Atargatis. Atargatis is plainly a deity behind whose name and attribures stand at least two, originally distinct, deities. Hence we turn now to a discussion of the origin and etymology of Atargatis.

The Identity of Atargatis

Variant Forms of the Name Atargatis

In neither Greek nor Aramaic is the tradition unanimous as to the form of this goddess' name; and there is much to be learned from the divergent spellings of Atargatis. The various Greek forms are less instructive than the alternate Aramaic spellings, but still significant. In Greek, the form 'Αταργάτις is the most common,[52] though 'Αταργάτη is almost equally popular.[53] Other forms are 'Ατταγάθη[54] and 'Αταράτη.[55] Both of these forms are significant variations: the first because it may preserve the memory of an original doubling in the first half of the name; and the second because it may preserve a tradition in which the second part of the composite name Atargatis began with an Aramaic consonant which could be represented either by Greek γ or by no Greek letter at all. These possible conclusions from the forms 'Ατταγάθη and 'Αταράτη are both

---

52. Van Berg, *Répertoire*, p. 79, n.1 to no. 100.

53. Cumont, "Atargatis," in *PW*, vol. 2, col. 1896.

54. Hesychius, *Lexicon*, 8178 (Latte ed., vol. 1, p. 276), reprinted in van Berg, *Répertoire*, no. 59 (p. 42); van Berg notes that the emendation of ἀτταγάθη to ἀτταργάθη is certain from the word's place in the *Lexicon* (*Répertoire*, p. 43, n.2 to no. 59). Six had explained ἀτταγάθη as "Atta la bonne" ("Monnaies d'Hiérapolis," 107), understanding the second element as an adjective; but the likely emendation to ἀτταργάθη removes the basis for this understanding.

55. Baethgen, *Beiträge*, p. 69; and Fauth, "Dea Syria," in *Der Kleine Pauly*, vol. 1, col. 1401.

confirmed by the Semitic etymology of Atargatis, which we will discuss after reviewing the various Aramaic spellings of the goddess' name.

In Aramaic there are witnesses to the goddess' name spelled with three different initial consonants, *ʾaleph*, *ʿayin*, and *taw*. Much the most common Aramaic form is *ʿtrʿth*, or some variation of this form with a different *mater lectionis* at the end of the name. The Palmyra tesserae witness this form *ʿtrʿth*;[56] and such is the normal form of Atargatis in Palmyrene,[57] for example, on a Palmyrene inscription dated to A.D. 140.[58] A similar spelling is found on an *ʿbd hdd* coin from Hierapolis itself from the fourth century B.C., on the reverse of which is inscribed *ʿtrʿt*.[59] But alongside of this form *ʿtrʿth* and from evidence nearly contemporaneous with most of the witnesses to this form with initial *ʿayin* is the form *ʾtrʿtʾ* (again, with variations in the final vowel letter), with initial *ʾaleph*. The goddess' name is spelled *ʾtrʿtʾ* in Nabataea,[60] far to the south of Hierapolis, and at Hatra, east of Hierapolis. On a series of Aramaic inscriptions of the second and first centuries B.C. from Hatra, which are discussed in a superb series of articles by Caquot,[61] we find the forms *ʾtrʿtʾ*[62] and *ʾtrʿt*.[63]

---

56. Ingholt, Seyrig, and Starcky, *Recueil des tessères de Palmyre*, p. 182.

57. A. Caquot, "Nouvelles inscriptions araméennes de Hatra," *Syria* 29 (1952) 115, n.2.

58. Cooke, *NSI*, p. 267.

59. The coin is pictured in Cumont, "Syria Dea," in *Dictionnaire des antiquités*, vol. 4, pt. 2, fig. 6698 (p. 1591). The inscription also helps to confirm the identity of the goddess of Hierapolis with Atargatis. For a comprehensive discussion of the *ʿbd hdd* coinage, see S. Ronzevalle, S.J., "Les monnaies de la dynastie de ʿAbd-Hadad et les cultes de Hiérapolis-Bambycé," *MUSJ* 23 (1940) 1-82.

60. *CIS*, vol. 2, nos. 422-423, discussed by Lidzbarski (*Eph.*, vol. 1, pp. 195-196) and noted by Caquot ("Nouvelles inscriptions araméennes," 115, n.2).

61. "Nouvelles inscriptions araméennes de Hatra," *Syria* 29 (1952) 89-118; "Nouvelles inscriptions araméennes de Hatra," (II) *Syria* 30 (1953) 234-244; "Nouvelles inscriptions araméennes de Hatra," (III) *Syria* 32 (1955) 49-58; "Nouvelles inscriptions araméennes de Hatra," (IV) *Syria* 32 (1955) 261-272;

In the Talmud and in Syriac, Atargatis' name becomes simply *trʿth* (or *trʿtʾ*), with neither *ʾaleph* nor *ʿayin* at the beginning of the name.[64] But the most instructive variation in the spelling of Atargatis from Aramaic sources remains that between *ʿtrʿth* and *ʾtrʿtʾ*, that is, the forms with initial *ʿayin* and those with initial *ʾaleph*.

The Etymology of Atargatis

Already in the third century A.D. an attempt was made to supply an etymology for the name of the Syrian Goddess by Athenaeus (8.37). His explanation, which assumes that Atargatis is a Greek name, is as follows: there was a Syrian queen named Gatis (Γάτις), who allowed none of her subjects to eat fish apart from her presence; this is, fish were not to be eaten ἄτερ Γάτιδος ("apart from Gatis") and the phrase ἄτερ Γάτιδος was corrupted by the people of her realm into the divine

---

and "Nouvelles inscriptions araméennes de Hatra," (V) *Syria* 40 (1963) 1-16.

62. Caquot, "Nouvelles inscriptions araméennes," *Syria* 29 (1952) 92, no. 5 (= *KAI*, no. 239). Note the misprint of *ʾdtrʿtʾ* for *dʾtrʿtʾ* in Caquot's transcription of the inscription. This same form occurs again in inscription no. 29 ("Nouvelles inscriptions araméennes," (II) *Syria* 30 [1953] 235 = *KAI*, no. 247).

63. Caquot's inscription no. 30 ("Nouvelles inscriptions araméennes," (II) *Syria* 30 [1953] 236 = *KAI*, no. 248).

64. Noted by Baethgen, *Beiträge*, p. 69; by Cumont, "Syria Dea," in *Dictionnaire des antiquités*, vol. 4, pt. 2, p. 1591, and p. 1591, n.28; by Paton, "Atargatis," in Hastings' *Encyclopaedia of Religion and Ethics*, vol. 2, pp. 164-165; and by Caquot, "Nouvelles inscriptions araméennes," *Syria* 29 (1952) 115, n.2. These forms are to be found, for example, in Talmud *Aboda Zara* 2b and in the Syriac work of Jacob of Sarug entitled "On the Fall of the Idols," l. 55 in the edition of Martin, "Discourse de Jacques de Saroug sur la chute des idoles." The loss of initial *ʾaleph* is not a phenomenon expected in Syriac and Aramaic, but is witnessed in Phoenician. Thus the name of Israel's ally is *ʾḥrm* or *ḥrm* (see *PPG*, para. 94) and "handmaid" is *ʾmt* or *mt*. Hence, the form *trʿth* may well reflect the goddess' name from a Phoenician, rather than an Aramaic, source.

name 'Αταργᾶτις.[65] Three centuries later, Simplicius offered an alternate interpretation of the name, this time based upon the assumption that the name was to be explained as natively Semitic. According to Simplicius, "Atargatis in Syrian means 'divine sanctuary'" (διὸ καὶ τὴν Συρίαν 'Αταργάτην τόπον θεῶν).[66] Simplicius must have understood the first half of the name as Aramaic *'tr*, "place," "sanctuary," and the second half as a divine name.[67] Though neither Athenaeus nor Simplicius approaches a correct etymology, it is significant that the latter recognizes the Semitic origin of Atargatis and that he agrees with the evidence from Nabataea and Hatra in spelling Atargatis' name in Aramaic with an initial *'aleph*.

In the nineteenth century a consensus was reached about the etymology of Atargatis; and one still finds this opinion, which is at best half correct, repeated today. This view sees behind the first part of the name ('Αταρ-) the goddess ʿAštart, Greek Astarte, and behind the second part (-γάτις) either Attis or some unknown, but probably Anatolian, deity. Cooke gives a classic formulation of the old view: "The name is compounded of עתר = עתתר = עשתרת and עתה.... whether עתה was a male or female deity is not clear....it is possible that ʿAtheh was the Phrygian god Attis - Adonis..; ʿAthar-ʿatheh will then represent a union between the Syrian goddess and the youthful god of foreign origin."[68]

There was undivided opinion that 'Αταρ- represented ʿAštart; and this view cannot be contradicted, though it is to be supplemented. Already in 1887, Robertson Smith wrote that Atargatis was "a name in which the first element is the

---

65. Athenaeus' interpretation is discussed by R. A. Stewart Macalister, *The Philistines*: Their History and Civilization, The Schweich Lectures, 1911 (London: British Academy, 1914), p. 97, and by van Berg, *Répertoire*, no. 109 (pp. 84-85), where the text of Athenaeus' statement is reproduced.

66. *Corollarium de loco* 150r, printed in van Berg, *Répertoire*, no. 123 (pp. 98-99).

67. Simplicius' etymology is discussed by Baethgen, *Beiträge*, p. 73; by Albright, "The Evolution of the West-Semitic Divinity ʿAn-ʿAnat-ʿAttâ," 101; and by van Berg, *Répertoire*, p. 99, n.1 to no. 123.

68. *NSI*, pp. 269-270.

specifically Aramaic form of the Phoenician Astarte."[69] By "specifically Aramaic," Robertson Smith implies, quite correctly, that the Greek 'Αταρ- and the Aramaic *ʿtr-* represent the name in a language in which earlier *ṯ* had merged with *t*, as it does in Aramaic, rather than the name in Hebrew or Phoenician, where *ṯ* merged with *š* and is represented by the grapheme ש.[70] At about the same time, Baethgen concurred in asserting, "der erste Theil עתר ist das arämaische Aequivalent für phönicisch-hebraisches עשתר[ת] ohne Femininendung";[71] and the view was echoed by Paton,[72] and Cumont,[73] and has since become a resounding chorus.[74]

About the second element (-γάτις) there was less unanimity, but a general consensus that it represented Attis or some unknown god. Among earlier scholars, Baudissin calls "Ate...eine andere Form des Namens Attis."[75] The same identification is urged by Baethgen,[76] and by Cumont, who flatly says that *ʿth* is "l'équivalent de l'Attis phrygien."[77] Even within the past quarter century, James A. Montgomery writes of Atargatis, "the name, like the deity, is composite = עתר + עתה, the latter the Greek "Αττις."[78] Others have been less certain about the identity of -γάτις/-*ʿth*. Macalister found *ʿth* "obscure" but "possibly of Lydian origin."[79] Strong and Garstang argued that both parts of the name Atargatis are different names for the

69. "Ctesias and the Semiramis Legend," 313.

70. Thus, for example, "bull" is *ṯr* in Ugaritic, *šwr* in biblical Hebrew, *twrʾ* in Aramaic.

71. *Beiträge*, p. 69.

72. "Atargatis," in Hastings' *Encyclopaedia of Religion and Ethics*, vol. 2, p. 165.

73. "Atargatis," in *PW*, vol. 2, col. 1896.

74. See Goossens, *Hiérapolis de Syrie*, p. 59.

75. *Adonis und Esmun*, p. 158, n.l.

76. *Beiträge*, pp. 71-72.

77. "Syria Dea," in *Dictionnaire des antiquités*, vol. 4, pt. 2, p. 1591; in his "Atargatis" article in *PW*, Cumont says again that the name shows Astarte as "Frau des Gottes ʿatē" (vol. 2, col. 1896).

78. *A Critical and Exegetical Commentary on the Books of Kings*, ICC, ed. Henry Snyder Gehman (Edinburgh: T. & T. Clark, 1951), p. 474.

79. *The Philistines*, p. 95.

same goddess; the name is, then, "a compound of the Syrian and Cilician form."[80] Paton was willing to venture only that *'th* is probably a male deity,[81] while Goossens came closest to the truth in claiming the "Até est une déesse araméenne, qui a succédé à Anat dans le panthéon syrien."[82]

The general view, thus, has been that Atargatis was an androgynous deity, or one whose sex was at least "flexible."[83] But, though this view still finds supporters, or, better, those still willing to accept its conclusions uncritically,[84] Albright conclusively demonstrated its shortcomings in a long article entitled "The Evolution of the West-Semitic Divinity 'An-'Anat-'Attâ,"[85] published fifty years ago. "Atargatis," concluded Albright, "is no longer to be regarded as an androgynous compound of a goddess and her *paredros*, but as the blend of two sister-goddesses with practically identical cults and characteristics."[86] According to Albright and those who with him have abandoned the position of Baethgen, Robertson Smith, Baudissin, and others, the second half of the name Atargatis (-γάτις/-*'th*) represents not Attis, or some unknown Anatolian deity, but the goddess 'Anat who plays such a significant role in the Ugaritic

---

80. *The Syrian Goddess*, p. 1; their argument here is as obscure as is their Cilician goddess 'Ate.

81. "Atargatis," in Hastings' *Encyclopaedia of Religion and Ethics*, vol. 2, p. 165.

82. *Hiérapolis de Syrie*, p. 61; Goossens seems thus to distinguish between "Até" and "Anat," rather than to see the former as a later form of the latter's name.

83. Baudissin cites the view of Ed. Meyer, that Atargatis' sex was "schwankend" (*Adonis und Esmun*, p. 158, n.1).

84. Written but fifteen years ago, the dissertation of Morin repeats the position that *'th* is of unknown sex and identity ("The Cult of Dea Syria," 5-6).

85. *AJSL* 41 (1925) 73-101, with "Further Observations on the Name *'Anat-'Attah*," *AJSL* 41 (1925) 283-285, and "Note on the Goddess 'Anat," *AJSL* 43 (1927) 233-236. Though Albright gave the definitive and much the best documented statement to the position that *'th* is an Aramaic spelling of the goddess 'Anat, he was anticipated by others; see, for example, Six, "Monnaies d'Hiérapolis," 108-110.

86. "The Evolution of the West-Semitic Divinity 'An-'Anat-'Attâ," 90-91.

myths. Thus, "the Aramaeans replaced the Canaanite-Hebrew name *ʿAnat* with the Aramaeized form *ʿAttâ* and later amalgamated the sister-deities ʿAttar and ʿAttâ into the *dea syria*, Atargatis."[87] Both parts of the compound name *ʿtrʿth* are seen, correctly according to this position, as the later Aramaic reflexes of Canaanite ʿAštart and ʿAnat: *ʿAṯtart* > *ʿAttar(t)* becomes Greek ʼΑταρ-, and *ʿAnat* > *ʿAttâ* becomes Greek -γάτις. In both cases, Albright claims, "the reduction of the doubling [*ʿAttar* > *ʿAtar*, *ʿAttâ* > *ʿAtâ*] is a normal phenomenon in early Aramaic."[88]

Though it was Albright who gave fullest expression to the view that ʼΑταργάτις is compounded from ʿAštart and ʿAnat, others have joined him in combatting the nineteenth-century view that the deity was androgynous. René Dussaud almost directly translates the view of Albright when he writes, "ʿAnat (sous la forme araméenne ʿAtté) et ʿAshtart s'unissent en une entité Atargatis";[89] and André Dupont-Sommer offers a similar formulation: Atargatis "est formé de deux mots: Atar (=ʿAttar), qui désigne la grande déesse de la fécondité, identique à l'Ishtar mésopotamienne, à la ʿAštart-Astarté des Phéniciens; et Gatis, transcription grécisée de ʿAttâ, qui n'est autre que l'antique déesse cananéenne ʿAnat (> ʿAntâ > ʿAttâ)."[90] There is, then,

---

87. Albright, "The Evolution of the West-Semitic Divinity ʿAn-ʿAnat-ʿAttâ," 101; cf. *YGC*, p. 133.

88. *YGC*, p. 133, n.58; the claim is seductive in its resolution of the doubling problem, though one would like some evidence for it. The representation of *ṯ* by Aramaic *t*, and the syncope of *ʿAnat* > *ʿAntâ*, are clearly characteristic Aramaic developments. For the latter, note Albright's formula, "*ʿAnat* : *ʿAttâ* :: *šanat*, 'year' : *šattâ*" ("The Evolution of the West-Semitic Divinity ʿAn-ʿAnat-ʿAttâ," 88), repeated by André Dupont-Sommer, "L'inscription de l'amulette d'Arslan Tash," *Revue de l'histoire des religions* 120 (1939) 150. See the discussion of the problematic ending on *ʿAtâ* in n.95 below.

89. "Temples et cultes de la triade héliopolitaine à Baʿalbeck," *Syria* 23 (1942-1943) 43, n.2; cf. also Dussaud, "Peut-on identifier l'Apollon barbu de Hiérapolis de Syrie?" 140.

90. "Une stèle araméenne d'un prêtre de Baʿal trouvée en Égypte," *Syria* 33 (1956) 85; cf. also Dupont-Sommer, "L'inscription de l'amulette d'Arslan Tash," 146-150 and Ronzevalle, "Les monnaies," 26-27.

a new consensus, which retains the ʿAštart-ʾΑταρ identification of the older consensus,[91] but replaces Attis (or some unknown deity) with ʿAnat as the goddess represented by the second half of the name. This view fits nicely with the by-forms ʾΑτταγάθη and ʾΑταράτη which were noted above; ʾΑτταγάθη may preserve the memory of the older Aramaic form with the doubling *(ʿAttar)*, while ʾΑταράτη reflects the general situation in which Semitic *ʿayin* was sometimes represented by Greek γ and sometimes by zero.[92]

This new consensus about the etymology of Atargatis is greatly indebted to the discovery of the Ugaritic texts, even though Albright's position was articulated before their discovery, for at Ugarit we see for the first time the major role played by ʿAnat in the Canaanite pantheon. "Vor der Entzifferung der mythologischen Texte aus Ugarit," notes Stadelmann, "wusste man verhältnismässig wenig über die Göttin ʿAnat aus dem

---

91. For further arguments in support of *ʿṯtrt/ʿAštart* = ʾΑταρ-, see Ronzevalle, "Les monnaies," 29-31; Fitzmyer, "The Phoenician Inscription from Pyrgi," 287; and Morin, "The Cult of Dea Syria," 4.

92. To be sure, one still finds those who claim, like Goossens, that γ always represents Proto-Semitic *ǵ*, while Ø (zero) represents Proto-Semitic ʿ, and hence that *ʿtrʿth* must go back to a form *"ʿatar-ǵatah"* (*Hiérapolis de Syrie*, pp. 58-59). Aside from the fact that the name occurs as ʾΑταράτη, this argument is without basis, since a study of Greek transcriptions of *ʿayin* reveals no pattern such that Proto-Semitic *ǵ* yields ʿ, while Proto-Semitic ʿ yields Ø. The evidence is contradictory; and one cannot claim for those transcribing a Semitic word into Greek any knowledge of whether the ʿ they were transcribing was etymological *ǵ* or ʿ. Note, for example, thet the transcription of Hebrew עלומיו in the Mercati fragment of the second column of the Hexapla is αλουμαυ; see Einar Brønno, *Studien über hebräische Morphologie und Vokalismus*, auf Grundlage der Mercatischen Fragmente der zweiten Kolumne der Hexapla des Origenes, Abhandlungen für die Kunde des Morgenlandes, 28 (Leipzig: Deutsche Morgenländische Gesellschaft, 1943), p. 315. According to the hypothesis γ < *ǵ*, but φ < ʿ, the ʿ of עלם ought to be etymological ʿ, yet we know from Ugaritic *ǵlm* that this is not the case.

kanaanäischen Bereich."[93] But when one combines the material from Ugarit with what is known about the Canaanite deities from other sources (the Old Testament and the material from Egypt and the Phoenician-Punic world), there emerge not one or two but three major Canaanite goddesses: 'Ašerah, ʿAnat, and ʿAštart. Since each of these goddesses is clearly a major figure in the Canaanite pantheon, and since one cannot claim for any one goddess an ascendency over the other two in the total ancient Near Eastern picture, we must go beyond the new consensus, which sees ʿAštart and ʿAnat combined in Atargatis, and ask if we do not have in Atargatis rather a conflation of all three major Canaanite goddesses.

That such is the case, that Atargatis is a composite of ʿAštart, ʿAnat, *and* 'Ašerah, is especially clear from an examination of the characteristics of the three goddesses and the attributes of Atargatis, to which we will devote the major part of this section of the present study. But the role of 'Ašerah in the composition of Atargatis is already arguable from the Greek and Aramaic spellings of her name and clearer still from the identification of Atargatis with a goddess called Δερκετώ by the Greeks. Greek 'Αταρ- can with little difficulty represent the Aramaic spellings of either 'Ašerah or ʿAštart, for just as Ugaritic *ʿṯtrt*, Hebrew-Phoenician *ʿštrt*, is *ʿtr* in Aramaic, so too Ugaritic *'ṯrt*, Hebrew *'šrh*, is *'tr* in Aramaic. Already in the seventh century B.C., an Aramaic plaque from Arslan Tash, a site very near Hierapolis, witnesses 'Ašerah's name spelled *'šr*, as has been noted by Frank Moore Cross and Richard J. Saley: "The spelling *'šr* for *'aširo* is interesting. Usually the form in Phoenician is *'Aširt*. The dialect of the plaque at this point has an isogloss with Hebrew."[94] So similar are the Aramaic forms *'tr* (= 'Ašerah) and *ʿtr* (= ʿAštart) that it is difficult not to see in the Aramaic *ʿtr*- and Greek 'Αταρ- a congeneric assimilation of *'tr* and *ʿtr* and a conceptual assimilation of 'Ašerah and ʿAštart. Since the forms *ʿtr* and 'Αταρ- preserve no ending, the distinction between the endings

---

93. Stadelmann, p. 88. He adds "aus dem kanaanäischen Bereich" because more was known, before the discovery of the Ugaritic texts, of ʿAnat's role in Egypt, as we will see below.

94. "Phoenician Incantations on a Plaque of the Seventh Century B.C. from Arslan Tash in Upper Syria," *BASOR* 197 (1970) 45, n.17.

of Hebrew ʿAštart and ʾAšerah (Aramaic *ʾašero*) presents no problem; indeed the form ʾΑταραγάτις from Dura-Europos noted above, the only spelling which does preserve an ending on ʾΑταρ-, is closest to Hebrew ʾAšerah. It is also to be noted that when it stands independently or as the second part of a compound name, ʿAnat's name is usually written *ʿth* or *ʿtʾ*, with the article presumably, but that the name is written *ʿt*, with no grammatical ending, when the name occurs as the first element in a compound name.[95] The second vowel of Greek ʾΑταρ- argues that the indistinct short *i* of *ʾtr-* yielded to the *a* of *ʿtr* if the two names were assimilated into one.

It is also possible to argue that the Aramaic by-form *ʾtrʿtʾ*, with initial *ʾaleph*, preserves the memory of ʾAšerah's place in the compound name Atargatis. This has been done by Michael C. Astour, who uses the evidence of *ʾtrʿtʾ* to claim that ʿAštart has no original role in the composition of the name Atargatis: "The first half of the compound name of Atargatis did not originally represent the Aramaic form of Astarte, as it is supposed, but derived in straight line from Asherah: W-S *ʾṡ̌r(t)* Aram. *ʾtr*, still preserved in the older variant *ʾtrʿth* instead of the later, more common, syncretistic *ʿtrʿth*."[96] But Astour has no basis for his claim that *ʾtrʿth* is older than

95. See the forms listed by Albright ("The Evolution of the West-Semitic Divinity ʿAn-ʿAnat-ʿAttâ," 89). Independently and as the second element in a compound name, ʿAnat's name is usually (but not always, note the Hatra form *ʾtrʿt*) written *ʿAtâ*. If this *-â* is the article, the memory of the etymological origin of ʿAnat's name may have been preserved in Syria, which would be unexpected though not without parallel. The word *ʿnt* was still understood as a noun in Egypt, according to Albright and others. Albright also argued that the "spelling עתה can surely not be explained otherwise than as a feminine absolute, in which the original feminine *t* has been taken as a stem consonant, and a second feminine ending affixed" ("The Evolution of the West-Semitic Divinity ʿAn-ʿAnat-ʿAttâ," 90), which is "clearly shown by the constant writing with *he* and not with *alef*" ("Further Observations on the Name *ʿAnat-ʿAttah*," 283); but we have now forms with a final *ʾaleph*. Ultimately, one has to admit that the ending on ʿAtâ remains a puzzle for which no satisfactory solution has been adduced.

96. *Hellenosemitica* (Leiden: E. J. Brill, 1965), p. 206.

ʿtrʿth,[97] nor for his dismissal of ʿAštart as an original component of Atargatis. The form *ʾtrʿth/ʾtrʿtʾ* is more often seen as a dissimilation of the spelling *ʿtrʿth*, and not as an independent witness for ʾAšerah's place in the composite name Atargatis. Lidzbarski, in defending the equation of Nabataean *ʾtrʿtʾ* with *ʿtrʿth*, thus analyzed the Nabataean form at the beginning of this century: "Hier wie in אתעקב kann der Übergang durch das zweite ע veranlasst sein. אתרעתא wäre dann ein Mittelglied zwischen עתרעתה and ܬܪܥܬܐ."[98] Similar analyses are offered by Albright, who sees Simplicius' etymology (τόπος θεῶν) "on the basis of the dissimilated pronunciation,"[99] by Caquot,[100] and most recently by Donner and Rollig: "Der Name [Atargatis] ist zusammengesetzt aus *ʿAstart* > *ʿAttar* > *ʾAttar* und *ʿAnat* > *ʿAttā*."[101] Especially in later material, both this dissimilation and the confusion of *ʾaleph* for *ʿayin* or *ʿayin* for *ʾaleph* are widely evidenced,[102] so that the argument that *ʾtrʿtʾ* is simply a dissimilation from *ʿtrʿth* is not unreasonable. However, the form *ʾtrʿtʾ* with initial *ʾaleph* is hardly a single aberration but occurs in material as widely separated as that from Nabataea and from Hatra; and it is at least intriguing that one never finds a spelling *ʿtrʾth*, with the second *ʿayin*

---

97. The form *ʿtrʿth* occurs already on the *ʿbd hdd* coins noted above, which cannot be later than the Nabataean and Hatra form *ʾtrʿth/ʾtrʿtʾ*. In his comprehensive study of this coinage, Ronzevalle dates all the Hierapolis *ʿbd hdd* coins prior to 312 B.C. ("Les Monnaies," 58); and René Dussaud ("Notes de mythologie syrienne," *Revue archéologique* 4th series, vol. 4 [1904] 240) dates the same coinage to 332 B.C. or soon thereafter.

98. *Eph*., vol. 1, p. 196. The same argument is voiced by Ronzevalle, who calls *ʾtrʿtʾ* "un stade intermédiaire" ("Les monnaies," 12).

99. "The Evolution of the West-Semitic Divinity ʿAn-ʿAnat-ʿAttâ," 101.

100. "Nouvelles inscriptions araméennes," *Syria* 29 (1952) 115, n.2.

101. *KAI*, vol. 2, p. 296.

102. *ʾAleph* for *ʿayin*: *ʾntḥn*, "veillecht fur עַנתחן* ''ʿAnat hat sich erbarmt'" (*KAI*, vol. 2, p. 106); or *ʾwlm* for *ʿwlm* (*KAI*, no. 128). *ʿAyin* for *ʾaleph*: *ʿdr* for *ʾdr* (*KAI*, no. 162); *ʿbn* for *ʾbn* (*KAI*, no. 166); or *ʿlnm* for *ʾlnm* (*KAI*, no. 117). For further examples of both errors, see Benz, *Personal Names*, p. 203.

dissimilated to *ʿaleph*, though this phenomenon is witnessed elsewhere.[103] While one would not wish to base an argument alone on the Aramaic spelling *ʾtrʿtʾ*, the claim that the form is always a result of the dissimilation of two *ʿayin*'s is suspiciously facile. In some cases the spelling *ʾtrʿtʾ* may well represent a composite divine name whose first element was still seen clearly to designate the goddess ʾAšerah; and the clue presented by this evidence is one substantiated by the use of ʾAšerah epithets for, and the presence of ʾAšerah attributes in, the goddess Atargatis.

The argument that *ʾtrʿtʾ* represents a legitimate and significant variant of *ʿtrʿth*, and not one based alone on dissimilation or confusion, is not, in any case, a key link in the present discussion, which, if broken, would destroy the entire chain of argument. The Aramaic forms *ʿtr* for Canaanite ʿAštart and *ʾtr* for Canaanite ʾAšerah might easily have merged, so that the spelling *ʿtrʿth* alone can preserve the place of all three major Canaanite goddesses in the one figure. A stronger link in this argument is the identification of Atargatis with Derceto, along with the latter's identification with ʾAšerah. Lucian mentions the goddess Δερκετῶ of whom there is "in Phoenicia" (ἐν Φοινίκῃ) an image which is partly a woman and partly a fish (ἡμισέη μὲν γυνή, τὸ δὲ ὁκόσον ἐκ μηρῶν ἐς ἄκρους πόδας ἰχθυός οὐρὴ ἀποτείνεται, para. 14). This image he distinguishes from that of Hera in Hierapolis which is "all woman" (πᾶσα γυνή); and hence he denies that the Hierapolis Hera is the same as Derceto (para. 14). But Lucian's own explanation of the distinction is based alone upon the difference between a single image of Derceto and a single image of Atargatis; and we will see both that Lucian, and others, associate the Hierapolis Atargatis with fish and that other representations of Atargatis picture the goddess in the company of fish. Strabo, in noting the barbarians' habit of giving alternate names to the same deity, says such people call "Athara Atargatis, while Ctesias calls the same one Derceto" (ʾΑταργάτιν δὲ τὴν ʾΑθάραν, Δερκετὼ δʾαὐτὴν Κτησίας καλεῖ).[104] Pliny says of Hierapolis, which, he

---

103. Note, for example, the personal name *ʿbdʾnt* for *ʿbdʿnt* (Benz, *Personal Names*, p. 382).

104. Strabo 16.4.27. The passage and its importance are noted by René Dussaud, "Peut-on identifier l'Apollon barbu de Hiérapolis de Syrie?" 140, n.6.

notes is natively *Mabog*, "there is worshipped the marvelous Atargatis, whom the Greeks call Derceto" *(ibi prodigiosa Atargatis, Graecis autem Derceto dicta, colitur; Historia Naturalis* 5.19 [81]). Other sources lead to the same conclusion in identifying Derceto with the Syrian Goddess. A third-century A.D. scholium to the phrase κατὰ Βαμβύκην in Germanicus' *Aratea* explains that there is worshipped "Derceto...whom the Syrians name a goddess" *(Derceto...quam Syri deam nominaverunt)*.[105] A work of perhaps the same era attributed to Eratosthenes says of the deity Derceto at Hierapolis that the goddess is she "whom those living in the area name the Syrian Goddess" (ἣν οἱ περὶ τοὺς τόπους οἰκοῦντες Συρίαν θεὸν ὠνόμασαν).[106] And a scholium to the *Iliad* reads "Derceto is called Atargatis by the Syrians" (ἡ δὲ Δερκετὼ παρα Σύροις καλεῖται 'Αταργατῖς).[107]

The identification of the Syrian Goddess/Atargatis with Derceto is, then, indisputable. Indeed, Derceto has been explained almost universally as a direct Greek transcription or slight corruption of *ʿtrʿth* or the Syrian form *trʿtʾ*. Thus, nearly a century ago, Robertson Smith stated flatly, "Derceto is a corruption of Atargatis."[108] A quarter century later Cooke wrote of the name Atargatis, "it is often Δερκετώ, Derceto";[109] and E. S. Bouchier agreed in affirming that Derceto was "assimilated to the indigenous Atargatis, of whom her name is clearly a corruption."[110] The hypothesis was long unquestioned and the list of those who repeated it is both lengthy and impressive: Macalister,[111] Cumont,[112] Paton,[113] Harmon,[114] Clemen,[115]

---

105. Cited in van Berg, *Répertoire*, no. 22 (pp. 19-20).

106. Pseudo-Eratosthenes, *Catasterismi* 38, reprinted in van Berg, *Répertoire*, no. 26 (p. 22).

107. *Scholia in Homeri Iliadem* B 461 c.-d., reprinted in van Berg, *Répertoire*, no. 61 (p. 43).

108. "Ctesias and the Semiramis Legend," 313.

109. *NSI*, p. 270.

110. *Syria as a Roman Province*, p. 268.

111. *The Philistines*, p. 95.

112. "Syria Dea," in *Dictionnaire des antiquités*, vol. 4, pt. 2, p. 1591, and "Atargatis," in *PW*, vol. 2, col. 1896.

113. "Atargatis," in Hastings' *Encyclopaedia of Religion and Ethics*, vol. 2, pp. 164-165.

114. *Lucian*, vol. 4, p. 356, n.3.

115. *LSSG*, p. 41.

Goossens,[116] Dupont-Sommer,[117] Höfer,[118] Montgomery,[119] Morin,[120] and, just over ten years ago, Fauth, who again merely notes that from *ʿtrʿth* developed "apokop. *Tarʿata̱*, woraus griech. Δερκετώ."[121]

This derivation of Derceto left unasked the question of a possible Semitic etymology for the name. There is, however, a Semitic root *drk*, "to tread," from whence comes the Ugaritic *darkatu*, "dominion." In the Keret epic, ʾĒl asks the bereaved Keret if he desires "The kingship of Bull, his (Divine-)father / Dominion like the Father of man" *(mulka ṯôri ʾabihu / darka*[*ta*] *ka-ʾabi ʾadami)*;[122] and in the Baʿl-Yamm epic, Baʿl's magic club is to "drive out Sea from his throne / River from the seat of his dominion" *(garriš yamma la-kussiʾihu / nahara la-kaḥṯi darkatihu)*.[123] For the initial recognition of the possible relation of this word to the name Derceto, we are, again, indebted to Albright. In 1934, Albright suggested tentatively, "it is not impossible that the name *Derketo*, variant of *Atargatis*, is really an appellation of the latter, meaning primarily 'dominion.'"[124] Albright subsequently abandoned his initial tentativeness.[125] While Albright felt that the title *darkatu* was an appellation of ʿAnat,[126] Cross is surely correct in countering that "*darkatu*, 'dominion' like *mulk* or *milkat*, 'royalty,' 'queen,' is appropriately applied to any one of the three great goddesses."[127]

It is possible to go beyond viewing *darkatu* as the Semitic origin of Greek Derceto and as a possible title for ʿAštart,

---

116. *Hiérapolis de Syrie*, p. 58.

117. "L'inscription de l'amulette d'Arslan Tash," 152, n.3.

118. "Syria," in Roscher's *Ausführliches Lexikon*, vol. 4, col. 163.

119. *The Book of Kings* (ICC), p. 474.

120. "The Cult of Dea Syria," 23, n.50.

121. "Dea Syria," in *Der Kleine Pauly*, vol. 1, col. 1401.

122. *CTCA* 14.41-43, omitting the verb.

123. *CTCA* 2.4.12-13.

124. "The North-Canaanite Poems of ʾAlʾêyên Baʿal and the 'Gracious Gods,'" *JPOS* 14 (1932) 130, n.153.

125. "The Oracles of Balaam," *JBL* 63 (1944) 219, n.82; and "Islam and the Religions of the Ancient Orient," 300, n.58.

126. *YGC*, p. 130.

127. *CMHE*, p. 31.

ʿAnat, or ʾAšerah, and to see *darkatu*/Derceto as best identified specifically with ʾAšerah, a step taken already by Cross.[128] This identification rests primarily on the link between both Ugaritic *ʾAṯiratu* and Greek Δερκετῶ with the sea and with fish. ʾAšerah's "marine connections"[129] are clear already from her full name in the Ugaritic texts, where the goddess is "The Lady Who Treads Upon (the) Sea" *(rabbatu ʾaṯiratu yammi)*, and these connections will be documented fully below. For Derceto's links with the sea we have not only Lucian's statement that the Phoenician Derceto was portrayed as half fish (*D.S.D.*, para. 14), but also the instructive testimony of Diodorus Siculus; Diodorus tells of the Ascalon deity "whom the Syrians call Derceto" (ἣν ὀνομάζουσιν οἱ Σύροι Δερκετοῦν), whose shrine is near "a large, deep lake, full of fish" (λίμνη μεγάλη καὶ βαθεῖα πλήρης ἰχθύων) and who is herself half fish (Diodorus Siculus 2.4.2). Ovid also relates a tale of a goddess *Derceti* who becomes a fish (*Metamorphoses* 4.44-47).

The identification of Derceto with ʾAšerah together with the use of Derceto as a title of, or in place of the name of, Atargatis, allows one to reach a conclusion already suggested by the alternate forms *ʿtrʿth* and *ʾtrʿtʾ*: Atargatis is a composite deity, as long believed, but the evidence demands that one see in her not just Aštart, as did the nineteenth-century discussion, or just ʿAštart and ʿAnat, as did Albright and others following him, but ʿAštart, ʿAnat, and ʾAšerah. In short, Atargatis is a conflation of all three major Canaanite goddesses. Thus far, this is a conclusion based primarily upon etymological speculation, though buttressed by the Derceto identification. But a summary of our knowledge of ʿAštart, ʿAnat, and ʾAšerah, set alongside what Lucian and others tell

---

128. *CMHE*, p. 31. The step has also been taken by Astour, who derives the name Derceto from a verb "*dārak*, 'to trample, to press (grapes)'" (*Hellenosemitica*, p. 187, n.9), and who also claims that Atargatis is "a slightly modified form of the great mother-goddess of the old Canaanite pantheon, Lady Asherah of the Sea *(Rbt Aṡrt Ym)* of Ugaritic myths" (*Hellenosemitica*, p. 206). Though Astour is correct in associating Derceto with ʾAšerah, one finds his insistence on some link between the root *drk* of the goddess' title and pressing of grapes somewhat bizarre.

129. The phrase is that of Cross (*CMHE*, p. 31).

us of the worship of Atargatis, makes firm this conclusion; and it is to such a summary that we turn now.

The Three Great Goddesses of the Canaanite Pantheon

ʿAštart[130]

Akkadian ^{d}*As-tar-tú*[131] and Greek 'Ἀστάρτη, Latin *Astarte* leave no doubt as to the correct pronunciation of the fertility goddess whose place of primacy among the goddesses of Syria-Palestine long seemed unchallengeable. Yet the discovery and publication of the Ugaritic texts issued just this challenge, for in the Ugaritic myths *ʿAṯtartu* plays a minor role, far surpassed by the goddesses *ʿAnatu* and *ʾAṯiratu*.[132] Even here, however, ʿAštart does have, in the words of John Gray, "a definite place in the pantheon since her name appears in offering

---

130. For summary descriptions of ʿAštart, see Cooke, *NSI*, p. 27, n.1; Albright, *YGC*, pp. 132-134; *KAI*, vol. 2, pp. 16-17; Fitzmyer, "The Phoenician Inscription from Pyrgi," 287-288; John Gray, *The Legacy of Canaan:* The Ras Shamra Texts and their Relevance to the Old Testament, Supplements to *VT*, 5, 2d ed. (Leiden: E. J. Brill, 1965), pp. 175-177; and Stadelmann, pp. 96-101.

131. The name occurs thus in the treaty between Esarhaddon and Baʿal of Tyre; see the ed. of Riekele Borger, *Die Inschriften Asarhaddons Königs von Assyrien*, Beihefte zum *Archiv für Orientforschung*, 9 (Graz, 1956), para. 69.4.18 (p. 109).

132. So too Albright, *YGC*, p. 132; James B. Pritchard, *Palestinian Figurines*, in Relation to Certain Goddesses Known Through Literature, American Oriental Series, 24 (New Haven: American Oriental Society, 1943), p. 65; and Stadelmann, p. 32 (ʿAštart's is "eine fast unbedeutende Rolle"). On the basis of the number of occurrences alone, note that while the name *ʾaṯrt* occurs in the Ugaritic texts sixty-two times (to say nothing of the occurrences of ʾAšerah under different epithets, e.g., *ʾilt* or *qdš*), and while the name *ʿnt* occurs one hundred and twenty-eight times, *ʿṯtrt* occurs but forty-six times; these counts are based upon Richard E. Whitaker's *A Concordance of the Ugaritic Literature* (Cambridge, Mass.: Harvard University Press, 1972) - see p. v for a list of the texts included in this concordance.

lists."[133] When ʿAštart does take part in the drama of the Ugaritic myths, she usually acts alongside of ʾAšerah, ʿAnat or some other deity. Twice she seems to appear as a war goddess, acting in concert with Ḥôrān. The Keret epic breaks off with Keret invoking the following curse against his son, who has used the occasion of the king's illness to consider usurping his father's throne: "May Ḥôrān break, oh my son / May Ḥôrān break your head / May ʿAštart name-of-Baʿl (break) your skull" *(yaṯbura ḥôrānu ya-binī / yaṯburu ḥôrānu riʾšaka / ʿaṯtartu šim baʿli qudqudaka).*[134] Her action here with Ḥôrān seems typical, since the curse, in broken form, occurs again at the outset of the Baʿl Yamm epic.[135] Beyond activities carried out together

---

133. *The Legacy of Canaan*, p. 175.

134. *CTCA* 16.6.54-57.

135. *CTCA* 2.1.7-8. The *De Syria Dea* contains a hint that Ḥôrān's identification with Greek Atlas, proposed by Albright and others, may be correct. To his description of the side temple in which sits the image of the bearded Apollo, Lucian appends a note that beside this Apollo are the images of Atlas, Hermes, and Eileithyia (μετὰ δὲ τὸν ʼΑπόλλωνα ξόανόν ἐστιν ῎Ατλαντος, μετὰ δὲ ʽΕρμέω καὶ Εἰλειθυίης, para. 38). The pairing of Hermes, who is usually the equivalent of Nabu (see Ingholt, "Parthian Sculptures," 31 and 41, and the references there), with Eileithyia makes little sense; and Lucian may well have misconstrued the arrangement of the idols. If the correct pairing is to set Atlas alongside of Eileithyia, this is a significant piece of evidence for the identification of Ḥôrān with Atlas. Eileithyia is the divine midwife in Greek tradition (Harmon, *Lucian*, vol. 4, p. 392, n.2 and Rose, *Religion in Greece and Rome*, p. 30), as Lucian himself notes in his *Dialogi Deorum* 225, and as seen clearly in Diodorus Siculus 5.73.4: "Eileithyia received the charge of those giving birth and the care of those suffering the pains of childbirth; hence, those who are thus endangered call especially upon this goddess" (Εἰλείθυιαν δὲ λαβεῖν τὴν περὶ τὰς τικτούσας ἐπιμέλειαν καὶ θεραπείαν τῶν ἐν τῷ τίκτειν κακοπαθουσῶν. διὸ καὶ τὰς ἐν τοῖς τοιούτοις κινδυνευούσας γυναῖκας ἐπικαλεῖσθαι μάλιστα τὴν θεὸν ταύτην). Now, as Albright has ingeniously and convincingly demonstrated, the consort of Ḥôrān according to Philo Byblios is "*Thūrō* (= *Tĕwūre*, later *Thŏēris*), name of the Egyptian goddess of childbirth....expressly identified by Philo with

with other deities, however, ʿAštart acts too seldomly at Ugarit for her character to receive any memorable stamp.

In Egypt, ʿAštart is, with the goddess ʿAnat especially, a deity of love and of war.[136] In a representation from the New Kingdom, ʿAštart is seen playing both roles, for she is here "a naked girl, with immature breasts, astride a galloping stallion... armed either with bow and arrows or with shield and javelin."[137]

Chūsarthis (= *Kûšart*, singular of the word which appears in Hebrew as *Kôšārôt*)" (*YGC*, p. 138, n.73, cf. p. 248); and Ḥôrān's association with the birth goddess is now clearer in the incantation text RS 24.244. For the *kṯrm/kṯrt* assisting at childbirth at Ugarit, see *CTCA* 2.3.20; 11.6; 14.16; and 17.2.26-40. One could hardly claim that the pairing of Atlas with Eileithyia, which is apparently present in the description in the *D.S.D.*, together with the pairing of *ḥrn* with *kṯrt* from Phoenician lore proves the identification of Ḥôrān with Greek Atlas; the evidence does, however, add strength to this identification as argued on grounds wholly independent of Lucian's description. See Cross and Saley, "Phoenician Incantations on a Plaque of the Seventh Century from Arslan Tash in Upper Syria," 47-48, for a statement of the evidence associating Ḥôrān with Atlas. But note the arguments against this identification in Clapham, "Sancuniathon," 163 (Ḥôrān is not, in Sakkunyaton, of the correct generation to be Atlas), and in R. B. Coote, "The Serpent and Sacred Marriage in Northwest Semitic Tradition" (unpublished Ph.D. dissertation, Harvard University, 1972), 14, n.9 (Albright's etymology for Ḥôrān as "'One of the Pit'" seems unlikely in "the light of etymological *ḫ in *ḫr, 'pit'"). Stadelmann rejects both Albright's view that Ḥôrān is Atlas and John Gray's position that Ḥôrān is ʾEšmun, to conclude pessimistically, "mir scheint, das vorliegende Material ist zu dürftig" (Stadelmann, p. 79, n.6).

136. Stadelmann (pp. 101-110) summarizes the evidence for ʿAštart's role in Egypt. Note too the briefer summary in Wolfgang Helck's monumental *Die Beziehungen Ägyptens zu Vorderasien im 3. und 2. Jahrtausend v. Chr.*, 2d ed., Ägyptologische Abhandlungen (ed. Wolfgang Helck und Eberhard Otto), vol. 5 (Wiesbaden: Otto Harrassowitz, 1971), pp. 456-458.

137. Albright, *YGC*, p. 133; cf. p. 133, n.60 for another similar portrayal which combines ʿAštart and ʿAnat, and see also *FSAC*, p. 177, and Pritchard, *Figurines*, pp. 67-68.

Her role as a war goddess in Egypt is seen with especial clarity in a group of stelae pictured and described in Jean Leclant's lengthy article, "Astarté à cheval d'après les représentations égyptiennes."[138] When inscribed with the goddess' name, these stelae prove the identity of ʿAštart with the series of war goddess representations in Egypt showing the goddess armed and riding a horse; thus, a stele from Memphis is read by Leclant, "'Astarté maîtresse du ciel, régente de tous les dieux,'"[139] while another is inscribed, "'Astarté, dame des combats, déesse des Asiatiques.'"[140] ʿAštart's portrayal as a war goddess does not come to an end with the second millennium; "noch in der Ptölemaerzeit is ihre Eigenschaft als 'Herrin der Pferde und des Streitwagens' lebendig."[141] As goddess of love, ʿAštart is combined with ʿAnat, and the two are referred to as "'the two great goddesses who were pregnant but did not bear.'"[142] This too is a tradition which continued into later times, when ʿAštart was identified with Isis; thus a Memphis stele of the first or second century B.C. is dedicated "To my lady, the awesome deity Isis, the deity ʿAštart" *(lrbty lʾlm ʾdrt ʾs ʾlm ʿštrt)*.[143]

In the Phoenician-Punic world, the cult of ʿAštart is witnessed by a great many sources, of diverse date and from the entire Mediterranean basin;[144] and it was upon the basis of these sources that ʿAštart was claimed as the preeminent Canaanite goddess before the discovery of the Ugaritic texts. Evidence for the worship of ʿAštart at Sidon is especially impressive.

---

138. *Syria* 37 (1960) 1-67. Leclant's conclusions are endorsed by Stadelmann (pp. 99-101).

139. Leclant, "Astarté à cheval, " 12 and fig. 1.

140. Leclant, "Astarté à cheval," 25, quoting G. Bénédite.

141. Stadelmann, p. 102.

142. From the Papyrus Harris, as cited in Pritchard, *Figurines*, p. 79; cf. W. F. Albright, "The North-Canaanite Epic of ʾAlʾêyân Baʿal and Môt," *JPOS* 12 (1932) 193, and *FSAC*, p. 177.

143. *KAI*, no. 43; cf. Benz, *Personal Names*, p. 271. In Egyptian sources, Isis is identified with both ʿAštart and Aphrodite (*KAI*, vol. 2, p. 65); the latter is, as we will see, ʿAštart's usual Greek equivalent.

144. For lists of sites where evidence for the worship of ʿAštart has come to light, see Cooke, *NSI*, p. 27, n.1; *KAI*, vol. 2, p. 18; and Benz, *Personal Names*, p. 386.

Lucian himself bears witness to ʿAštart's cult at Sidon: "There is another great shrine in Phoenician, which belongs to the Sidonians; they say themselves that it is Astarte's" (ἔνι δὲ καὶ ἄλλο ἱρὸν ἐν Φοινίκῃ μέγα, τὸ Σιδώνιοι ἔχουσιν, ὡς μὲν αὐτοὶ λέγουσιν, Ἀστάρτης ἐστίν, *D.S.D.*, para. 4). Tabnit, a sixth-century B.C. king of Sidon, labels both his father ʾEšmunʿazōr and himself priests of ʿAštart *(khn ʿštrt)*.[145] A descendant of Tabnit, who bears the name ʾEšmunʿazōr again, mentions that his mother is named *ʾmʿštrt*,[146] a name which is surely to be translated "ʿAštart is (Divine-)mother," rather than emended to *ʾmtʿštrt* and translated "'*serva Astartes*,'" as is done by the editors of the *Corpus Inscriptionum Semiticarum*.[147]

Though her cult is especially well attested at Sidon, ʿAštart was worshipped elsewhere in Syria-Palestine and the surrounding lands. A second-century B.C. inscription from Tyre is dedicated "to ʿAštart" *(lʿštrt)*,[148] as is a third-century B.C. inscription from Maʿṣūb, south of Tyre.[149] And a box from the seventh-century B.C. found at Ur records a "gift" *(mtt)* "to ʿAštart" *(lʿštrt)*.[150]

Some scholars have found evidence for ʿAštart's cult at Byblos by identifying ʿAštart with the "Lady of Byblos" *(bʿlt gbl)*, a title which occurs on several inscriptions from the tenth century and later,[151] and already in the Amarna Letters as "^{iltu}*bêlit ša gubla*."[152] In the *D.S.D.* paragraph 6, Lucian

145. *KAI*, no. 13.

146. *KAI*, no. 14.

147. *KAI*, vol. 1, p. 17; the error is repeated by Cooke (*NSI*, p. 36), but Donner and Röllig correctly translate "'Mutter (ist) ʿAštart'" (*KAI*, vol. 2, p. 22).

148. *KAI*, no. 17.

149. *KAI*, no. 19.

150. *KAI*, no. 29.

151. The title occurs, for example, on the inscriptions of ʾElibaʿl (*KAI*, no. 6) and Sipiṭbaʿl (*KAI*, no. 7), and is restored from the reading *bʿl gbl* on the inscription of Yeḥimilk (*KAI*, no. 4) by W. F. Albright ("The Phoenician Inscriptions of the Tenth Century B.C. from Byblos," *JAOS* 67 [1947] 156, n.32) and by Donner and Röllig (*KAI*,,vol. 2, p. 7).

152. See the list in the glossary on p. 1583 (prepared by Erich Ebeling) in Jørgen Alexander Knudtzon, *Die El-Amarna-Tafeln* (Aalen: O. Zeller, 1964 [reprint of ed. of 1915]).

claims to have seen "a great shrine of Aphrodite of Byblos" (μέγα ἱρὸν Ἀφροδίτης Βυβλίης), which does add support for the identification of *bʿlt gbl* with ʿAštart, since the latter's usual Greek name was Aphrodite. Thus, Moscati[153] and, much earlier, Cooke make the identification of ʿAštart with *bʿlt gbl*, the latter claiming "there can be little doubt that the Baʿalath of Gebal was ʿAshtart."[154] However, there can be and is doubt. *Baʿlatu*, like *darkatu*, is a title appropriate for any one of the major Canaanite goddesses; and a text from *Ugaritica V* applies the title three times to ʿAnat rather than to ʿAštart.[155] In fact, the best hypothesis is that which sees in *bʿlt gbl* neither ʿAštart nor ʿAnat, but ʾAšerah.[156] Cross notes that *bʿlt* is "a favourite epithet of Canaanite Asherah."[157] Further, the links between Byblos and Egypt, and between the Lady of Byblos and Egyptian Ḥatḥor, are well established; and these too point to the identity of *bʿlt gbl* with ʾAšerah.[158]

There can be no doubt, however, that ʿAštart was worshipped on Cyprus and in the western Mediterranean. A Kition inscription copied by Pococke in 1738 is dedicated "To Lady ʿAštart" *(lrbt lʿštrt)*;[159] and another inscription from Cyprus witnesses the personal name "maid of Aštart" *(ʾmt štrt)*.[160] On Malta,

---

153. *WP*, p. 34.

154. *NSI*, p. 21.

155. RS 24.252 (*Ugaritica V*, no. 2); the titles are *bʿlt mlk*, *bʿlt drkt*, and *bʿlt šmm rmm*.

156. A suggestion made already in 1943 by Pritchard (*Figurines*, p. 71).

157. Frank Moore Cross, Jr., "The Origin and Early Evolution of the Alphabet," *Eretz Israel* 8 (1967) 8*.

158. Egyptian Ḥatḥor is identified with Qudšu (Stadelmann, p. 122), which is, as we will see, an epithet of Canaanite ʾAšerah. Further, Albright has restored the reading *tnt lb*[*ʿlt*] on a Proto-Sinaitic text from the Ḥatḥor temple (*The Proto-Sinaitic Inscriptions and Their Decipherment*, Harvard Theological Studies, 22 [Cambridge, Mass.: Harvard University Press, 1969], p. 17); and Cross has seen that *tnt* and *bʿlt* are here "parallel epithets" (*CMHE*, p. 32).

159. *KAI*, no. 33; see *CIS*, vol. 1, p. 11, for the story of Pococke's copying of the inscription, which was subsequently lost.

160. *KAI*, no. 35; cf. *NSI*, p. 36.

we hear of a "temple of ʿAštart" *(mqdš bt ʿštrt)*.[161] Inscriptions dedicated to ʿAštart have been discovered in Sicily,[162] and Sardinia;[163] and the recently published Pyrgi inscription bears the same dedication.[164] Names compounded with ʿAštart are found both often and over a wide area in the Mediterranean basin.[165]

The Old Testament confirms ʿAštart's major presence at Sidon and her character as a fertility goddess. As a divine name, ʿAštart is vocalized in the Old Testament usually as a plural *(ʿaštārôt)* but also as a singular *(ʿaštōret)*, the latter traditionally, though probably wrongly, explained as a contamination from the vocalization of the noun *bōšet*, "shame."[166] The Greek translators of the Hebrew Bible witness a similar ambiguity, rendering the goddess' name as Ἀστάρτη (for example, 1 Kings 11:33), but also as Ἀσταρῶθ (Judges 10:6; 1 Samuel 7:4), Ἀσταρτεῖον (1 Samuel 31:10), and even as τὰ ἄλση (1 Samuel 7:3; cf. 12:10), which is more often a translation of the symbols of the goddess ʾAšerah. 1 Kings 11:5, 11:33 and 2 Kings 23:13 all link ʿAštart with Sidon; and the singular form *(ʿaštōret)* is found only when connected with the Sidonians' worship (1 Kings 11:5, 11:33; 2 Kings 23:13). Baethgen claimed

---

161. *KAI*, no. 62.

162. *CIS*, vol. 1, no. 135.

163. *CIS*, vol. 1, no. 140.

164. *KAI*, no. 277; on ʿAštart's presence here, see Fitzmyer, "The Phoenician Inscription from Pyrgi," 287-288.

165. Benz, *Personal Names*, pp. 386-387. The great frequency of names with ʿAštart as the theophorous element was noted already by Baethgen in the last century (*Beiträge*, p. 36).

166. Otto Eissfeldt writes that ʿAštart's "Name in Alten Testament zu *ʿastōret* [*sic*] entstellt ist und damit (Vocale *o* und *e*!) an *bōšet* 'Schande' erinnern, die Göttin also als einen schändlichen Götzen brandmarken will" ("Zum geographischen Horizant der Ras-Schamra-Texte," *ZDMG* 94 [1940] 77, n.1). Cf. Montgomery, *The Books of Kings* (ICC), p. 245, Moscati, *WP*, p. 34, and Stadelmann, pp. 96-97. Though the biblical form *ʿaštōret* is difficult to explain, since one would not expect the *a* vowel to become *ō* in this position, the argument that the form is a contamination from *bōšet* is without evidence and is difficult to accept. Can the form be a result of a conformity to ʿAštōr?

"bei den Philistern war Astarte Kriegsgöttin";[167] but he substantiates this claim only by citing 1 Samuel 31:10, where we read that the Philistines placed the armor of the slain Saul in the "temple of ʿAštart" *(bêt ʿaštārôt)*. Still, this note does agree with the evidence from Ugarit and Egypt, where ʿAštart's martial role is clear. There is in the Old Testament also a noun formed from the goddess' name, which indicates her character as a fertility goddess. The noun occurs four times in the Book of Deuteronomy (7:13; 28:4, 18, 51), always in the phrase traditionally translated "increase of your flock" *(ʿaštĕrôt ṣōʾnekā)*, always accompanying and parallel to the phrase "offspring of your cattle" *(šĕgar(-)ʾălāpêkā)*. Though the root *šgr* occurs elsewhere in the Old Testament only in Exodus 13:12, the Aramaic verb *šĕgar*, "to drop," Pa. *šaggar*, "to drop (young)," "to give birth,"[168] establishes the meaning of *šĕgar(-)ʾălāpêkā* and hence the link between the noun *ʿaštĕrôt* and ʿAštart's fertility function.[169]

In keeping with her role as a fertility goddess is ʿAštart's frequent identification with Greek Aphrodite.[170] Evidence for this identification abounds, but especially instructive is a

---

167. *Beiträge*, p. 34; the same is suggested more tentatively by Pritchard (*Figurines*, p. 69).

168. On Aramaic *šgr*, see Marcus Jastrow, *A Dictionary of the Targumim, the Talmud Babli and Yerushalmi, and the Midrashic Literature* (New York: Judaica Press, 1971), p. 1522b, and S. R. Driver, *A Critical and Exegetical Commentary on Deuteronomy*, ICC, 3d ed. (Edinburgh: T. & T. Clark, 1902), p. 103.

169. Thus too Albright: the noun is used "in the sense of '(sheep) breeding'" (*ARI*, p. 75); and Pritchard (*Figurines*, p. 72). S. R. Driver argued that the noun "must have its origin in the name of the goddess *ʿAshtōreth*, and appears to show that this deity, under one of her types, had the form of a sheep" (*Deuteronomy* [ICC], p. 103); for the latter suggestion, that ʿAštart had the form of a sheep, there is no further evidence.

170. For general statements of, and summaries of evidence for, the ʿAštart-Aphrodite identification, see Baethgen, *Beiträge*, p. 34; Cooke, *NSI*, p. 27, n.1; *KAI*, vol. 2, p. 18; Fitzmyer, "The Phoenician Inscription from Pyrgi," 288; and Stadelmann, p. 97.

fourth-century B.C. Phoenician-Greek bilingual from Athens.[171] Here, the writer, who describes himself as an "Ascalonite" (*'šqlny*/'Ασκα[λωνίτης]), gives his father's name as *'bd'štrt*; and this name is rendered 'Αφροδίσιος in Greek, thus suggesting an identification of the Semitic 'Aštart with the Greek goddess of sexual love.

'Anat[172]

'Anat asserts her presence (whether or not her name means "Presence") in the mythological texts from Ugarit more often than either 'Ašerah or 'Aštart;[173] and it is a fair assumption that she maintained a role in Canaanite religion after the second millennium B.C., even if direct evidence for her subsequent role is scant.[174] At Ugarit, 'Anat's standard epithet is

---

171. *KAI*, no. 54; cf. Lidzbarski, *Eph.*, vol. 1, p. 150 and p. 151, n.1.

172. An especially good summary of 'Anat's functions and of the evidence attesting to her place in the Canaanite pantheon is to be found in Stadelmann, pp. 88-91. A lengthier treatment can be found in Arvid S. Kapelrud, *The Violent Goddess*: Anat in the Ras Shamra Texts (Oslo: Universitetsforlaget, 1969), but note the correctives in the review of Johannes C. de Moor, *Ugarit-Forschungen* 1 (1969) 223-227. Albright long argued that the etymology of 'Anat's name is to be sought in Akkadian *ettu/ittu*, biblical Hebrew *'ēt* and that the name originally meant "'sign, indication of purpose, active will'" (*ARI*, p. 75, n.14; cf. "The North-Canaanite Epic of 'Al'êyân Ba'al and Môt," 193 and n.24). For Albright, this etymological background surfaces in the divine name 'Anat-Bêt'el of the Elephantine papyri, which divine name Albright understands to mean "'Sign (of the Active Presence) of God'" (*ARI*, p. 174). While this view is attractive and might, as we noted above (n. 95), provide the basis for an explanation of the troublesome -*â* in the divine name *'Atâ*, there are problems with it; for example, the original initial consonant of Akkadian *ittu* need not be *'ayin*.

173. See the data collected in n.132 above.

174. Cf. the statement of Donner and Röllig: 'Anat "spielt...eine führende Rolle im ugaritischen und so wohl auch im gemeinkanaanäischen Pantheon" (*KAI*, vol. 2, p. 69). Evidence for 'Anat's subsequent role is given below.

batultu, "virgin."[175] Yet ʿAnat was no ordinary virgin. Both she and ʾAšerah are said to be divine wet nurses *(mšnqt)*, from whose breasts a child may suck;[176] and she had as mates certainly Baʿl Haddu and perhaps also ʾĒl, as we will see below. The "theological background" of ʿAnat's epithet *batultu* is, for de Moor, "that ʿAnatu, although she did have intercourse, never brought forth offspring."[177] But it seems equally important to assert that the epithet accented ʿAnat's sexual attractiveness; and many scholars would take issue with the claim that ʿAnat "never brought forth offspring."[178]

---

175. Soo too Pritchard, who translates both *btlt* and *rḥm* as "'maiden,' 'virgin'" (*Figurines*, p. 76), and Donner and Röllig (*KAI*, vol. 2, p. 59). Sakkunyaton calls both ʿAnat and ʿAštart virgins (Albright, *ARI*, p. 75).

176. *CTCA* 15.2.26-28, supplying a *t* after *mšnq* (see Herdner, *ad loc.*). ʿAnat's name is restored here by both H. L. Ginsberg (*The Legend of King Keret:* A Canaanite Epic of the Bronze Age, Bulletin of the American Schools of Oriental Research, Supplementary Studies, nos. 2-3 [New Haven: American Schools of Oriental Research, 1946], p. 23) and G. R. Driver (*Canaanite Myths and Legends*, Old Testament Studies Published under the Auspices of the Society for Old Testament Study, no. 3 [Edinburgh: T. & T. Clark, 1956], p. 37), as seems certain following *btlt*.

177. Johannes C. de Moor, "Studies in the New Alphabetic Texts from Ras Shamra I," *Ugarit-Forschungen* 1 (1969) 182.

178. For example, Stadelmann, who is in good company in asserting of ʿAnat "dass sie als Geliebte Baʿls bezeichnet wird und ihm einen Wildstier geboren hat" (p. 90). Stadelmann is certainly justified in reading *CTCA* 10 as the text of Baʿl and ʿAnat's mating; however, as Professor Cross has reminded me, the animal names here serve also as designations of classes of nobility, so it is not quite accurate to say that ʿAnat bears "einen Wildstier." We hear of an "ox" *(ʾlp)* and a "cow" *(ypt)* born to Anat (*CTCA* 10.3.3-4), a "stallion" *(ʾibr)* and a "wild bull" *(rʾum)* born to Baʿl (*CTCA* 10.3.34-35); but *ʾibr* and *rʾum*, for example, could as well be translated "prince" and "lord." The phenomenon is widespread in both Ugaritic and Hebrew. Thus, B. Mazar has seen in Psalm 57:5 a reference to "mercenaries called *l*^{e}*bāʾîm*, probably a military corps whose emblem was the lion-goddess" ("The Military Élite of King David," *VT* 13 [1963]

Regularly in the Ugaritic texts the consort of *batultu ʿanatu* is Baʿl, who bears the appellations *haddu* and *ʾalʾiyānu.*[179] ʿAnat is called Baʿl's "sister" *(ʾaḫt)*;[180] but she is so plainly also his consort that the term may mean merely "fellow deity," since all the deities of Ugarit can be called the offspring of ʾĒl and ʾAšerah, or is a term of endearment, as is true of Hebrew *ʾāḥôt.*[181] The two deities act often in concert. Thus, for example, ʾAšerah sees "the coming of Baʿl" *(halāka baʿli)*, then "the coming of Virgin ʿAnat" *(halāka batulti ʿanati)*,[182] as the two deities arrive to enlist ʾAšerah's help in obtaining from ʾĒl permission to build a palace for Baʿl: "ʾAlʾiyan Baʿl arrived / The Virgin ʿAnat arrived / The two beseeched {Lady} ʾAšerah of the Sea / The two entreated the Creatress of the gods" *(maǵaya ʾalʾiyānu baʿlu / maǵayat batultu ʿanatu /*

---

312). See Cross, *CMHE*, p. 4, n.6, and the comprehensive study of Patrick D. Miller "Animal Names as Designations in Ugaritic and Hebrew," *Ugarit-Forschungen* 2 (1970) 177-186. Miller writes of *ʾabbîr*, "every usage of *ʾabbîr* in Hebrew can be understood either as referring to bulls or horses or as a metaphorical designation for soldiers, princes, or leaders, except possibly for the idiom *ʾabbîrê lēb*" ("Animal Names," 180).

179. The old view that Baʿl and ʾAlʾiyānu are to be distinguished has found increasingly fewer supporters. With regard to the latter epithet, Albright originally argued that it was "a good elative, from some adjective meaning 'might,' derived from the stem *lʾy* 'to be mighty, able'" ("The North-Canaanite Epic of ʾAlʾêyân Baʿal and Môt," 189). But Albright later viewed *ʾalʾiyānu* as "an abbreviation of the full formula *ʾalʾiyu qurâdîma qâriyêya baʾarṣi malḥâmati*, 'I prevail over the heroes whom I meet in the land of battle'" (*ARI*, p. 73, n. 11). The epithet is, then, simply a first person singular imperfect, from an original liturgical phrase, onto which was added the ending *-ānu*, a common ending for hypocoristica (see Cross, *CMHE*, pp. 66-67, and p. 66, n.80); this seems the right understanding of *ʾalʾiyānu* even if Albright's "full formula" is too full.

180. E.g., in *CTCA* 3.4.83, or 10.2.15-20.

181. The usage is particularly clear in Canticles 4:12, where "sister" occurs alongside "bride" *(kallâ)*.

182. *CTCA* 4.2.13-15; the verbs are vocalized as infinite absolutes.

tamagginâni {*rabbata*} [*'a*]*ṯirata yammi / taǵẓiyâni qâniyata 'ilîma).*[183] It is quite correct to say, with Kapelrud, of ʻAnat's relationship to Baʻl, that she "is closely connected with this god, so closely that practically nothing is related about her when she is not in some way or other, working for Baal or doing his errands."[184] It is possible that ʻAnat is also one of 'Ēl's mates in the poem known as "The Birth of the Gracious Gods" (*CTCA* 23).[185] In this text, whose cultic function is indicated by occasional rubrics directed to the dramatic participants (for example l. 12, or ll. 18-19), 'Ēl's "wives" *('aṯṯatâmi)* or "daughters" *(bittâmi)* whom he "seduces" *(yapattî,* l. 39) are named *'Aṯiratu* and *Raḥmayu.*[186] Elsewhere, ʻAnat is called *rḥm*, so that the conclusion is enticing that 'Ēl's two wives in the poem are 'Ašerah and ʻAnat, unless *'atrt . wrḥmy* is to be seen as a designation of 'Ašerah alone.[187] The question

---

183. *CTCA* 4.3.23-26, vocalizing the latter two verbs as duals. If one omits *rabbata*, the quatrain yields a beautifully balanced syllable count of 9:9::11:11; see now the treatment of Frank Moore Cross ("Prose and Poetry in the Mythic and Epic Texts from Ugarit," *HTR* 67 [1974] 11-12), who also excises *rabbata*.

184. *The Violent Goddess*, p. 41. Indeed, Kapelrud continues, this close relationship "has made it hard to keep the deeds and victories of one from those of the other" (p. 48). Cf. the statement of Cross with respect to the defeat of a dragon and of Sea: "In the mixed tradition preserved at Ugarit, both Baʻl and his consort ʻAnat are credited with killing the seven-headed dragon. Both also are credited with victorious battles over Yamm-Nahar. Evidently we have in each case 'alloforms' of the basic cosmogonic myth" (*CMHE*, p. 149).

185. See the recent study of the poem as a type of *hieros gamos* text in Cross, *CMHE*, pp. 22-24.

186. *CTCA* 23.28, cf. 23.13. At least the line *šadu 'ilimi šadu 'aṯirati wa-raḥmayi*, "The field (=precinct?) of 'El, the field of 'Ašerah and Raḥmay," would seem to give the names of the three chief divine participants in the drama; see n.187 below.

187. See *CTCA* 6.2.27 for *rḥm ʻnt*. In his *Baal in the Ras Shamra Texts* (Copehhagen: G. E. C. Gad, 1952), Arvid S. Kapelrud finds "little doubt that the goddess *rḥm* or *rḥmy*...is identical with ʻAnat" (p. 70); and the same conclusion is reached

of the various pairings of the chief Canaanite deities in the Ugaritic myths, the Old Testament, and in Phoenician tradition is one to which we will return.

ʿAnat's most memorable role in the Ugaritic myths is that which she plays as a war goddess. Representations from Ras Shamra, one of which shows the enthroned goddess asserting her power with "a mace in her right hand and a spear and shield in her left hand,"[188] coincide with her character as revealed in the literary sources, in which she "shows her mettle on gods, men and primaeval monsters."[189] *CTCA* 3, the most extended and sanguine portrait of ʿAnat as warrior, shows the goddess swimming in blood, her continued happiness dependent upon shedding more. Not even before ʾĒl, the acknowledged head of the pantheon, does ʿAnat shrink, as she threatens him with characteristic violence should he refuse a palace to her consort Baʿl (*CTCA* 3.4.6ff.).

As was the case with the goddess ʿAštart, ʿAnat's portrait as sketched from the Ugaritic myths is filled out from Egyptian representations of and tales about this fearsome yet desirable goddess.[190] In a Canaanite myth preserved in Egypt, we see

---

by Clapham, "Sancuniathon," 103. However, the phenomenon of two appellations designating a single deity is widespread in Ugaritic, so *ʾaṯrt . wrḥmy* may well designate ʾAšerah alone, with ʾĒl's two wives unnamed and probably minor deities, like those whose birth this poem proclaims. *Rḥmy* will then be a name of ʾAšerah, *rḥm* ("maiden") an epithet appropriate for any goddess. However, note the word divider between *ʾaṯrt* and *wrḥmy*, though *kṯr wḫss*, a common dual name occurs both with and without a word divider between the two elements of the name.

188. The description is that of Marvin Pope in his review of Umberto Cassuto's *The Goddess Anath* [Hebrew] (Jerusalem: The Bialik Institute, 1951), describing the frontispiece to Cassuto's book, in *JCS* 6 (1952) 134. The frontispiece is reproduced in the English ed. of *The Goddess Anath* (Jersualem: Magnes Press, 1971).

189. John Gray, *The Legacy of Canaan*, p. 174.

190. There is, again, an excellent summary of ʿAnat in Egypt in Stadelmann, pp. 91-96; note too the briefer description in Helck, *Die Beziehungen*, pp. 460-463, and the discussion of ʿAnat's later role in Egypt compared with the earlier witnesses in Albert Vincent, *La religion des Judéo-Araméens d'Eléphantine* (Paris: Paul Geuthner, 1937), pp. 634-635.

"'Anath the Victorious, a man-like woman, dressed as a man but girded as a woman.'"[191] Nor are we dependent on literary evidence alone for her role in Egypt: "Auf ägyptischen Darstellungen erscheint sie nackt, Schild und Speer in Händen, rittlings auf einem Pferd."[192] These representations recall ʻAnat's role at Ugarit, but also the Egyptian portrayals of ʻAštart; and in Egypt especially it is difficult to distinguish between the two goddesses. Thus a Ramses III monument bears an inscription translated by Stadelmann, "'ʻAnat und ʻAstarte ein Schild für den König.'"[193] Both ʻAnat and ʻAštart are war goddesses along the Nile.[194]

We have noted already that in Egypt ʻAnat and ʻAštart are together called "'the two great goddesses who were pregnant but did not bear.'"[195] Yet in Egypt as in Ugarit ʻAnat is a virgin who can be a wet nurse: "In Ägypten ist ʻAnat die Amme des Königs, durch deren Milch der junge König Mut and Kraft erlangt."[196] Further, Ramses II calls her, in the translation of Stadelmann, "'Mutter'"; and she replies, "'ich bin Deine Mutter.'"[197] Stadelmann argues convincingly that this exchange implies not merely that Ramses II had an especial affection for this goddess, but also that ʻAnat is, in Egypt as in Syria, a "Fruchtbarkeitsgöttin."[198]

Little is heard of ʻAnat in Phoenician or Punic sources, upon which was based the formerly slight assessment of ʻAnat's role in Syria-Palestine. The inscription *ʻbd lb(ʾ)t* on the El-Khadr arrowheads of the twelfth century B.C. is translated by Cross "'servant of the Lion-Lady' (i.e. ʻAnat)";[199] but we

---

191. Albright, *YGC*, p. 129; cf. Dupont-Sommer, "Une stèle araméenne d'un prêtre de Baʻal trouvée en Egypte," 87.

192. *KAI*, vol. 2, p. 59. Similar descriptions of ʻAnat's representations in Egypt are given by Cooke (*NSI*, p. 81), by Albright ("The Evolution of the West-Semitic Divinity ʻAn-ʻAnat-ʻAttâ," 82), and by Stadelmann (p. 95).

193. Stadelmann, p. 95; Ramses' words were noted already by Baethgen (*Beiträge*, p. 52).

194. Albright, *FSAC*, p. 177.

195. See n.142 above.

196. Stadelmann, p. 90.

197. Stadelmann, p. 92.

198. Stadelmann, p. 94.

199. "The Origin and Early Evolution of the Alphabet,"

will see that lions are associated, almost equally, with all three great Canaanite goddesses. ʿAnat then fades from sight on the mainland, though this is doubtlessly a result of our localized and still very incomplete evidence. There is no certain occurrence of ʿAnat as a divine name in the Old Testament.[200] On Cyprus, ʿAnat's continued vitality is witnessed by two dedications, whose provenance (one is on a helmet, the other on a lance) suggests that ʿAnat continued her role as a war goddess.[201] The suggestion becomes plain statement on a fourth-century B.C. Phoenician-Greek bilingual text from Cyprus.[202] The deity to whom the inscription is dedicated is written *ʿnt ʿz ḥym,*[203]

13*. Cross notes that she is "goddess of war and probably patroness of archers. Her machinations to acquire a composite bow and arrow is a central thread of the Aqhat Epic" (13*, n. 33). Donner and Röllig are less certain, and willing only to see here either ʿAštart or ʿAnat (*KAI*, vol. 2, p. 29), while in his recently published *Canaanite Myth and Hebrew Epic*, Cross sees *labiʾtu* as an epithet of ʾAšerah (p. 33).

200. In Judges 3:31 we hear of *šamgar ben-ʿănāt*, which may witness such an occurrence. Albright argued that "*Shamgar ben-ʿAnat* means simply 'Shamgar of Bet- Anat'....In Punic inscriptions בן צר, 'son of Tyre,' means 'Tyrian'" ("The Evolution of the West-Semitic Divinity ʿAn-ʿAnat-ʿAttâ," 84). Recently, Robert G. Boling has questioned this and argued that "the Anathite" *(bn-ʿnt)* "may be merely a military designation" which identifies Shamgar as a mercenary (*Judges*, The Anchor Bible, 6A [Garden City, N.Y.: Doubleday, 1975], p. 89).

201. See J. Brian Peckham, S.J., *The Development of the Late Phoenician Scripts*, Harvard Semitic Series, 20 (Cambridge, Mass.: Harvard University Press, 1968), p. 17, n.24.

202. *KAI*, no. 42.

203. *ʿnt ʿz ḥym* is read here by Baethgen (*Beiträge*, p. 53), by the editors of *CIS* (vol. 1, no. 95), by Cooke (*NSI*, p. 88), by Baudissin (*Adonis und Esmun*, p. 18 and p. 23), by Albright ("The Evolution of the West-Semitic Divinity ʿAn-ʿAnat-ʿAttâ," 82), and by Cassuto (*The Goddess Anath*, p. 64). Donner and Röllig, however, read *ʿnt mʿz ḥym KAI*, no. 42), as do Charles-F. Jean and Jacob Hoftijzer (*DISO*, p. 205). There is no *m* visible on the plate in *CIS* (vol. 1, p. 14), nor does there appear to be room for a letter before the ʿ. See also the drawing in Lidzbarski, *NE*, tf. 6, no. 5. Has the biblical

"'Anat, the strength of the living," in Phoenician, and 'Αθηνᾷ Σωτείρᾳ Νίκῃ in Greek. No clearer statement of ʿAnat's martial role is available than this identification of the goddess with Athena. Though a full discussion of ʿAnat and Atargatis will follow the review of ʾAšerah below, in connection with this bilingual we do note an Aramaic personal name *ʿtrʿzh*, which seems to combine the *ʿtr* of the first half of Atargatis' compound name with the stem *ʿzz* used of ʿAnat/Athena,[204] and again in this connection, a third-century B.C. Greek inscription from Beroea,[205] dedicated to 'Αταργάτει Σωτείραι: both texts witness Atargatis' assumption of epithets used also of ʿAnat and thus suggest that the name Atargatis subsumes the name and attributes of ʿAnat. Finally, with respect to ʿAnat's worship beyond the second millennium B.C., there are a number of Punic names from Carthage and Hadrumetum (Sousse) containing ʿAnat as the theophorous element.[206]

ʾAšerah

Though the meaning of this goddess' name was long sought in Hebrew *ʾašrê*, "blessedness," her full title at Ugarit makes much more likely an alternate explanation. This full title is

---

phrase *māʿôz ḥayyay* ("the strength of my life," Psalm 27:1) crept in here?

204. *CIS*, vol. 2, no. 52; the name is explained here as *"ex nomine divino* עתר *et radice* עז *compositum"* (*CIS*, vol. 2, p. 56). There is an alternate explanation of the name *ʿtrʿzh*, suggested to me by Professor Cross, which is attractive for its suggested identification of *ʿtr* with the goddess ʾAšerah, also called *ʾilt*. This is that *ʿzh* is to be linked with the Arabic goddess al-ʿUzzā (see *WM*, pp. 475-476), Old South Arabic ʿUzzayān (*WM*, p. 548). The goddess is often identifies with Allāt (*WM*, p. 476), i.e. ʾAšerah/*ʾilt*, so the name may add evidence to the presence of the goddess ʾAšerah in the assimilated form *ʿtr-*.

205. 'Αναστ. Κ. 'Ορλάνδος, "Βεροίας ἐπιγραφαὶ ἀνέκδοται," 'Αρχαιολογικὸν Δελτιόν 2 (1916), no. 1 (144). Only the initial dedication of this inscription is preserved, so we can say no more of the incription's character.

206. For example, *ʿbdʿnt*, or *ʿbdʾnt*, in *CIS*, vol. 1, nos. 3781, 4562, 4563, and 5550. See also Benz, *Personal Names*, p. 382.

rabbatu 'aṯiratu yammi, which seems best taken as implying that 'Ašerah is both "'The Lady Who Traverses the Sea,'" and "'The Lady Who Treads on the Sea (Dragon).'"[207] Either translation of 'Ašerah's full title makes plain her status as a sea goddess, a status appropriate for the chief consort of 'Ēl, whose dwelling is at the source of water, and for a goddess who is seen as the mother of the gods. As a marine goddess, 'Ašerah has in her service a deity called a "fisherman" *(dgy)*, to whom is spoken the command, "Fisherman of Lady 'Ašerah of the Sea / Take a net in your hands..." *(daggayu rabbati 'aṯirati yammi / qaḥ raṯta bādêka...)*.[208]

Though the pairings of the deities at Ugarit are flexible, 'Ašerah is chiefly the consort of 'Ēl. As the consort of the head of the pantheon, she is appropriately called 'Ēlat; and the titles 'Ašerah and 'Ēlat can alternate in parallelism as follows: "He cries to 'Ašerah and her children / To 'Ēlat and the band of her kinsmen" *(yaṣīḥu 'aṯirata wa-banīha / 'ilata wa-ṣibburata 'arihīha)*.[209] 'Ašerah also bears the epithet

---

207. Albright, *YGC*, p. 121; cf. *ARI*, p. 77, and note the full statement of the ambiguities in the following formulation of R. B. Coote: "Whether Asherah treads *on* the Sea in the cosmogonic battle with the sea dragon, as does her younger counterpart Anat, or whether she treads *by* the sea as the consort of El who lives at the source of the double deep or as the goddess of any one of the several Canaanite towns, or whether she treads *through* the sea as the goddess represented as the serpent in the sea, the *yammu* of her epithet cannot be totally divorced from the *yammu* who is the sea dragon" ("The Serpent and Sacred Marriage," 111). Coote subsequently proposes that the *rbt* of her title means not, or at least not only, "lady," but is to be linked to Ugaritic *rb*, so that 'Ašerah's full title means "'The serpent goddess who goes in the sea'" (127). For a representative statement of the older argument that the goddess' name means "'die Glückliche '" see Baudissin, *Adonis und Esmun*, p. 208.

208. *CTCA*, 4.2.31-32; cf. also *CTCA* 3.6.10.

209. *CTCA* 4.4.48-50; the couplet occurs again in broken form in *CTCA* 4.1.7-9. For the identification of 'Ašerah with 'Ēlat, see Frank M. Cross, Jr., "The Evolution of the Proto-Canaanite Alphabet," *BASOR* 134 (1954) 20, n.17 (where 49.II,12 should read 49.I.12=*CTCA* 6.1.40), Pritchard, *Figurines*, p. 61, and Gray, *The Legacy of Canaan*, p. 177.

qudšu, "holiness." That ʾAšerah and the goddess called Qudšu are identical has been argued by Albright and others,[210] and is assured by the alternation of the two names in the parallelistic poetry of Ugarit. Thus, in the Keret epic we read, "To Qudšu, ʾA[šerah] of Tyre / And to ʾĒlat of Sidon" *(la-qudši ʾa[ṯirati] ṣurri-mi / wa-la-ʾilati ṣidyāni-mi)*.[211] The same identification of ʾAšerah with Qudšu is suggested by the pairing of *lṭpn wqdš*,[212] since *lṭpn* is a common name of ʾAšerah's consort ʾĒl. That *qudšu (simpliciter)* usually designates ʾAšerah does not mean that the epithet is inappropriate for other deities; on the Arslan Tash plaque, for example, we hear of *bʿl qdš*. But just as *bʿl* usually designates *bʿl haddu*, so *qdš* most often designates *ʾaṯiratu*.

In keeping with her role as a fecund sea goddess who is ʾĒl's mate, ʾAšerah appears in the Ugaritic myths as the mother of the gods. This role ʾAšerah plays often under yet another of her titles, "Creatress of the gods" *(qāniyatu ʾilīma)*.[213]

---

210. *YGC*, pp. 121-122. Albright proposed this translation and vocalization of *qdš* already in 1939; see W. F. Albright, "Astarte Plaques and Figurines from Tell Beit Mirsim," in *Mélanges syriens, offerts à monsieur René Dussaud*, vol. 1, p. 118, n.2. See also Cross, *CMHE*, p. 33, and "Prose and Poetry in the Mythic and Epic Texts from Ugarit," 9

211. *CTCA* 14.196-197; cf. 14.201-202. For discussions of this couplet, see W. F. Albright, "A Vow to Asherah in the Keret Epic," *BASOR* 94 (1944) 30, n.5 and 31, n.7, and the tentative discussion of Ginsberg, *The Legend of King Keret*, p. 40. Cross also vocalizes the name *ṣurri-mi* ("Prose and Poetry in the Mythic and Epic Texts from Ugarit," 9-10), though it is possible to vocalize *ṣurêmi*, a dual representing the two Tyres (mainland Tyre and the island city) familiar from other sources (e.g., the annals of Sennacherib). However, the *-mi* at the end of Sidon in l. 197 militates against this.

212. *CTCA* 16.1.10-11.

213. For a discussion of the root *qny* and the meaning "Creatress" for *qnyt*, see Albright, "The 'Natural Force' of Moses," 34, n.21, and cf. *YGC*, p. 121, and Pritchard, *Figurines*, p. 61. Gray writes that ʾAšerah "is probably entitled *qnyt ʾelm*, 'Creatrix of the gods,' though this meaning of the phrase is not certainly established" (*The Legacy of Canaan*, pp. 177-178); but this is unnecessarily tentative.

That this title belongs to 'Ašerah is proved, aside from its appropriateness, by couplets of Ugaritic poetry such as, "Gifts of Lady 'Ašerah of the Sea / Entreaty-presents for the Creatress of the Gods" *(magginī rabbati 'aṯirati yammi / maǵazī qāniyati 'ilīma).*[214] Like her name 'Ēlat, this is a title she bears as the consort of 'Ēl, who is called "Creator of Creatures" *(bāniyu banūwāti).*[215] Indeed, an alternate name for "the gods" *('ilūma)* is "the sons of 'Ašerah" *(banū 'aṯirati).*[216]

Like ʻAštart and ʻAnat, 'Ašerah is known in Egypt, where she appears under the name Qudšu.[217] Here too, she is portrayed in keeping with her character in the Ugaritic texts, for stelae show Qudšu holding in her hands "ein Bündel Schlangen und einen Strauss Lotusblumen, die sie als Göttin der Fruchtbarkeit und der Erotik charackterisieren."[218] Such representations of Qudšu often show the goddess standing on a lion.[219]

---

214. *CTCA* 4.1.22-23. The two titles are elsewhere parallel in *CTCA* 4.3.25-26; 4.3.34-35; 4.4.31-32; and 8.1-2.

215. A title that occurs, for example, in *CTCA* 4.3.32; see Albright, *YGC*, p. 121, though Albright vocalizes "creatures" *binawāti*, thus differing from my understanding of *banūwāti* as a passive participle. In a much later Nabataean inscription (*CIS*, vol. 2, no. 185) 'Ēlat appears again as the mother of the gods *('lt 'm 'lhy).*

216. See, for example, *CTCA* 4.5.63, or 2.1.37-38 (where *'ilūma* is parallel to *banū qudši*, adding evidence to the 'Ašerah-Qudšu identification).

217. Stadelmann, again, provides an exemplary summary of Qudšu in Egypt (pp. 113-123), though Stadelmann believes that "Qudšu, wie qdš demnach zu vokalisieren ist, stellt also eine bestimmte Kultform der Göttinnen ʻAṯirtu, ʻAnat und Astarte dar" (p. 113, cf. p. 115). Stadelmann bases this assertion that *qudšu* is an epithet equally appropriate for any of the three major Canaanite goddesses primarily upon the evidence of the Winchester College relief which names Qudšu, ʻAnat, and ʻAštart; we will return to a discussion of this important relief. That *qudšu* could be used of many deities is undeniable, but that it usually refers to 'Ašerah is as clear.

218. Stadelmann, p. 114.

219. Albright, *ARI*, p. 76 and *YGC*, pp. 121-122; J. T. Milik and Frank M. Cross, Jr., "Inscribed Javelin-Heads from the Period of the Judges: A Recent Discovery in Palestine," *BASOR* 134 (1954) 8; and Cross, *CMHE*, p. 33.

In Punic material, ’Ašerah appears often under the name Tannit,[220] though this has often been denied. Albright identified Tannit with ‘Anat,[221] and he is followed here by Benz.[222] More commonly, Tannit is identified with ‘Aštart.[223] Of course, one solution would be to claim that Tannit, like Atargatis, combines the attributes of all three Canaanite goddesses, so that the attempt to identify her with any one of them is misguided. But there is evidence that Tannit was distinguished from ‘Aštart.[224] A Carthage inscription of the third or second century B.C.[225] is dedicated "To the Ladies[226] ‘Aštart and Tannit" *(lrbt l‘štrt wltnt)*, and refers to the temples of these two deities.[227]

---

220. I vocalize the name as Tannit because this is the primitive form which accords best with the name's etymology. From El-Hofra come the Greek forms θινιθ (*EH*, no. 1.-Greek, p. 167) and θεννειθ (*EH*, no. 3.-Greek, p. 169); and on the basis of this evidence, and the Punic forms *tynt* and *tnyt*, Donner and Röllig argue that the name is to be spelled "*Tinnit* oder *Tennit*" (*KAI*, vol. 2, p. 90). André Berthier and René Charlier (*EH*, p. 26) and Fitzmyer ("The Phoenician Inscription from Pyrgi," 287-288) agree, but Peckham notes "the vocalization of Tinnit, with 'i' in the first syllable, is derived from the late Phoenician form" (*The Development of the Late Phoenician Scripts*, p. 129, n.74). No reasonable etymology is supplied for the forms Tennit or Tinnit (or the traditional Tanit with one *n*), while Cross has argued that Tannit "is the derived feminine of a *qaṭṭīl* which in Phoenician becomes regularly Qaṭṭiltu....The orthography *tnt* [which is found already in the Proto-Sinaitic texts], and the transcription (τεννιτ) reflects, following normal Canaanite shifts, *tennit*<**tannit*<**tannitu*<**tannintu*" ("The Origin and Early Evolution of the Alphabet," 12*, n.27). See below for a discussion of the name's meaning.

221. *YGC*, p. 135, and n.63.

222. *Personal Names*, pp. 429-430.

223. Thus Harden (*The Phoenicians*, p. 87) and Moscati (*WP*, p. 139 and p. 193).

224. The distinction was noted nearly a century ago by Baethgen (*Beiträge*, p. 36).

225. *KAI*, no. 81.

226. For arguments that *rbt* = *rabbōt* (plural) here, see Lidzbarski, *Eph.*, vol. 1, pp. 19-20, and *KAI*, vol. 2, p. 98.

227. Cross, *CMHE*, p. 30.

That narrows the field to ʿAnat and ʾAšerah; and the name and attributes of Tannit suggest strongly that she is ʾAšerah. *Tnt*, the spelling already in the Proto-Sinaitic corpus of the second millennium B.C., is explained by Cross as a feminine form derived from *tnn*, "'dragon,' 'serpent,'" meaning "'the one of the (sea) serpent' or 'the Dragon Lady.'"[228] This explanation not only makes good sense of the various forms of the epithet as it is spelled in Phoenician, Punic, and Greek,[229] but also yields the bonus of providing an epithet which corresponds to ʾAšerah's character as a sea goddess at Ugarit and ʾAšerah/Derceto's links with the sea as revealed in later sources. Further, Tannit is called "mother" both in Latin *(nutrix)*[230] and in Punic *([l]ʾm lrbt ltnt)*.[231] Finally, literally thousands of Punic stelae are dedicated to the pair *tnt* and *bʿl ḥmn*, the latter of whom has been identified with ʾĒl by Benno Landsberger and Cross.[232]

To return for a moment to the Near East before summarizing the data about the three great Canaanite goddesses, we note that ʾAšerah is present in the Old Testament and in an Aramaic inscription from Arslan Tash, near the Euphrates and Hierapolis. In the latter text, which dates to the seventh century B.C., she appears as *ʾšr*,[233] in the company of her familiar consort ʾĒl, here under his epithet "Eternal One" *(ʿlm)*. The Old Testament evidence will be assessed fully in chapter III below. Here, it is enough to observe that while the word *ʾăšērâ* in the

---

228. "The Origin and Early Evolution of the Alphabet," 12*, n.27; cf. now *CMHE*, p. 33, and R. B. Coote, "The Serpent and Sacred Marriage," 118.

229. See n.220 above.

230. *KAI*, vol. 2, p. 90.

231. *CIS*, vol. 1, no. 196. *lrbt lʾmʾ* occurs alone in *CIS*, vol. 1, no. 177; and this *ʾmʾ* Cooke plausibly identifies with Tannit (*NSI*, p. 131). We noted above that a Nabataean text (*CIS*, vol. 2, no. 185) refers to *ʾlt ʾm ʾlhy*, "ʾĒlat, the mother of the gods."

232. The material for this identification is now fully set out by Cross in *CMHE*, pp. 24-36. The pair *bʿl ḥmn* and *tnt*, then, will correspond to *lṭpn wqdš* in *CTCA* 16.1.10-11.

233. See Cross and Saley, "Phoenician Incantations on a Plaque of the Seventh Century B.C. from Arslan Tash in Upper Syria," 45, n.17. For *ʿlm* as an epithet of ʾĒl here, see Cross, *CMHE*, p. 17.

Hebrew Bible sometimes designates a cultic symbol, at other times it is undeniably the name of the Canaanite goddess ’Ašerah.[234]

‘Aštart, ‘Anat, and ’Ašerah

The preceding survey, which has skimmed over a millennium and a half, touching down at points from Mesopotamia to the western edge of the Mediterranean, has demonstrated that each of these three goddesses possesses a distinctive character, which character she maintained in the eyes of her worshippers throughout the chronological and geographical limits of our survey. ‘Aštart is the goddess of sexual love, in Syria-Palestine, in Egypt, and to the Greeks who called her Aphrodite. Though she plays many roles, ‘Anat is most often a war goddess, memorably at Ugarit, in Egypt, and still so on fourth-century B.C. Cyprus where she is identified with Athena. ’Ašerah is the goddess of fecundity, and is appropriately associated with the teeming sea; she is the mother of the gods in the Ugaritic myths, and is still called mother, and still retains her links with the sea, over a thousand years after the destruction of Ugarit.

Yet while the evidence demands the assignment of distinctive characters to each goddess, the same evidence shows that from the beginning each goddess played lesser roles on the stages dominated by her sisters. It is not hyperbole to say "from the beginning," since this overlap already obtains at Ugarit, though many have failed to see it. Here, ‘Aštart rarely acts alone, and most often in company with ‘Anat. When Ba‘l Haddu's dangerous rhetoric seems about to lead to reckless action, the two goddesses act together: "[‘An]at seized [his right hand] / ‘Aštart seized his left hand" *([yamīnahu ‘an]atu to’ḫ̮idu / šim’alahu to’ḫ̮idu ‘aṯtarartu)*.[235] ‘Aštart's assumption

---

234. See William L. Reed, *The Asherah in the Old Testament* (Fort Worth: Texas Christian University Press, 1949) for a full presentation of the Old Testament, and de Vaux, *Ancient Israel*, p. 286, for a brief summary of the same.

235. *CTCA* 2.1.40. See Herdner, *ad loc.*, for the restoration of *‘anatu*, which is proposed also by G. R. Driver (*Canaanite Myths and Legends*, p. 80). The balanced syllable count (10:10) adds plausibility to the restoration, assuming that ‘Aštart's name does not occur in both lines, which would be unusual.

of ‘Anat's martial role here in the Ba‘l-Yamm epic finds a counterpart in the Keret epic, where ‘Anat appears in a role more often assigned to the goddess ‘Aštart; the bride requested by Keret will be she "whose fairness is like the fairness of ‘Anat/ Her beauty like the beauty of ‘Aštart" *(dī-ka-nu‘mi ‘anati nu‘muha / kamā tôsami ‘aṯtarti tôsamuha).*[236] In a recently published symposium text (RS 24.258), ‘Aštart and ‘Anat arrive together for the banquet (ll. 9-11) and subsequently go off hunting together (ll. 22-23).[237] Still clearer evidence for the occasional merging of these two goddesses comes from the incantation text (RS 24.244) from *Ugaritica V*. Šapšu is directed here to carry a "message" *(qala)* to ’Ēl (l. 3), to Ba‘l (l. 9), to Dagnu (l. 15), and then "to ‘Anat-and-‘Aštart" (*‘im ‘anati-wa‘aṯtarti*, ll. 19-20); as R. B. Coote notes, of the divine pairs to whom Šapšu is to go, "the group *‘ntw‘ṯtrt* is the only one spelled without a word divider."[238] ‘Anat, however, is also associated closely with ’Ašerah. We noted above that ‘Anat and ’Ašerah are together wet nurses in the Keret epic;[239] and the two act in concert to obtain ’Ēl's permission for the building of Ba‘l's palace.[240] Moreover, in the Ugaritic myths all three of these goddesses are at various times the consorts of ’Ēl,[241] thus assuming roles which readily led to the

---

236. *CTCA* 14.291-293; cf. 14.145-146, which is, like many of the couplets in the Keret epic especially (though also throughout the Ugaritic myths), a repetition with slight variation, so slight in this case that one suspects an error in 14. 145-146.

237. On this text see de Moor, "Studies in the New Alphabetic texts from Ras Shamra I," 167-175, especially 174 where de Moor notes other texts wherein "both ‘Anatu and ‘Aṯtartu are depicted as hunting goddesses."

238. "The Serpent and Sacred Marriage," 29. The place to which Šapšu is to carry the message here is *‘nbb*, a site elsewhere associated with ‘Anat (Clifford, *The Cosmic Mountain*, p. 86, and p. 89, n.61).

239. *CTCA* 15.2.26-28.

240. See Stadelmann, p. 32.

241. Cross summarizes the pairings as follows: ’Ēl's "three important consorts are his two sisters Asherah and Astarte, and his daughter ‘Anat. Ba‘l also takes ‘Anat as consort, and ’Ēl shows particular favor to Astarte the divine courtesan" (*CMHE*, p. 43).

merging of ‘Aštart, ‘Anat, and ’Ašerah.

The same overlap in function and identity between the three goddesses is witnessed in Egypt. Each receives a title translated by Stadelmann "'Herrin des Himmels,'"[242] As goddess of war, ‘Anat and ‘Aštart are often indistinguishable in Egypt;[243] and it will be recalled that these two are called "'the two great goddesses who were pregnant but did not bear.'"[244] Again, "in Zaubertexten bilden Astarte und ‘Anat häufig ein Paar."[245] Indeed, as in RS 24.244, the two names are combined into one in Egypt too, for a treaty between Ramses II and Hattusilis names among the treaty's witnesses a Syrian goddess *‘ntrt*.[246] Most significantly, the Winchester College relief mentioned above gives the names Qudšu, ‘Aštart, and ‘Anat to a typical Qudšu (’Ašerah) representation.[247] The most natural interpretation

---

242. ‘Anat: Stadelmann, pp. 92-95; ‘Aštart: p. 106; ’Ašerah/Qudsu: p. 120. A recently published text on a stone bowl from Egypt labels Qudšu "lady of the stars of Heaven," and ‘Aštart "lady of heaven," while ‘Anat is "lady of truth" (Donald B. Redford, "New Light on the Asiatic Campaigning of Ḥoremheb," *BASOR* 211 [1973] 37, and 43-46).

243. Baethgen, *Beiträge*, p. 52; Albright, *ARI*, p. 76, and *FSAC*, p. 177; and Pritchard, *Figurines*, p. 68.

244. Pritchard, *Figurines*, p. 79.

245. Stadelmann, p. 108.

246. Albright, "The Evolution of the West-Semitic Divinity ‘An-‘Anat-‘Attâ," 83, n.7, and *ARI*, p. 74. S. Langdon and Alan H. Gardiner suggest here an emendation to *‘-s-ṯ-r-t* ("The Treaty of Alliance Between Ḫattušili King of the Hittites and the Pharaoh Ramesses II of Egypt," *The Journal of Egyptian Archaeology* 6 [1920] 194, n.6 and 196). But Albrecht Goetze finds this suggestion "impossible" and hardly preferable to "the curious Egyptian *‘ntrt*" (*ANET*, 1st ed., p. 201, n.16; see now the note of John A. Wilson in *ANET*, 3d ed., p. 201, n.16). Dupont-Sommer also agrees with Albright here ("L'inscription de l'amulette d'Arslan Tash," 147, n.2).

247. The relief was published by I. E. S. Edwards, "A Relief of Qudshu-Astarte-Anath in the Winchester College Collection," *JNES* 14 (1955) 49-51, and pls. 3-5, and can now be seen conveniently in *ANEP*, no. 830. See also the comments by Cross, *CMHE*, pp. 33-34, and Stadelmann, p. 113, though the latter sees Qudšu as an epithet of the other two deities.

here is that the goddess portrayed on the relief *is* Qudšu, ʻAštart, and ʻAnat, and not that the relief portrays one of the three goddesses while the inscription names, in a spirit of comprehensiveness, all three. Thus, in Egypt the three major Canaanite goddesses were easily combined into a single figure; but the graphic mingling of the Winchester relief is only a clear statement of what was suggested on Canaanite soil.

The Old Testament, both in Hebrew and in Greek dress, exhibits a confusion between the names and roles of ʼAšerah and ʻAštart;[248] and this confusion, when combined with the conflate forms *ʻntwʻṯtrt* (Ras Shamra) and *ʻntrt* (Egypt), suggests the early mingling of all three major goddesses. I Kings 11:5, 11:33, and 2 Kings 23:13 concur with late Phoenician evidence in associating ʻAštart with Sidon, a city which is, in the Keret epic, associated with ʼĒlat/ʼAšerah. A reference to ʼAšerah *(laʼăšērâ)* in the Hebrew text of 2 Chronicles 15:16 is a reference to ʻAštart (τῇ ʼΑστάρτῃ) in the Greek text, while ʼAšerah's cultic symbols are *hāʼăšērîm* in Hebrew but ταῖς ʼΑστάρταις in Greek in 2 Chronicles 24:18. Demonstrating that the confusion worked in both directions, ʻAštart is *hāʻaštārôt* in the Hebrew text of 1 Samuel 7:3 and 12:10, but τὰ ἄλση (7:3) or τοῖς ἄλσεσιν (12:10) in the Greek text, phrases usually reserved for ʼAšerah's cultic symbols.[249] Both ʻAštart and ʼAšerah are mentioned in the same breath with Baʻl; yet, assuming the Baʻl of the Old Testament is Baʻl Haddu,[250] neither ʻAštart nor ʼAšerah

---

248. There is a good summary of the Old Testament presentation of ʼAšerah and ʻAštart in Pritchard, *Figurines*, pp. 61-63.

249. The Greek text for all of these readings is taken from the Codes Vaticanus (B), as printed in both the smaller (Swete) and larger (Brooke-McLean) Cambridge Septuagints. In both 1 Samuel 7:3 and 12:10, later recensions substitute, or simply add, ἀσταρῶθ; but the point of importance here is that in the Old Testament there is a general confusion about the identities of the goddesses of Canaan.

250. Otto Eissfeldt argues ingeniously that "der von Ahab in Israel eingeführte tyrische Baʻal kein anderer als Baʻal Šamēm ist" ("Baʻalšamēm und Jahwe," *ZAW* 57 [1939] 22, and *passim*). If Eissfeldt's argument holds up, then the pairing of ʼAšerah with Baʻl (Šamem) in the Old Testament might yet correspond to the regular marriage of ʼAšerah with ʼĒl in the

is primarily the consort in the Ugaritic myths of Baʿl, whose mate is regularly ʿAnat. Indeed, the variable pairings of the Canaanite deities[251] is itself impetus for the fusing of the three great goddesses into a single figure. And this variety obtains not only in the Old Testament, but also, and already, in the texts from Ras Shamra. Most intriguingly, there is now an inscription from the Phoenician mainland which records the dedication of a "statue" *(sml)* to the conflate goddess "Tannit-ʿAštart."[252] ʾAšerah (Tannit) and ʿAštart are here merged, as ʿAnat and ʿAštart are in the names *ʿntwʿṯtrt* and *ʿntrt*. The conclusion is therefore inevitable that, in the words of Dupont-Sommer, though ʾAšerah, ʿAštart, and ʿAnat are "primitivement distinctes," yet they are figures "qui ont tendu à se confondre et à s'identifier les unes avec les autres."[253]

Atargatis and the Three Major Canaanite Goddesses

When Lucian describes the image of the goddess he calls Hera, he calls upon a dazzling array of deities to explain this Hera's attributes. Atargatis at Hierapolis is, to Lucian, plainly Hera; but others call her Derceto (*D.S.D.*, para. 14), and Lucian himself notes that she shares characteristics with Athena, Aphrodite, Selene, Rhea, Artemis, and the Fates (para. 32). Though Lucian may have let his rhetorical list extend itself beyond the bounds of objective reporting, the accuracy of his description has been confirmed by our summary of ʾAšerah, ʿAštart, and ʿAnat: Lucian calls the Hierapolis Hera by various names and describes her with reference to the attributes of various deities because Atargatis is not just Derceto (ʾAšerah) or Aphrodite (ʿAštart) or Athena (ʿAnat) but rather a goddess

---

Ugaritic myths, since there is evidence that *bʿl šmm/šmn* is a title of ʾĒl.

251. The situation is well stated by Conrad Elphège L'Heureux: "The three chief goddesses of Canaanite religion, i.e., Asherah, Astate and Anat, exhibit an astonishing tendency to merge, become confused and shift in their marital associations" ("El and the Rephaim: New Light from *Ugaritica V*" [unpublished Ph.D. dissertation, Harvard University, 1971], 90).

252. The inscription reads here, *ltnt⟨ʿ⟩štrt*. I was informed by Professor Cross of this important inscription, which is as yet unpublished.

253. "L'inscription de l'amulette d'Arslan Tash," 147.

whose name and attributes combine the names and attributes of the three chief Canaanite goddesses.

Atargatis and ’Ašerah

The Aramaic spelling *’tr‘t’*, if not a product of dissimilation, and the identification of Atargatis with Derceto indicate that Atargatis' character subsumes that of Canaanite ’Ašerah; and further investigation confirms this. Both deities have clear marine associations. Canaanite ’Ašerah is "The Lady Who Treads Upon (the) Sea" *(rabbatu ’aṯiratu yammi)*, with whom is associated a "fisherman" *(daggayu)*, while evidence from wherever she is worshipped links Atargatis with fish and with sacred ponds.[254] "There is also a lake," writes Lucian, "not very far from the temple, in which are reared many holy fish of different kinds" (ἔστι δὲ καὶ λίμνη αὐτόθι, οὐ πολλὸν ἑκὰς τοῦ ἱροῦ, ἐν τῇ ἰχθύες ἱροὶ τρέφονται πολλοὶ καὶ πολυειδέες, *D.S.D.*, para. 45); and as late as 1939, H. Stocks could write of the same pond near the Hierapolis temple, "noch heute gibt es...im See kleine Fische."[255] In 1697, Henry Maundrell reported seeing at "Bambych" a figure "in Basso Relievo" of "two Syrens, which twining their fishy Tails together, made a Seat, on which was placed sitting a naked Woman, her Arms and the Syrens on each side mutually entwined."[256] At Khirbet et-Tannûr in Nabataea, where the goddess' name occurs as *’tr‘t’*, Glueck reports a bust of a fish goddess whom he calls Atargatis, with wavy hair like rippling water and with two fish above her hair.[257] Noting

---

254. Collections of evidence for the Atargatis-fish association can be found in Baethgen, *Beiträge*, p. 75; Baudissin, *Adonis und Esmun*, p. 21; Cumont, "Syria Dea," in *Dictionnaire des antiquités*, vol. 4, pt. 2, p. 1593; Goossens, *Hiérapolis de Syrie*, p. 64; Höfer, "Syria," in Roscher's *Ausführliches Lexikon*, vol. 4, col. 1633; and Henri Seyrig, "La triade héliopolitaine et les temples de Baalbek," *Syria* 10 (1929) 320.

255. "Studien," 6.

256. *A Journey From Aleppo*, p. 154. This relief supports the argument above that Lucian's denial of Hera's identification with Derceto (represented as half fish) rests on his report of a single Atargatis image (that in the central shrine at Hierapolis) and is not to be taken as a refutation of this certain identification.

257. "A Newly Discovered Nabataean Temple of Atargatis

that "no sanctuary of hers was complete without having attached to it a sacred pond, in which untouchable fish swam about," Glueck later expressed his conviction "that there may have been a sacred pond in the center of the outer courtyard at Khirbet Tannur."[258] Closer to Hierapolis, Atargatis' worship assumed the same shape at Palmyra. A tessera from the city portrays Atargatis with a "large figure of a fish";[259] and Henri Seyrig identifies with Atargatis the goddess with two fish about her feet represented in relief in the Bēl temple at Palmyra.[260] Greek evidence makes the same association of Atargatis with fish. Fish ponds have been identified near the temple of Atargatis on the island of Delos[261] and at the sanctuary of the Syrian Goddess at Rome.[262] As early as the fourth century B.C., Xenophon writes of fish that "the Syrians call them gods" (οὓς οἱ Σύροι θεοὺς ἐνόμιζον).[263] Other Greek writers agree with Xenophon and with the evidence from Hierapolis, Nabataea, and Palmyra, in making firm the association of Atargatis with the sea and with its life.[264]

Nor is the marine association the only evidence for identifying 'Ašerah with a component in Atargatis' character. In

---

and Hadad at Khirbet et-Tannûr, Transjordania," *AJA* 41 (1937) 368.

258. *Deities and Dolphins*, p. 391. Since Glueck substantiates his belief with no direct evidence, the belief must arise solely from the nature of other Atargatis cult sites. In a review of *Deities and Dolphins*, Jean Starcky argues that Glueck's "dolphins" are in fact fish, with unfortunate consequences for the accuracy of the book's title ("Le temple nabatéen de Khirbet Tannur. A propos d'un livre récent," *RB* 75 [1968] 215 and 228).

259. Rostovtzeff, "Hadad and Atargatis at Palmyra," 59.

260. "Antiquités syriennes," *Syria* 15 (1934) 170-171. More recently, Seyrig has discussed a Mesopotamian relief portraying Atargatis with fish ("Antiquités syriennes," *Syria* 49 [1972] 106 and pl. 1).

261. Morin, "The Cult of Dea Syria," 102, and 124-125.

262. P. V. C. Baur, *et al.*, *Dura-Europos, Preliminary Report of the Third Season*, p. 108, n.35.

263. *Anabasis* 1.4.9.

264. For example, Cornutus, *Theologiae Graecae compendium* 6, reprinted in van Berg, *Répertoire*, no. 84 (p. 53).

keeping with ’Ašerah's role at Ugarit as mother and "Creatress" *(qāniyatu)* of the gods, a role also played by ’Ašerah in the Punic world where she receives the title "mother" *(nutrix, ’m)* under her title Tannit, is evidence which portrays Atargatis in a similar role. A Roman inscription to the Syrian goddess calls her "mother of the gods and of Syria" *(mater deor. et mater syriae)*;[265] and a bronze object from the second century A.D. inscribed κυρία 'Αταργάτις has been described by Paul Perdrizet as a representation of a female breast, appropriate for "la déesse de l'universelle fécondité."[266] Lucian says the statue of the goddess at Hierapolis holds a "spindle" (ἄτρακτον) in one hand, which probably prompted his association of the goddess with Artemis.[267] ’Ašerah at Ugarit also holds a spindle *(plk)*; "She grasps her spindle... / The spindle...in her right hand" *(’aḫadat pilkaha... / pilka...ba-yamīniha)*.[268] Finally, Tannit (’Ašerah) was identified with Hera in the western Mediterranean;[269] and we have seen that Hera is the

---

265. Cited by Höfer, "Syria," in Roscher's *Ausführliches Lexikon*, vol. 4, col. 1641.

266. "A propos d'Atargatis," *Syria* 12 (1931) 268 and 271. The object is probably best seen as an *ex-voto* offering, representing a diseased organ, fittingly in Atargatis' domain.

267. So Harmon, *Lucian*, vol. 4, p. 386, n.1; note, however, that the phrase ἄτρακτον τῶν Μοιρῶν (*LS*, p. 245) may imply rather that the spindle suggested the Fates to Lucian.

268. *CTCA* 4.2.3-4. The bearer of the spindle here can only be ’Ašerah, who sits waiting the approach of Ba‘l and of ‘Anat (*CTCA* 4.2.12-15). For the translation of *plk* as "spindle" (Akkadian *pilakku/pilaqqu*, Aramaic *pilkâ*), see Albright, "The North-Canaanite Poems of ’Al’êyân Ba‘al and the 'Gracious Gods,'" 117, n.62. Theodor H. Gaster calls the spindle the "traditional weapon" of ‘Anat (*Thespis:* Ritual, Myth and Drama in the Ancient Near East, rev. ed. [New York: Harper Torchbook, 1966], p. 117, cf. pp. 175-176); but it is undeniably ’Ašerah's in the above passage.

269. See *WM*, p. 311, and Cross, *CMHE*, p. 29, with the references cited there. Avi-Yonah argued that Atargatis "is identified with Tannit of Carthage by the common epithet ἐπήκοος" ("Syrian Gods at Ptolemais-Acco," 11); the identification is sound, but the very wide use of this epithet (summarized by McCown, "The Goddesses of Gerasa," 144) renders precarious the attempt to use it to identify the two goddesses.

Greek goddess Lucian chooses to identify with Atargatis at Hierapolis.

Atargatis and ʿAštart

There are also grounds upon which to see Canaanite ʿAštart within the cult of Atargatis. In addition to fish, doves also were sacred in Hierapolis. Lucian observes, "of birds, the dove seemed to them [the residents of Hierapolis] an especially holy thing" (ὀρνίθων τε αυτεόισι περιστερὴ χρῆμα ἱρότατον, *D.S.D.*, para. 54). Others too mention the place of doves in the Atargatis cult.[270] Elsewhere in Syria-Palestine, however, doves are associated with Astarte, or with Aphrodite (=Astarte) by the Greeks. Aelian, for example, calls "doves the playthings of Aphrodite" (ἀθύρματα γὰρ 'Αφροδίτης περιστερὰς).[271] Hence, the presence of doves in the worship of Atargatis points toward ʿAštart as an element in Atargatis' makeup. The same might be said of the calathos, which is almost always shown atop Atargatis' head but which is linked by the Greeks with Astarte,[272] though it also appears on representations of Qudšu and Tannit. There is more direct evidence. The site called *ʿaštĕrōt qarnayim* in Genesis 14:5 ('Ασταρῶθ καρνάιν in the Greek text) has become τὸ Καρνιον καὶ τὸ 'Ατεργατειον in 2 Maccabees 12:26.[273]

---

270. For example, Cornutus, *Theologiae Gracae compendium* 6, printed in van Berg, *Répertoire*, no. 84 (p. 53).

271. *De Natura Animalium* 4.2. For further evidence of the presence of doves in the cult of Astarte/Aphrodite, see Robertson Smith, "Ctesias and the Semiramis Legend," 305; Baudissin, *Adonis und Esmun*, p. 38; Goossens, *Hiérapolis de Syrie*; and Donner and Röllig, *KAI*, vol. 2, p. 18.

272. Thus Henri Seyrig, "Antiquités syriennes," *Syria* 36 (1959) 40-41. Albright also notes that a type of "Astarte figurine" has a "feather headdress," in place of the usual "Ḥathor coiffure," and that, "it is sometimes hard to distinguish the feather headdress, especially in inferior pieces, from the rilled calathus....Both forms persisted into the Iron Age in Cyprus and Greek lands generally" ("Astarte Plaques and Figurines from Tell Beit Mirsim," p. 118). The calathos, then, may well have been associated with the fertility goddess long before Lucian wrote.

273. This has been noted by Baethgen, *Beiträge*, p. 74, and by Höfer, "Syria," in Roscher's *Ausführliches Lexikon*, vol.

Further, Lucian calls the queen who is indirectly responsible for Kombabos' fate Στρατονίκη; and elsewhere the element Στρατων is a "truncation" (Verstümmelung) of the element ʿAštart in the names of Sidonian kings.[274] Finally, in Greek literature the Syrian Goddess Atargatis is frequently identified directly with Astarte, or with Astarte's usual equivalent Aphrodite. Inscriptions from Phistyon, Thuria, Philippopolis, Beroea, Mylasa, Skyros, and Nisyros all call Atargatis Aphrodite;[275] and we noted at the outset that on Delos we have the notable collocation Ἁγνῇ Ἀφροδίτῃ Ἀταργάτι καὶ Ἀδάδου.[276] Plutarch writes that the goddess of Hierapolis is known variously as Hera and as Aphrodite (*Crassus* 17). Artemidorus ascribes the worship of fish to the cult of Astarte, with whom he implicitly identifies Atargatis.[277] As early as the fifth century B.C., Aeschylus calls northern Syria "the land of Aphrodite, rich in grain" (χθόνα καὶ Ἀφροδίτης πολύπυρον αἶαν).[278] Certainly, none of these references alone proves either that Atargatis was identified with Aphrodite/Astarte or that ʿAštart necessarily is a part of the composite character of Atargatis. But the literary and epigraphic evidence, when combined with that which links Atargatis and Astarte to doves and the calathos, and when seen in the light of the normal Semitic spelling *ʿtrʿth*, is of

---

4, col. 1640. Cf. also τὸ τεμενος ἐν Καρνάιν (1 Maccabees 5:43), noted by Paton, "Atargatis," in Hastings' *Encyclopaedia of Religion and Ethics*, vol. 2, p. 166.

274. Baethgen, *Beiträge*, p. 32; cf. Lidzbarsky, *Eph.*, vol. 1, p. 251, n.1, and Astour, *Hellenosemitica*, p. 258, and n.3.

275. Morin, "The Cult of Dea Syria," 17, where Morin also notes, "if some equation with a Greek divinity was required at all, 'Aphrodite' was the likely choice"; cf. also 82.

276. Hauvette-Besnault, "Fouilles de Délos," 497 (no. 15); cf. Cumont, "Syria Dea," in *Dictionnaire des antiquités*, vol. 4, pt. 2, p. 1592, and Morin, "The Cult of Dea Syria," 119.

277. *Onirocriticon* 1.8, printed in van Berg, *Répertoire*, no. 97 (pp. 77-78).

278. *Supplices* ll. 554-555. On the identification of the land mentioned by Aeschylus with "la Syrie du nord, au vaste pays agricole entre l'Oronte et l'Euphrate," see Perdrizet, "A propos d'Atargatis," 273, where Perdrizet also identifies Aeschylus' Aphrodite with Atargatis. Morin ("The Cult of Dea Syria," 132) argues the same.

undeniable force in establishing the role of ʿAštart in the character of Atargatis.

Atargatis and ʿAnat

The evidence from the cult of Atargatis that the goddess also subsumes the attributes of Canaanite ʿAnat is less compelling than that which bore witness to the role of ʾAšerah and ʿAštart in this cult. On the other hand, the etymological evidence is here the strongest, since the writing of the second half of the name Atargatis as -*ʿth*/-*ʿtʿ* can hardly reflect any known Semitic goddess but ʿAnat. Still, we are not dependent on etymology alone even in the case of ʿAnat. We noted above the Aramaic personal name *ʿtrʿzh* and the application of the same epithet to Athena/ʿAnat and to Atargatis. Zeus/Hadad is everywhere the consort of Atargatis; in the words of Seyrig, Atargatis is "la parèdre inséparable du dieu."[279] Although the shifting marriage alliances of the Canaanite deities have been noted, ʿAnat is regularly the consort of Baʿl Haddu; hence, Atargatis' mate is ʿAnat's mate. At Ugarit, ʿAnat's full title is often *batultu ʿanatu*, "Virgin ʿAnat." In Beroea, Atargatis too bears the appellation παρθένος.[280] Interestingly, neither Atargatis nor ʿAnat is an ordinary virgin, for three inscriptions from Phistyon (in Aetolia) are dedicated to the Syrian Goddess as ταῖ ματέρι τῶν θεῶν καὶ ταῖ παρθένοι.[281] In our review of Atargatis' iconography at the outset, we saw that lions support her throne in reliefs and on coins portraying the

---

279. "La triade héliopolitaine et les temples de Baalbek," 315, and cf. 320 (Seyrig is speaking of Atargatis and Hadad).

280. Ὀρλάνδος, "Βεροίας ἀπιγραφαὶ ἀνέκδοται," no. 2 (145) and no. 3 (147).

281. Guenther Klaffenbach, ed., *Inscriptiones Graecae*, consilio et auctoritate academiae litterarum Borussicae editae, vol. 9, pt. 1, fascicule 1 (Berlin: Walter de Gruyter, 1932), nos. 96b, 105, and 110b. The Phistyon inscriptions mentioning the goddess date from the first three centuries B.C. and all "are official acts of manumission" in which the "Dea Syria takes the part of the chief witness and guarantor of the manumission" (Morin, "The Cult of Dea Syria," 46). It is, of course, possible that the cult here combines Atargatis with the *magna mater* Cybele; but we have seen already that Atargatis can be called "mother."

goddess; and this datum too might reveal an association with ʻAnat. It must be admitted that none of the three major Canaanite goddesses is free from associations with the lion. In explaining the name *ʻbd lb(ʼ)t* on the twelfth-century B.C. El-Khadr arrowheads, Milik and Cross wrote:

> As for the lioness-goddess there is an embarrassing choice between the three chief Canaanite goddesses: *ʼAṯirat*, *ʻAṯtart* and *ʻAnat*. The first seems preferable, as she, under the epithet *Qudšu*, is represented standing on a lion in the numerous Egyptian stelae dedicated to her....But Asherah is rather mother and fertility-goddess, and in names of bowmen one might perhaps expect a war divinity. Usually ʻAṯtart and ʻAnat are characterized as goddesses of war in the Canaanite and Egyptian texts and representations. For example, they are the patronesses of chariot-warriors: it would be quite as appropriate in the case of archers. The interest of ʻAnat in the composite bow is vividly depicted in the ʼAqhat epic. In later times, Astarte is represented as lion-headed, or in the form of a sphinx, and assimilated to Sekhmet. She, or ʻAnat, appears on a Ras Shamra cylinder, sitting between two lions.[282]

The lions are, then, fitting companions for ʻAnat, called Athena in Greek, but also for her two sister goddesses. Disentangling which of three goddesses, all associated with the lion, is best seen in the lion of Atargatis, herself a composite of the same three goddesses, is best left as an impossible and probably misdirected task. Like the shifting marriage alliances, the association of all three goddesses with the lion doubtlessly aided their mingling into a single figure.

Conclusion

James B. Pritchard concludes his *Palestinian Figurines* monograph with a statement equally fitting here: "At a particular place and time one female deity seems to be predominant as the divine lady of that particular time and place."[283] Although

---

282. "Inscribed Javelin-Heads from the Period of the Judges: A Recent Discovery in Palestine," 8. We noted above that Cross identified *labīʼtu* ("Lion-Lady") with ʻAnat in 1967 ("The Origin and Early Evolution of the Alphabet," 13*), but with ʼAšerah in 1973 (*CMHE*, p. 33).

283. P. 85.

our view is doubtlessly distorted by the fragmentary nature of the evidence, that evidence we have suggests that 'Ašerah, 'Aštart, or 'Anat surpassed her sister goddesses in importance at different times and places, but also that each continued to be worshipped as a distinct goddess somewhere until at least the beginning of the present era. 'Aštart dominates in the names of Phoenicians on the mainland in the first millennium B.C., as she shares a place of honor among the references to foreign worship in the Old Testament. 'Ašerah is heard of more often than 'Aštart in the Ugaritic texts, and, under the epithet Tannit, again plays a role of major importance in Carthage and elsewhere in the western Mediterranean. Except for as the theophorous element on a few names and several inscriptions from Cyprus, the name 'Anat is little heard in the first millennium B.C., yet hers is the preeminent role in the Ugaritic texts.

But if these three deities retained their distinct identities over the entire period we have covered, they also began to share attributes and to be mingled together in their worshippers' eyes already at Ugarit. Because of the early date of this mingling, the claim of de Moor that "the pairing of the great goddesses 'Aṯtartu and 'Anatu is doubtlessly a late development in the theology of the Ugaritic priests, which after the complete identification of the two and the subsequent dropping of the conjunction would lead ultimately to the name of the Syrian goddess Atargatis"[284] is forced and without basis. This claim is unfounded, not merely because de Moor is incorrect in seeing behind Atargatis only 'Aštart and 'Anat, but also because of his imposition of an evolutionary scheme upon what he styles "the theology of the Ugaritic priests." The three major goddesses of Canaanite religion are associated in numerous ways at Ugarit; they share not only functions but even husbands. And the Qudšu relief now in Winchester College identifies one figure as all three goddesses in the time of Ramses III.[285]

The figure of Atargatis as described in the *De Syria Dea*

---

284. "Studies in the New Alphabetic Texts from Ras Shamra I," 170-171. De Moor is discussing RS 24.258 (*Ugaritica V*, no. 1), which he considers late also because of the "dishonourable" treatment of 'Ēl (168, and 168, n.2), thus applying the standards of an abstainer to the lordly drunk 'Ēl.

285. For the date of the relief, see Stadelmann, p. 115.

and by other visitors to Hierapolis bears astonishing resemblance to a situation that obtained over a thousand years before Lucian's visit. There are, as there must inevitably have been, changes brought about by the passage of these years and especially by the location of Hierapolis; one is hard put to imagine a location more vulnerable to a wide assortment of ancient Near Eastern powers with their different religions than Hierapolis' place in northern Syria near the Euphrates. Yet Atargatis still retains the attributes of ʾAšerah, ʿAštart, and ʿAnat, as her name still comprehends all of theirs. To study the figure of Atargatis is to vindicate the accuracy and comprehensiveness of Lucian's reporting, and to see at first hand the Canaanite background of the religion of north Syria shortly after the turn of the era.

Chapter III

Σημήιον

The Problem

In paragraph 33 of the *De Syria Dea* Lucian describes the object in the inner chamber (θάλαμος) of the Hierapolis temple, between the images of Zeus and Hera. This object he calls only σημήιον; and from his description of the object there has arisen a torrent of scholarly controversy in the past century. Indeed, one might be well advised to take the safer path and skirt "l'épineuse question du *semeion* décrit par Lucien,"[1] were it not for the central importance of this object which is placed in the position of preeminence in the Hierapolis temple. Whatever the identity of the σημήιον, it clearly played a major role in the cult; and hence an explanation of its significance is a prerequisite to understanding the religion of Hierapolis.

Lucian's description is as follows:

> In between the two [images of Hera and Zeus] there stands another golden image, not at all like those other images. It has no form[2] of its own, but bears the qualities[3] of

---

1. A. Caquot, "Note sur le *semeion* et les inscriptions araméennes de Hatra," *Syria* 32 (1955) 59; cf. Stocks' statement, "die mittelfigur der Triad (33) hat noch keine allseitig befriedigende Erklärung gefunden" ("Studien," 15), though we will see that Stocks' assumption of a divine triad in this scene is unnecessary.

2. Comte du Mesnil du Buisson translates here, "Elle n'a pas de forme [humaine?] propre" ("L'étendard," 76), which is surely correct since the force of Lucian's words is to distinguish this object from the anthropomorphic statues of Hera and Zeus. The word ξόανον probably has the same force here (even though it is applied to all three "images"), since in para. 2 Lucian distinguishes between ἀγάλματα and ξόανα and in para. 33 he introduces Zeus' statue as an ἄγαλμα.

3. For the translation of εἶδος as "quality," see *LS*, sub voce (p. 482b). Harmon also renders "qualitees" here (*Lucian*, vol. 4, p. 389). It would not be tendentious and

the other gods. Even the Assyrians themselves call it a σημήιον, and they have given it no name of its own; nor do they talk about its origin or form. Some hold that it is Dionysos, others that it is Deucalion, still others that it is Semiramis. There is, indeed, a golden dove placed upon its apex,[4] for which reason they say that this σημήιον is of Semiramis. Twice each year it goes on a journey to the sea for the conveyance of the water of which I have spoken.[5]

ἐν μέσῳ δὲ ἀμφοτέρων ἕστηκε ξόανον ἄλλο χρύσεον οὐδαμὰ τοῖσιν ἄλλοισι ξοάνοισιν ἴκελον. τὸ δὲ μορφὴν μὲν ἰδίην οὐκ ἔχει, φορέει δὲ τῶν ἄλλων θεῶν εἴδεα. καλέεται δὲ σημήιον καὶ ὑπ' αὐτῶν 'Ασσυρίων, οὐδέ τι οὔνομα ἴδιον αὐτῷ ἔθεντο, ἀλλ' οὐδὲ γενέσιος αὐτοῦ καὶ εἴδεος λέγουσι· καί μιν οἱ μὲν ἐς Διόνυσον, ἄλλοι δὲ ἐς Δευκαλίωνα, οἱ δὲ ἐς Σεμίραμιν ἄγουσι· καὶ γὰρ δὴ ὦν ἐπὶ τῇ κορυφῇ αὐτοῦ περιστερὴ χρυσέη ἐφέστηκε. τοὔνεκα δὴ μυθέονται Σεμιράμιος ἔμμεναι τόδε σημήιον. ἀποδημέει δὲ δὶς ἑκάστου ἔτεος ἐς θάλασσαν ἐς κομιδὴν τοῦ εἶπον ὕδατος.

From Lucian's description one concludes that the σημήιον is an architectural form of some sort, rather than an anthropomorphic statue, which carries with it devices suggestive of divine symbols. Among these there is certainly a dove, and probably also something which reminded Lucian of Dionysos, perhaps a device which could be interpreted as a pole or phallus on which was hung cult objects. Happily, we are not dependent upon Lucian's account alone for our knowledge of the σημήιον,

---

probably more in keeping with Lucian's description to translate εἴδεα here as "symbols."

4. While κορυφή can be used of the head of a man or an animal, it is more often used of the summit of a mountain or, as here, the apex of a triangle, and thus again distinguishes the σημήιον from a statue in human form; see *LS*, sub voce (p. 983a).

5. Lucian's reference is to para. 13, the end of his telling of the Deucalion story. The most natural explanation of this rite is that it is associated, like the city's name Mabbug, with the belief in a chasm or spring at Hierapolis as an outlet of the source of all earthly water, and that the rite is an apotropaic gesture to prevent the recurrence of the deluge.

for coins from the era and area portray the assembly of images in the Hierapolis θάλαμος, including the σημήιον between Hadad and Atargatis. Among these is a coin of Hierapolis issued in the early third century A.D. under Caracalla (figure 1).[6] Several scholars describe the reverse of this coin; and their descriptions merit repetition here. Imhoof-Blumer writes,

> Front eines kleinen Giebelgebäudes mit Legionszeichen zwischen den beiden Säulen und einer Taube? auf dem Akroterion. Zu beiden Seiten die zwei grossen syrischen Gottheiten (die θεοὶ Συρίας der Kupfermunzen), und zwar links Baal Kevan [sic] mit Kalathos und Sceptar von vorn auf oder zwischen zwei Stieren sitzend, rechts Atergatis [sic] mit denselben Attributen und einer Spindel? von vorn auf oder zwischen zwei Löwen sitzend.[7]

A. B. Cook, whose drawing of the Caracalla coin plainly shows a crescent in the pediment of the structure, offers a description which is virtually a translation of Imhoof-Blumer's:

> a god with *kálathos* and sceptre seated on or between two bulls and a goddess with the same attributes and a spindle (?) seated on or between lions. The two deities are grouped on either side of a small gabled structure, in which is an object resembling a military standard and on which rests a dove.[8]

---

6. Drawings of the Caracalla coin may be found in the following collections or discussions: Joseph Pellerin, *Mélange de diverses médailles*, vol. 1 (Paris: H. L. Guerin & L. F. Delatour, 1765), pl. 8, no. 12; A. B. Cook, *Zeus*, vol. 1, p. 586 (fig. 448); Stocks, "Studien," pl. 1, no. 5; and Ingholt, "Parthian Sculptures," pl. 4, no. 2. Unless one has escaped my attention, no photograph of this coin is available, and all representations of it are based on Pellerin's eighteenth-century drawing.

7. F. Imhoof-Blumer, *Griechische Münzen*, Abhandlungen der k. bayer. Akademie der wiss. I. cl. 18, vol. 3 (Munich: Verlag der k. Akademie, 1880), p. (759), no. 772. The obverse of the coin is a portrait of Caracalla. The inscription to which Imhoof-Blumer refers is that on the coins described immediately below.

8. *Zeus*, vol. 1, p. 586. I emphasize the crescent within the pediment of the "gabled structure" because none of the commentators takes note of it, though it is plainly to be seen on Pellerin's drawing from which the others are taken.

The same arrangement, except for the presence of a disk or a disk and crescent within the pediment,[9] appears on a Hierapolis coin issued under Alexander Severus a few years after the Caracalla coin (figure 2).[10] The Severus coin bears the legend ϑεοὶ Συρίας Ἱεροπολίτων. Ingholt describes accurately the Severus and Caracalla coins together:

> In the center of both appears a narrow gabled structure topped by a bird and inside it a pole or standard decorated with three (Caracalla) or four (Severus) disks. To the left of the structure is a male divinity seated between two bulls and to the right a goddess, seated between two lions.[11]

The same representations appear on a near contemporary coin of Julia Mamaea.[12]

Representations from sites near Hierapolis show objects which are similar to that in the center of the coins and which have been compared justly with the Hierapolis σημήιον. The

---

9. The drawing in Garstang and Strong, *The Syrian Goddess*, fig. 7, p. 70, shows the disk topped by a crescent-shaped object, though none of the photographs of the coin is clear enough to assert this with absolute confidence, even with the photographs enlarged several times.

10. Again, the obverse is a portrait of Severus, the reverse portrays the shrine of Hierapolis. Photographs of the coin's reverse appear in: Imhoof-Blumer, *Griechische Münzen*, p. 14, no. 7 (coin no. 773); Garstang and Strong, *The Syrian Goddess*, frontispiece, fig. 1; P. V. C. Baur, *et al.*, *Dura-Europos, Preliminary Report of the Third Season*, pl. 18, no. 7; Stocks, "Studien," pl. 1, no. 1; Ingholt, "Parthian Sculptures," pl. 4, no. 2; and Henri Seyrig, "Antiquités syriennes," *Syria* 49 (1972) fig. 4 (105). There are drawings of the coin in A. B. Cook, *Zeus*, vol. 1, fig. 449 (p. 586); Langdon, *Semitic Mythology*, fig. 21 (p. 36--this is the least precise of the drawings); and Comte du Mesnil du Buisson, "L'étendard," fig. 2 (77).

11. "Parthian Sculptures," 18. Again, Ingholt does not mention the crescent and disk, or disk alone, within the pediment.

12. The coin is described by Imhoof-Blumer, *Griechische Münzen*, pp. (759-760) (no. 775) and by A. B. Cook, *Zeus*, vol. 1, p. 586.

Hadad-Atargatis relief from Dura-Europos now in the Yale University Art Gallery, which was discussed in the previous chapter, shows a standard between the two deities.[13] The standard consists of three disks, as in the Caracalla coin, topped by a crossbar from which streamers or ribbons descend at each end, above which is an upturned crescent;[14] the major difference between this standard and that from Hierapolis is that "the special aedicula of the coins is missing."[15] A coin from Carrhae portrays a similar object, this time with the aedicule or "gabled structure," including a large upturned crescent in the pediment.[16] From Hatra come several altars on which are again standards; and some of these altars even bear inscriptions apparently labeling the object *smy'*, which word we will discuss later.[17] The Hatra device consists of a pole topped by a crescent, below which are a bas-relief, a bust of a god (presumably), a plain disk, and three rings. In the last number in his "Antiquités syriennes" series, Henri Seyrig published a relief now in the Beirut Museum,[18] to which it was brought from

---

13. Again, the relief is pictured in P. V. C. Baur, *et al.*, *Dura-Europos, Preliminary Report of the Third Season*, pl. 14; Comte du Mesnil du Buisson, "L'étendard," pl. 27a; Ingholt, "Parthian Sculptures," pl. 4, no. 1; and a full page photograph in Ann Perkins, *The Art of Dura-Europos*, pl. 38.

14. The standard is described by Baur (in P. V. C. Baur, *et al.*, *Dura-Europos, Preliminary Report of the Third Season*, pp. 100-101), who ascribes the crescent to "Atargatis as Selene" (pp. 120-121), by Comte du Mesnil du Buisson ("L'étendard," 78), and by Ingholt ("Parthian Sculptures," 18).

15. Ingholt, "Parthian Sculptures," 18.

16. The Carrhae coin is pictured in P. V. C. Baur, *et al.*, *Dura-Europos, Preliminary Report of the Third Season*, pl. 18, no. 8, and in Comte du Mesnil du Buisson, "L'étendard," fig. 2 (77).

17. See, for example, Javier Teixidor, "The Altars Found at Hatra," *Sumer* 21 (1965) pl. 4, no. 1 (=Hatra inscription no. 200, discussed by Teixidor in 88-89), and Ingholt, "Parthian Sculptures," pl. 7, no. 1. Below we will argue that both Lucian's σημήιον and the word *smy'* from Hatra mean simply "sign" or "symbol."

18. *Syria* 49 (1972) pl. 1. Seyrig discusses the provenance of the relief in 104-105.

somewhere in upper Mesopotamia, which portrays "les dieux de Hiérapolis,"[19] including a central object which is a pole decorated with five disks from the top of which descend eight ribbons conveying the impression of the pediment of an aedicule.[20] Finally, Seyrig mentions in the same article "une intéressant intaille, découverte par M. du Mesnil du Buisson au Cabinet des médailles de Paris," which portrays an object much like that in the center of the Hierapolis coins, including "une columbe au sommet."[21] Significantly, there is in the pediment of the structure here a goddess with prominent breasts, in place of the usual crescent or disk and crescent, thus suggesting that the crescent or crescent and disk in the Hierapolis structure is a symbol of a goddess; this is a suggestion to which we will return.

The object between Hadad and Atargatis on representations from Dura-Europos, Carrhae, Hatra, and elsewhere is never precisely the same as, though clearly reminiscent of, the structure on the Hierapolis coins of Caracalla and Severus. That this last structure is Lucian's σημήιον is undeniable. Both are non-anthropomorphic images placed between the great goddess and the great god of northern Syria; both contain objects which probably symbolize the traits of some deity; and both have a pediment on top of which sits a dove. It would be hypercritical to question this identification; and of all the recent students of the *De Syria Dea* only Strong and Garstang raise this question. They affirm that the σημήιον "is hardly to be explained by the later structure of Roman character" on the Severus coin but is rather an "altar, with pedestal and flat round top."[22] But there is nowhere in the *D.S.D.* the suggestion that the σημήιον functioned as or resembled an altar; and the suggestion of Strong and Garstang arises from their desire to deny Syrian parallels for the Hierapolis cult in favor of Anatolian influences alone. Other than this tendentious

---

19. Seyrig, "Antiquités syriennes," *Syria* 49 (1972) 105.

20. Seyrig, "Antiquités syriennes," *Syria* 49 (1972) 106, and n.3.

21. *Syria* 49 (1972) 106 and fig. 6. Seyrig guesses that there was also on the Beirut Museum relief a dove, which is now broken off (107).

22. Garstang and Strong, *The Syrian Goddess*, p. 73, n.43; cf. p. 24.

hypothesis, the scholarly community is correctly united in equating the σημήιον described in paragraph 33 of the *D.S.D.* with the device on the Hierapolis coins.[23] We have, then, pictorial and verbal representations of the σημήιον, and can fairly ask what role the σημήιον played in the religious life of Hierapolis.

Is Σημήιον a Divine Name?

Though many have despaired of arriving at any conclusion on the basis of the evidence now available, an answer to the question of the meaning of Lucian's σημήιον has often been that the word is to be seen as a divine name, or as a form only slightly altered from that of a divine name.[24] Among the first, if not the first, to suggest this explanation was Movers, who wrote in 1856, "der Name Simi, ܣܝܡܝ (σημεῖον mit der in Syrischen gewöhnlichen Aussprache des η als ι, im Rabb. סימן), wie hier[25] die Semiramis heisst, erklärt sich aus der Stelle von dem Bilde der Semiramis bei Lucian §33."[26] René Dussaud,

---

23. See, for example, A. B. Cook, *Zeus*, vol. 1, pp. 586-587 (Cook notes that "the word used here for the 'top' *(koryphê)* is the word applied in late Greek to the apex of a triangle. Hence the coin, which shows a bird sitting on the pediment of the *aedicula*, aptly illustrates the text"); Seb. Ronzevalle, S.J., "Inscription bilingue de Deir el-Qalaʿa," *Revue archéologique*, 4th series, vol. 2 (1903) 39, n.1 ("L'exactitude matérielle de cette précieuse information est...confirmée par les monuments numismatiques d'Hiérapolis"); du Mesnil du Buisson, "L'étendard," 76; Ingholt, "Parthian Sculptures," 18 ("two coins from Hierapolis portray without a doubt the divine triad mentioned by Lucian"); Goossens, *Hiérapolis de Syrie*, p. 65; and Walton, "Atargatis," in *Reallexikon für Antike und Christentum*, vol. 1, col. 854. Note too in support of the conclusion drawn from Lucian's use of κορυφή here, that in para. 32 he uses the usual word for "head" (κεφαλή) in describing the statue of Hera.

24. Much the best summary presentation of this problem and the various solutions suggested is offered by Clemen, in "Miszellen," pp. 100-103.

25. Movers' reference is to the *Apology* attributed to Melito of Sardis, which will be discussed at length below.

26. F. C. Movers, *Die Phönizier*, vol. 2, part 3 (Berlin: Ferd. Dümmler's Verlagsbuchhandlung, 1856), p. 137, n.47.

in company with others, added the refinement that σημήιον is "ein Name, der nach dem Muster von Adonion oder Balanion gebildet ist";[27] and Vincent, arguing that "le *sêmeion* est incontestablement une divinité,"[28] echoes Dussaud with, "il est visiblement construit sur la form ἡραῖον, le sanctuaire ou l'idole de Héra, βαλάνιον, le sanctuaire ou l'idole de Ba'al à Héliopolis."[29] A slight variation on this hypothesis is the argument that σημήιον as it stands in the *D.S.D.* means just "symbol" or "image," but that as such it represents Lucian's auditory error for a divine name. Thus Clemen writes that while Lucian "versteht unter σημήιον...ein Bild, keinen Eigennamen," a proper name may yet lurk behind the term σημήιον.[30]

The standard corollary to this explanation of σημήιον is that the Hierapolitans worshipped a divine triad, consisting of Hadad, Atargatis, and a deity whose name is represented by σημήιον, though the variety in the identifications proposed for this last deity is already a major weakness in this argument. Cumont states that the Hierapolis triad is Semitic Hadad, Atargatis and "Simios" = Roman Jupiter, Venus, and Mercury,[31] Ronzevalle that the triad is "Hadad, Atargatis et Sémiramis,"[32] and Dussaud, who has devoted many discussions to this problem, suggests yet another explanation; there is, Dussaud affirms unequivocally, "kein Zweifel, dass man in Hierapolis eine göttliche Dreiheit verehrte, bestehend aus Hadad, Atargatis, seiner Beisitzerin, und ihrer Tochter Sime oder Simea."[33] Baudissin

---

27. "Simea und Simios," in *PW*, 2d series, vol. 3, col. 137.

28. *La religion des Judéo-Araméens d'Eléphantine*, p. 656.

29. *La religion des Judéo-Araméens d'Eléphantine*, p. 666; cf. Ingholt, "Parthian Sculptures," 20: "In order to designate the *image* of Semea the Syrians could just add the suffix --ân to the name of the deity, a most common nominal ending both in Jewish-Aramaic and in Syriac" (this statement, which is itself not the same as claiming σημήιον is a divine name as it stands, does not represent Ingholt's ultimate position, which will be reviewed below).

30. "Miszellen," p. 101.

31. "Syria Dea," in *Dictionnaire des antiquités*, vol. 4, pt. 2, p. 1593.

32. "Inscription bilingue," 44.

33. "Simea und Simios," in *PW*, 2d series, vol. 3, col. 138. Dussaud's position on this question is often difficult to

merely mentions in passing "die Trias von Hierapolis bei Lucian, *De Syria dea* §33: Here, Zeus und σημήιον."[34] Clemen too constructs a triad from the *De Syria Dea*, seeing the third member as either a goddess Simia, or, since "die dritte Person in den Triaden...immer eine männlich Gottheit ist," a god identical with ʾEšmun.[35] The same indecision is witnesses in the arguments of Walton, who sees "Simios oder Simea" as a part of the Hierapolis "göttliche Trias,"[36] and of Astour, who states, "in the Hellenistic age Ešmun-Asclepios was identified with a Syrian deity who was sometimes Hadad's son Simios, sometimes Hadad's daughter Semia or Sima."[37] Most recently, Donner and Röllig explain the personal name *ʿbdsmyʾ* from Hatra, as "'Der Sklave des Semios.' Die Gottheit masc. Simios / fem. Simia ist im hellenist. Orient weit verbreitet gewesen. In Hierapolis-Bambyke begegnet Simia als Tochter der Arargatis und des Hadad; vgl. Lukian, Dea Syria 33."[38]

What is the evidence that a deity Simios or Simia is "weit verbreitet" in the Hellenistic Near East? There is some evidence to this effect; but it is as confusing and contradictory as the explanations noted above. In the *Corpus Inscriptionum*

---

sort out. Thus, earlier he had argued that the Hierapolis triad was Hadad, Atargatis and "Simios = Mercure = Nebo," while Simea was Nebo's consort "Tašmet" ("Notes de Mythologie syrienne," *Revue archéologique*, 4th series, vol. 4 [1904] 258). In an article entitled "Temples et cultes de la triade héliopolitaine à Baʿalbeck," Dussaud listed the triad of Hierapolis as "Hadad, Ashérat (Atargatis) et Simios" (76), the last being the same as "Aliyan, fils de Baʿal" (77), though today no one would claim that *ʾalʾiyān* is other than an appellation of Baʿl Haddu himself. The position presented in the quotation given in the text above is also that in Dussaud's article "Peut-on identifier l'Apollon barbu de Hiérapolis de Syrie?," where he asserts that "le fameux *séméion*" is "la déesse Simia" (130-131).

34. *Adonis und Esmun*, p. 16, n.l.

35. *LSSG*, p. 43.

36. "Atargatis," in *Reallexikon für Antike und Christentum*, vol. 1, col. 854.

37. *Hellenosemitica*, p. 162.

38. *KAI*, vol. 2, p. 297; the name *ʿbdsmyʾ* occurs in their inscription no. 242.

Latinarum, under the heading "Berytus," we find the inscription *Iononis fil. Iovis Sim...*,[39] which is completed and understood by Th. Mommsen on the basis of the Syriac *symy brt hdd* (of the *Apology* attributed to Melito) as *"Sime filia Hadad respondet Iunoni Iovis filiae."*[40] Ronzevalle compares with this inscription a Latin-Greek bilingual found at Deir el Qalaʿa, near Beirut, which he reads as *I(unoni) S(imae)* = θε[ᾷ] Σίμᾳ.[41] Dussaud, however, argues that little is to be gained from this apparent assertion that Sima is Hera's daughter, since "ce texte emploie *Jupiter* et *Juno* comme de simples équivalents de θεός."[42] It thus seems that the lineage, at least, of Sima is unclear from these brief occurrences of the name. A god Simios is apparently mentioned in a Greek inscription dated to A.D. 223 from Kefer Nebo in Syria. This inscription reads Σειμίῳ καὶ Συμβετύλῳ καὶ Λεόντι θεοῖς πατρῴοις.[43] To Lidzbarski, this represents a triad of Simi (= Συμβετύλῳ), "ein männlicher Simios" (= Σειμίῳ) constructed "aus der Göttin Simi," and Atargatis (= Λέοντι) since "das dritte Glied der Trias das Tier der Atargatis ist."[44] Dussaud also finds both Simios (= Σειμίῳ) and Simia (= Συμβετύλῳ) here,[45] the latter "'die symbetyle

---

39. *CIL*, vol. 3, no. 159. This inscription does not appear in *Inscriptions grecques et latines de la Syrie*, Bibliothèque archéologique et historique, vol. 12- (Paris: Paul Geuthner, 1929-); but it is mentioned in the notes to *Inscriptions grecques et latines de la Syrie*, no. 376, where the *CIL* reading is repeated.

40. *CIL*, vol. 3, no. 6669.

41. "Inscription bilingue," 29-30. The Greek section reads in full θεῷ ἁγίῳ Βάλ καὶ θεᾷ Ἥρᾳ καὶ θε[ᾷ] Σίμᾳ καὶ νεωτέρα Ἡρᾳ. The inscription is read the same by Wilhelm Dittenberger, *Orientis graeci inscriptiones selectae* (Leipzig: S. Hirzel, 1903), no. 590 (vol. 2, pp. 281-282), and by Lidzbarski, *Eph*, vol. 2, p. 325; see also Ingholt, "Partian Sculptures, " 21.

42. "Notes de Mythologie syrienne," 252.

43. *Inscriptions grecques et latines de la Syrie*, no. 376; also in Lidzbarski, *Eph.*, vol. 2, pp. 323-324.

44. *Eph.*, vol. 2, pp. 323-324; cf. "Seimios ou Seimos un doublet masculin de Σημέ(α), Σίμα ou Σιμία" (*Inscriptions grecques et latines de la Syrie*, no. 376).

45. "Notes de Mythologie syrienne," 256-257.

Gottheit,' d.h. Simia."[46] Clemen equates this male deity Simios with the figure "Simmas" mentioned by Diodorus Siculus in the latter's account of Semiramis (2.4.6.).[47] Ingholt would like to keep the Kefer Nebo triad the same as that which many have claimed to find in *D.S.D.* paragraph 33, and hence sees Hadad-Zeus, rather than a goddess Simia or Simi, behind the apparently enigmatic Συμβέτυλος.[48] Another inscription, found near Homs, contains the name σημεδ which Perdrizet emends to σημέᾳ (seeing, presumably and reasonably, an error in writing Δ for Α), thus adding another witness to the list of occurrences of a goddess Simia.[49] Finally, Simia or Simios has been seen in the personal names Βαρσημέα, 'Αβεδσιμίος, and 'Αμασσημία.[50]

Taking their cue from this Greek and Latin evidence, many scholars have gone on to find evidence for a goddess Simia in Semitic sources. Among the deities worshipped in Samaria is said to be ’Ašima *(’ăšîmā)*, a product of the "men of Hamath" *(’anšê ḥămāt)* according to 2 Kings 17:30; and this ’Ašima has been compared to Simia and other similar names. Ronzevalle equates the *S(imae)* / Σίμᾳ of the Deir el Qala‘a bilingual with (Pseudo-)Melito's *symy*, with ’Ašima, and with "la personnalité mythique connue sous le nom de *Sémiramis*";[51] and in his

---

46. "Simea und Simios," in *PW*, 2d series, vol. 3, col. 139.

47. Clemen writes, Σείμιος "is vielleicht auch [in addition to the Kefer Nebo reference] in dem bei Diodor (II 4 6) als Pflegevater der Semiramis erscheinenden Simmas zu erkennen" ("Miszellen," p. 102); without elaboration, this argument reads oddly.

48. "Parthian Sculptures," 22. As we will see, Συμβέτυλος is the Greek equivalent of the Elephantine אשמביתאל, and is not so problematic as the scholarly discussion would indicate.

49. Paul Perdrizet, "Syriaca," *Revue archéologique*, 3d series, vol. 32 (1898) 39.

50. See Dittenberger, *Orientis graeci inscriptiones selectae*, vol. 2, p. 282, and Ronzevalle, "Inscription bilingue," 33. The last name is apparently from a form 'Αματ (= *’mt*, "handmaid") -σημία.

51. "Inscription bilingue," 36 and 38-40. Ronzevalle's proposed etymology for Semiramis, Sîmâ (divine name) plus *rwm* ("to be high") is refuted by Dussaud ("Notes de Mythologie syrienne," 256). For a recent discussion of the still unsolved problem of the etymology of Semiramis, see Wilhelm Eilers,

commentary on 2 Kings 17:30, Montgomery puzzlingly combines the already confusing data and writes, "the name Ashima appears in that of the golden image described by Lucian, §33, 'called by the Greeks [sic] σημήιον,...Simi is to be identified with Atargatis....Simios was her son."[52] Others equate the divine name *'šmbyt'l* from Elephantine with both 'Ašima and the name Simia.[53]

But the key Semitic source for those who wish to identify Lucian's σημήιον with a goddess Simi/Simia is the *Apology* attributed to Melito of Sardis. This work, entitled *An Oration of Meliton the Philosopher, which was Given Before Antoninus Caesar (m'mr' dmylytwn pylswp' dhw' qdm 'anṭwnynws qsr)*, is found in a Syriac manuscript of the sixth or seventh century, which is now in the British Museum,[54] and was published in the mid-nineteenth

---

Semiramis (Wien: Kommissionsverlag des Österreichischen Akademie der Wissenschaften, 1971), especially pp. 42-46. Eilers rejects all the proposed etymologies as unsatisfactory.

52. *The Book of Kings* (ICC), p. 475. Since Lucian clearly says that the ξόανον was "called a σημήιον by the Assyrians themselves" (καλέεται δὲ σημήιον καὶ ὑπ' αὐτῶν 'Ασσυρίων), it is difficult to see where Montgomery derives his statement "'called by the Greeks σημήιον.'" Equally obscure is the parentage he gives to Simios. 'Ašima is probably best seen either as an error for the name 'Ašerah, or as an intentional corruption of 'Ašerah; the latter is the understanding of John Gray, who translates the phrase in 2 Kings 17:30 "'the men of Hamath made Asherah" (*I & II Kings:* A Commentary, Old Testament Library, 2d ed. [London: SCM, 1970], p. 653), calling the Hebrew "an orthodox Jewish parody (*'ᵃšēmā*, 'guilt') of 'ᵃšērā" (p. 653, n. e).

53. For summaries of these proposed identifications, see Vincent, *La religion des Judéo-Araméens d'Eléphantine*, p. 656, and Stanley A. Cook, *The Religion of Ancient Palestine in the Light of Archaeology*, The Schweich Lecture of the British Academy, 1925 (London: Oxford University Press, 1930), pp. 150-152. Cook calls Simē/Sima "the goddess of Hierapolis, daughter of Zeus-Hadad and of Hera-Atargatis" (p. 151).

54. The manuscript is dated to the seventh century by Rubens Duval (*Anciennes littératures chrétiennes*, vol. 2: La littérature syriaque, 2d ed. [Paris: Victor Lecoffre, 1900], p. 167), and to the sixth or seventh century by Otto Bardenhewer (*Geschichte der altkirchlichen Litteratur* [Freiburg: Herdersche Verlagshandlung, 1902], p. 553).

century by Cureton (with an English translation),[55] and by Renan (with a Latin translation).[56] For many, this work's mention of "Simi the daughter of Hadad" *(symy brt hadd)*, who is linked with Mabbug *(mbwg)*,[57] provides irrefutable proof that Lucian's σημήιον represents a divine name. Six writes of this term as used in the *De Syria Dea*, "c'est Simi, la fille de Hadad du fragment de Méliton";[58] and about the same time Nöldeke says with similar finality, "nun bestätigt aber noch dazu die Apologie des PseudoMeliton das nur in der Endung etwas gräcisierte σημήιον als Lucian's Namen der Göttin durch ܣܡܝ ܒܪܬ ܗܕܕ."[59] In this century, Harmon found proof in Melito's *Apology* "that Lucian's 'token' (semeion) rests upon a misunderstanding of the name of a goddess Simi, Simia, Semea."[60] And for Vincent too the remarks in this *Apology* "apportent avec elle la preuve que le σημήιον d'Hiérapolis est bien Simia et que cette déesse est une divinité syrienne."[61]

Before turning to a detailed discussion of the presupposition common to all of these views, that σημήιον is primatively a deity who makes up a part of a divine triad at Hierapolis, we will note other hypotheses which similarly rest upon the

---

55. William Cureton, *Spicilegium Syriacum:* Containing Remains of Bardesan, Meliton, Ambrose and Mara Bar Serapion (London: Rivington, 1855).

56. E. Renan, "S. Melitonis, Fragmenta Apologiae ad Marcum Aurelium Imperatorem," in *Spicilegium Solesmensa*, complectens sanctorum patrum scriptorumque ecclesiasticorum anecdoto hactenus opera, vol. 2, ed. J. B. Pitra (Paris: Firmin Didot Fratres, 1855), pp. XXXVII-LXI.

57. In the edition of Cureton, p. 25, ll. 9-20.

58. "Monnaies d'Hiérapolis," 121.

59. "Baethgen's *Beiträge*," 473. Nöldeke's comment comes in response to the proposal offered by Baethgen in solution to the problem of the σημήιον (that Lucian confused *'t'* with *'t'*), which will be discussed below, as will the question of the authorship of the *Apology* under Melito's name.

60. *Lucian*, vol. 4, p. 388, n.2.

61. *La religion des Judéo-Araméens d'Eléphantine*, p. 666. The evidence from this *Apology* is also cited in confirmation of the presence of a goddess in the word σημήιον by Clemen, *LSSG*, p. 43, and by Dussaud, "Peut-on identifier l'Apollon barbu de Hiérapolis de Syria?" 131.

assumption that Lucian's σημήιον represents a divine name. Since many scholars identify the σημήιον with 'Ešmun, the question arises whether σημήιον itself is a transcription of 'Ešmun. This question was answered negatively already by Baudisson in his *Adonis und Esmun*; while 'Ešmun does occur as *šmn* alone, "für die Aussprache des Namens ist durch alle überlieferten umschreibungen in der zweiten Silbe u (oder o) bezeugt."[62] Another suggestion is that of H. Zimmern, who derives the name Sima/Simea, Melito's *symy*, from Akkadian *šimtu*, "'Geschick'.... auffälliger Weise ganz als Synonym von Ištar, 'Göttin,'" and finds both "vielleicht auch in dem σημήιον bei Lucian, *De Dea Syria*, §33, mit der goldenen Taube auf dem Kopf."[63] Finally, Ingholt translates σημήιον "image of the god Heavens,"[64] and finds in the word *smy'* which occurs below the Hatra standards and which he equates with σημήιον, "a dialectical variant of the common Aramaic word shemayyâ, 'heavens,'" with a *s* for the usual *š* because of possible Arabic influence.[65] This suggestion has been decisively countered by Caquot, who argues (with respect to *smy'*) that no Aramaic dialect would represent "heaven" with a *s* instead of a *š*, and that if σημήιον were related to *šĕmayyâ* the first vowel would not be η.[66]

Basic problems remain in the assumption that Lucian's σημήιον represents a third deity alongside Hadad and Atargatis, both because the identity of this presumed third deity is not one upon which scholars can agree, and, more fundamentally, because the assumption that the shrine in the Hierapolis θάλαμος represents a triad is unnecessary. As for the identity of this presumed third deity, we have already seen that both a female Simia/Sima and a male Simios are evidenced by the Greek and Latin material; and hence one witnesses different groups of scholars arguing for a triad of either two females and a male (Simia, Atargatis, and Hadad) or a female and two males (Atargatis, Hadad, and Simios), yet both groups maintaining that their triad's composition touches upon some fundamental

---

62. P. 203.

63. *"Šimāt, Sīma, Tyche, Manāt," Islamica* 2 (1926) 547-577. As we will see, Zimmern later changed his mind and denied the identity of Lucian's σημήιον with any divine name.

64. "Parthian Sculptures," 43.

65. "Parthian Sculptures," 25-26.

66. "Note sur le *semeion*," 67-69.

principle of divine worship in the Phoenician or Syrian mind. Stocks approaches the correct answer when he notes that witnesses to a deity Simios or Simia are found only "an der Grenze des semitischen Sprachgebietes."[67] In fact, not only is neither grouping of two females and a male deity nor two males and a female deity basic to Phoenician religion, but also the notion of a divine triad of whatever composition plays no significant role in Phoenician and Syrian religion. Twenty years ago Caquot first argued that the often repeated "triade hiérapolitaine" including Simia or Simios is pure scholarly invention;[68] and in a brilliant piece entitled "Les dieux de Hiérapolis," in his "Antiquités syriennes" series, Seyrig decisively refuted the argument that a triad of some sort must be found at Hierapolis.[69] Seyrig notes the fashion of discovering at Hierapolis "une triade formée d'un grand-dieu, d'une grande-déesse, et d'un parèdre mineur - ou, s'il faut employer la terminologie courante, d'un dieu-fils";[70] but, almost alone, Seyrig further notes that the evidence for the σημήιον-Simios equation is far from clear, and that the identity of the latter is even cloudier. If Simios is a deity, he is, for Seyrig, "probablement l'équivalent de Hadad,"[71] which leaves us without the third member of the fashionable triad. There does seem to be a triad of Hadad, Atargatis, and a third deity called Asclepios on Delos; but we nowhere hear of this at Hierapolis, and hence Seyrig labels the Delos triad "une phénomène local."[72] Further, the argument that all the Phoenician cities worshipped a triad of deities is based solely on evidence from the second century A.D. and later, while we have seen that the *D.S.D.* describes a religion remarkable for its similarity to Canaanite religion of a much earlier date. And the triads of Palmyra "sont d'un tout autre type les phéniciennes, et rappellent plutôt certaines triades babyloniennes."[73] Finally, Seyrig's conclusion also deserves notice here: "D'après les monuments accessibles aujourd'hui, le culte de Mabog s'adressait à Hadad et à Atargatis, sans adjonction

---

67. "Studien," 16.
68. "Note sur le *semeion*," 66.
69. *Syria* 37 (1960) 233-252.
70. "Antiquités syriennes," *Syria* 37 (1960) 241.
71. "Antiquités syriennes," *Syria* 37 (1960) 244.
72. "Antiquités syriennes," *Syria* 37 (1960) 247.
73. "Antiquités syriennes," *Syria* 37 (1960) 250.

d'un parèdre mineur."[74]

We would, of course, not press this argument to include the claim that Canaanite/Phoenician deities were never pictured in groups of three. Text RS 24.252 from *Ugaritica V*, for example, portrays ʾĒl (father), flanked by Baʿl Haddu (son), and ʿAštart (mistress); and the same three deities appear together in Sakkunyaton's account of Phoenician religion.[75] Further, the Punic *cippi* representations often portray three idols within the frame of a stele, though there are also portrayals of two or of one idol.[76] Nor would we claim that Hadad and Atargatis were the only deities worshipped at Hierapolis. In paragraphs 34-38 of the *De Syria Dea*, Lucian notes the images of several more deities, the most important of whom is the one he calls Apollo. Lucian's description of this Apollo's image (para. 35-37), the accuracy of which is confirmed by the description of the same image given by Macrobius,[77] demonstrates clearly that the deity represented is not the Greek Apollo, for this is an "image of a bearded Apollo" (Ἀπόλλωνος γενειήτεω ξόανον), who is clothed (Ἀπόλλωνα εἵμασι κοσμέουσι) unlike the nude young Apollo of Greek representations. The Hierapolis bearded Apollo has been identified with Nabu/Nebo,[78] and with Hadad;[79] but the god's iconography and function (that of issuing

---

74. "Antiquités syriennes," *Syria* 37 (1960) 251.

75. As preserved in Eusebius' *Praeparatio Evangelica* 1. 10.31.

76. These *cippi* may be conveniently studied in Anna Maria Bisi's excellent study, *Le Stele Puniche*, Studi Semitici, no. 27 (Rome: Istituto di Studi del Vicino Oriente, Università di Roma, 1967). Examples of *cippi* representations with three idols are figs. 16, 60, 112, and 114-116, pls. 6 (no. 1), 7 (nos. 1 and 2), 9 (nos. 1 and 2), 21 (no. 2), 25 (no. 2), and 54; with two idols are figs. 18, 66, 97, 105, and 123, and pls. 2 (no. 1), and 13 (no. 1); and with one idol are fig. 23, and pls. 10 (no. 1) and 47.

77. *Saturnalia* 1.17.66-70. Macrobius says the Hierapolitans call the deity Apollo *(Apollinem appellant)* and notes that the image is bearded *(huius facies prelixa in acutum barba figurata est)*.

78. Harmon, *Lucian*, vol. 4, p. 390, n.2. But this Babylonian deity is the god of "Schreibkunst" (*WM*, p. 106).

79. Hauvette-Besnault, "Fouilles de Délos," 481-482;

oracles) as described by Lucian correspond neither to those of Nabu and Hadad, nor to those of Rešep, who is the usual Semitic equivalent of Greek Apollo.[80] But the portrait of a seated, bearded deity who issues oracles does correspond beautifully with the portrait of ʾĒl in the Ugaritic myths.[81] Thus Dussaud, alone, identifies the Hierapolis bearded Apollo with ʾĒl,[82] and argues that "le choix d'Apollon par le clergé de Hiérapolis est une flatterie à l'adresse de la dynastie des Séleucides dont le fondateur se prétendait issu d'Apollon."[83] Dussaud is surely correct; and he might have added that the practice at Hierapolis of human sacrifice (*D.S.D.*, para. 58) strongly suggests a cult of ʾĒl/Kronos at the city.[84] As a deity whose cult seems of

---

Bouchier, *Syria as a Roman Province*, p. 261; and Walton, "Atargatis," in *Reallexikon für Antike und Christentum*, vol. 1, col. 855. But Hadad is already portrayed in the θάλαμος, and in a way very different from the bearded Apollo.

80. The equivalence is made directly on a fourth-century B.C. trilingual inscription from Idalion, where Phoenician Rešep is Greek Apollo (*KAI*, no. 39). But, as his name indicates, Rešep was "the god of the underworld, of pestilence and war, like the Babylonian Nergal" (Roger T. O'Callaghan, S.J., "The Great Phoenician Portal Inscription from Karatepe," *Orientalia* NS 18 [1949] 202-203). For similar descriptions of Rešep, see *KAI*, vol. 2, p. 24, and Stadelmann, p. 49; and note the representation of Rešep on a New Kingdom stele (*ANEP*, no. 476).

81. For ʾĒl as the god who issues oracles *(tḥm)*, see *CTCA* 4.4.40-43; and for ʾĒl's "gray beard" *(šbt dqn)*, see *CTCA* 4.5.66. The literary descriptions of ʾĒl are supplemented by representations of ʾĒl from Ras Shamra and of Baʿl Ḥamōn from the Punic world (see Cross, *CMHE*, pp. 35-36).

82. "Peut-on identifier l'Apollon barbu de Hiérapolis de Syrie?" 147-148.

83. "Peut-on identifier l'Apollon barbu de Hiérapolis de Syrie?" 148. Note the third-century B.C. Seleucid coin published by A.-R. Bellinger and E.-T. Newell ("A Seleucid Mint at Dura-Duropus," *Syria* 21 [1940] 81, and pl. 14, no. 20) representing Antiochus on the obverse, Apollo on the reverse. The oracle giving function alone may have been sufficient to identify ʾĒl with Apollo, though ʾĒl's usual Greek equivalent is Kronos.

84. As Cross notes, "Diodorus Siculus [20.14.4-7]

minor significance compared to the attention devoted to Hadad and Atargatis, and yet as a deity without whose "divine decrees" (θέσφατα) nothing was done at Hierapolis (para. 36), this bearded Apollo is astonishingly like 'Ēl at Ugarit, for 'Ēl too plays a lesser role in the Ugaritic myths than do Ba'l and 'Anat, yet his assent is a prerequisite for any action. Thus, there was a third major deity worshipped at Hierapolis; but he did not constitute the third member of a triad with Hadad and Atargatis, and Lucian's description of his duties and worship reminds us again of the close relationship between the religion of Hierapolis and that of the Canaanites of a millennium and a half before, for whom the divine triad was of no theological significance.[85]

Beyond an insistence on discovering at Hierapolis a triad, further arguments for identifying σημήιον with a deity rest on equally shaky ground. The first half of the divine name *'šmbyt'l* from Elephantine is best explained as the equivalent of *šm*, "name," despite Vincent's assertion that theophorous names with *šm* are never preceded by a prothetic *'aleph*.[86] Lidzbarski equates *'šm-* here with *šm*, the former with a "Vorstazaleph," and concludes "die Urform אשם kein eigentlicher Gottesname, sondern nur Ersatz eines Namens ist."[87] Grimme too explains *'šmbyt'l* as "nur eine besondere Erscheinungsform des ביתאל,"[88] in which explanation he is followed by A. Šanda,[89]

---

specifically observes that the cult of human sacrifice was limited to worship of Kronos, that is, of 'Ēl" (*CMHE*, p. 26). For the Kronos-'Ēl identification, see also Donner, "Ein Orthostatenfragment," 81. A city named after the presence of a spring in its midst is also an appropriate city for a cult of 'Ēl who dwells at the *mabbūkê naharêmi*.

85. The likelihood of the bearded Apollo-'Ēl identification also detracts from the arguments of those who have claimed to have witnessed the demise of 'Ēl at Ugarit in the second millennium B.C. 'Ēl lived on, as indeed we should expect of one entitled the "Eternal One" (*'lm*), even if his continued vitality is witnessed by references to him not under the name 'Ēl but under the epithets *'lm* (Arslan Tash), *b'l ḥmn*, and *b'l šmm/šmn*.

86. *La religion des Judéo-Araméens d'Eléphantine*, p. 656.

87. *Eph.*, vol. 3, pp. 263-265.

88. Herbert Grimme, "Die Jahotriade von Elephantine," *Orientalistische Literaturzeitung* 15 (1912) 14.

and by Albright who adds that the Greek Συμβέτυλος contains "the Aramaic form *šum* of the Hebrew-Phoenician *šem/ešem*, 'name.'"[90] Rešep's name too is written *ʾršp* on a fifth-century B.C. Ibiza stele;[91] and already in the eighth-century B.C. Panammuwa I inscription we find *ʾšm hdd*, "name of Hadad," with a prothetic *ʾaleph*.[92] Thus disappears a name claimed as the equivalent of a name Simia/Simios and of σημήιον.

That leaves us with the phrase *symy brt hdd* from the *Apology* under the name of Melito of Sardis.[93] If this work were an originally Syriac composition from the second century, its witness would be formidable; but there is evidence against a date in the second century and against Syriac as the language of composition, at least of the section of the *Apology* in which *symy brt hdd* occurs. To be sure, Cureton's initial publication of this document argued for its genuineness; but Cureton stands alone in his view that the *Apology* is from Melito's hand "a short time before the death of Antoninus Pius."[94] In a review published in 1856 of Cureton's edition, Jacobi noted that nowhere in the work was to be found the name of Christ, that fragments of Melito's Greek *Apology* quoted by Eusebius find no place in this Syriac text, and that the name Melito occurs only in the heading given the text; therefore, concluded Jacobi, the work is not Melito's and the Antoninus of the title is more

---

89. Šanda writes, "Συμβέτυλος ist אשמביתאל der aram. Papyri von Elephantine," *Die Bücher der Könige*, Exegetisches Handbuch zum alten Testament, vol. 9, 2d half (Münster: Aschendorff, 1912), p. 230.

90. "The Evolution of the West-Semitic Divinity ʿAn-ʿAnat-ʿAttâ," 93; cf. *FSAC*, p. 286.

91. *KAI*, no. 72; see *KAI*, vol. 2, p. 88.

92. *KAI*, no. 214.

93. Recent summaries of Melito's life and works are to be found in Campbell Bonner, *The Homily on the Passion by Melito Bishop of Sardis*, with some Fragments of the Apocryphal Ezekiel, Studies and Documents ed. by Kirsopp Lake and Silva Lake, no. 12 (Philadelphia: University of Pennsylvania, 1940), pp. 3-5, and in Othmar Perler, *Méliton de Sardis: Sur la pâque et fragments*, Sources Chrétiennes, no. 123 (Paris: les Editions du Cerf, 1966), pp. 7-15.

94. *Spicilegium Syriacum*, p. x.

likely to be Caracalla or Elagabalus.[95] By the end of the nineteenth century, Seeberg could assert "mit absoluter Sicherheit" that Melito was not the author of this Syriac *Apology*;[96] and in this century almost no one is willing to grant the work to Melito or to the second century.[97]

The question of the original language of the *Apology* is answered less uniformly; but, as we will see below, this is because the text contains a distinct euhemeristic section whose concerns and style are different from what precedes and follows. Altaner and Stuiber label the work "eine wohl original-syrisch geschriebene *Apologie*";[98] and Quasten asserts, again without argument or supporting data, that the *Apology* "was written in Syriac and not translated from the Greek."[99] In his *Geschichte der syrischen Literatur*, Anton Baumstark claims that the text "ist anscheinend vielleicht überhaupt nicht aus dem Griechischen

---

95. J. L. Jacobi, rev. of W. Cureton, *Spicilegium Syriacum* (London, 1855), *Deutsche Zeitschrift für chrisliche Wissenschaft und christliches Leben*, 7th year, no. 14 (1856) 105-108. Cureton himself had observed that Eusebius' quotations did not occur in the text he was editing; but he postulated two *Apologies* to account for this problem (*Spicilegium Syriacum*, pp. vii-x).

96. R. Seeberg, "Die Apologie des Aristides untersucht und wiederhergestellt," in *Forschungen zur Geschichte des neutestamentlichen Kanons*, ed. Th. Zahn (Erlangen und Leipzig: Georg Böhme, 1893), p. 238, n.l.

97. The following all argue that the *Apology* is ungenuine and from the third century or later: Duval, *Anciennes littératures chrétiennes*, vol. 2, p. 168; Bardenhewer, *Geschichte der altkirchlichen Literatur*, pp. 553-555; Felix Haase, "Untersuchungen zur bardesanischen Gnosis," *Texte und Untersuchungen zur Geschichte der altchrislichen Literatur* 24 (1910) 67-72; Berthold Altaner--Alfred Stuiber, *Patrologie:* Leben, Schriften und Lehre der Kirchenväter, 7th ed. (Freiburg: Herder, 1966), p. 63; Johannes Quasten, *Patrology*, vol. 1: The Beginnings of Patristic Literature (Utrecht-Antwerp: Spectrum, 1950), p. 247; Seyrig, "Antiquités syriennes," *Syria* 37 (1960) 243; and J. T. Milik and J. Teixidor, "New Evidence on the North-Arabic Deity Aktab-Kutbâ," *BASOR* 163 (1961) 24.

98. *Patrologie*, p. 63.

99. *Patrology*, p. 247.

übersetzt, sondern ein Original" whose unknown author probably came from Hierapolis-Mabbug,[100] though the claim is unsupported and the author's presumed familiarity with Hierapolis is illusionary, as we will see. As categorically, Salmon labeled the work a "Greek original."[101] Nöldeke, though he ultimately decides the work is "doch ein griechisches Original,"[102] first noted the problem in attributing the entire work either to an original Syriac or an original Greek composition. If addressed to an emperor, as the title claims, the work must have been composed in Greek: Yet, "das Syrisch ist so fliessend, dass man die Schrift, ohne jenen Umstand, sicher als ein syrisches Original ansähe."[103] The solution to this impasse is to distinguish between the euhemeristic section near the work's beginning and the "flowing Syriac" sections which preceded and follow it.[104] This section records the objects of worship of several lands; thus, "the Egyptians worship Joseph the Hebrew" *(sgdw mṣryʾ ˋlywsp ʿbryʾ)*, "the Athenians worship Athena" *(sgdw ʾtnyʾ lʾtnʾ)*, "the Phoenicians worship Balti, queen of Cyprus" *(sgdw bny pwnyqʾ lblty mlktʾ dqwprws)*, while "the Syrians worship ʿAti of *ḥdybytʾ*" who cured "Simi, the daughter of Hadad, king of Syria" *(sgdw swryyʾ lʿty ḥdybytʾ...lsymy brt hdd mlkʾ dswryʾ)*. Jacobi,[105] Seeburg,[106] and Duval[107] all comment on

100. (Bonn: Marcus und Webers, 1922), p. 27.

101. George Salmon, "Melito," in *A Dictionary of Christian Biography*, ed. William Smith and Henry Wace, vol. 3 (London: John Murray, 1882), p. 895.

102. Th. Nöldeke, "Ueber die Apologie unter Meliton's Name in Cureton's Spirilegium [sic] Syriacum," *Jahrbücher für protestantische Theologie* 13 (1887) 346.

103. Nöldeke, "Ueber die Apologie," 345-346. Bardenhewer also observed that "der syrische Ausdruck ist gewandt und fliessend und weist keinen Spuren einen Übersetzung auf" (*Geschichte der altkirchlichen Literatur*, p. 554), though we will see that there are a number of "traces" for a translation from the Greek.

104. In the edition of Cureton, the euhemeristic section runs from p. 24, l. 21, to p. 25, l. 23.

105. Rev. of Cureton, *Spicilegium Syriacum*, 106.

106. "Die Apologie des Aristides," p. 238, n.1 (the author "zeigt im weiteren Vorlauf der Darstellung kein besonderes Interesse an syrischer Religion").

107. *Anciennes littêratures chrêtiennes*, vol. 2, p. 169.

the distinctiveness of this section; but it was Lidzbarski who first noted the relevance of this distinctive section to the question of the language(s) of composition: "Die Frage, in welcher Sprache die Apologie ursprünglich abgefasst sei, ist noch nicht entschieden, aber im Abschnitt über die heidnischen Götter zeigt sich der Autor von einer euhemeristischen Quelle abhängig, die am ehesten griechisch geschrieben war."[108] Moreover, in this euhemeristic section there are several clear traces of the text's reliance upon a Greek original. Thus the text refers to ʿAti *(ʿty)*, a divine name which is surely the same as the *ʿth* or *ʿtʾ* of the second part of Atargatis' composite name; but the spelling *ʿty* is without parallel in Semitic sources and thus represents, as Dupont-Sommer has noted, "la transcription du grec αθη ou αθης."[109] In discussing the religion of the Mesopotamians *(bny byt nhryn)*, the *Apology*'s author refers to the "*ʿbyʾ* of Edessa," which Cureton translates "the patrician of Edessa";[110] and Duval has observed that *ʾbyʾ* is "un mot artificiel, formé de *abâ* 'père,' et que rend littéralement le grec πατρίκιος *(Patrice)*."[111] Finally, the city from which ʿAti hails is most sensibly explained as based upon a textual error possible only in Greek. This city is given as *ḥdybytʾ* in our Syriac text. While Cureton despairs of translating this word,[112] most students of the text translate "Adiabene." Renan does so only tentatively *("Adoraverunt Syri Ati Adiabensum(?)")*,[113] but Six,[114] Payne Smith,[115] Fauth,[116] and Milik and Teixidor[117] all render the word "Adiabene" without

---

108. *Eph.*, vol. 3, p. 264.

109. "L'inscription de l'amulette d'Arslan Tash," 151, n.1; Dupont-Sommer also explains *ʿty* as the equivalent (through a Greek medium) of *ʿth* or *ʿtʾ*.

110. *Spicilegium Syriacum*, p. 44, l. 32.

111. *Anciennes littératures chrétiennes*, vol. 2, p. 169.

112. *Spicilegium Syriacum*, p. 90.

113. "S. Melitonis, Fragmenta Apologiae," p. XLIII, l. 13.

114. "Monnaies d'Hierapolis," 107 ("un personnage mystique de l'Adiabene").

115. *Thesaurus Syriacus*, vol. 1, col. 1202 *("nom. mulieris ex Adiabene")*.

116. "Dea Syria," in *Der Kleine Pauly*, vol. 1, col. 1401.

117. "Aktab-Kutbâ," 24 ("The Syrians worshipped *ʿTY* of Adiabene").

question. However, Adiabene, the district from east of the Tigris to Lake Urmia, makes little sense as the home of the goddess worshipped by the "Syrians" *(swryy')*, whose "king" is Hadad, who are said to reside in the area around Hierapolis-Mabbug, and who are distinguished from the "Mesopotamians" *(bny byt nhryn)*. Stocks has also noted the inappropriateness of Adiabene; but he proposes an unlikely series of textual errors *(ḥdybyt' < ḥrybyt' < ḥrnyt')*, so that ʿAti's home becomes Harran.[118] There is a more economical solution. If we assume a Greek source in which the town was given as Χαλέπ, "Aleppo," then the textual error of ΧΑΔΕΠ for ΧΑΛΕΠ represents only the confusion of Δ for Λ, one of the commonest Greek textual errors;[119] and since the form *ḥdbyt'* would make no sense, the anomalous form was doubtless altered to *ḥdybyt'* and understood as Adiabene. The cult of "Hadad of Aleppo" *(hdd ḥlb)* is widely attested in ancient sources;[120] and it would be as natural to hear of a cult in the same city of Hadad's consort ʿAnat (= ʿAti).

There is, then, evidence that this Syriac *Apology* is a document not from the hand of, and probably later than, Melito, whose section on the pagan deities was derived from a Greek source. Further, the author has no real knowledge of the cults he is discussing. At one point he speaks of "the Thracian Magus Orpheus" *('rpws mgwy' trqy')* at Mabbug; and Lidzbarski

---

118. "Studien," 12, n.37. The error of *d* for *r* is common in Syriac (dependent as it is only upon one diacritical mark) as in other Semitic scripts; but the disappearance of the *n* and the origin of the *b* in Stocks' formula are less readily explained.

119. On the frequency of this Greek error, see Clapham, "Sanchuniathon," 83, n.6.

120. See the Sefire Treaty, I, A, ll. 10-11, where *hdd ḥlb* is reconstructed by both Joseph Fitzmyer (*The Aramaic Inscriptions of Sefîre*, Biblica et Orientalia, 19 [Rome: Pontifical Biblical Institute, 1967], pp. 12-13) and by Donner and Röllig (*KAI*, vol. 2, p. 246). Hadad of Aleppo is also mentioned in a treaty of Aššurnirāri V, and Adad of Aleppo in an inscription of Šalmaneser III (Fitzmyer, *Sefîre*, p. 36). For a discussion of the various Semitic, Egyptian, and Greek forms of the city's name, see H. Th. Bossert, "Zur Vokalisation des Luwischen," *Orientalia* NS 30 (1961) 319-320.

properly asks, "sollten die Priester von Mabbûg dies wirklich gesagt haben?"[121] Therefore, the *Apology*'s witness to a goddess *symy* carries little weight as an independent Semitic witness, and the Greek source here may rest upon a misunderstanding of σημήιον or a similar Greek term. With Caquot we can conclude, "les conclusions tirées de ce passage du pseudo-Méliton sur la signification 'réelle' du mot *semeion* et sur la présence de Semia dans une 'triade hiérapolitaine' me paraissent injustifiées."[122]

Σημήιον = *"Symbol," "Image"*

Though, as we have seen, there are both new pieces of evidence and strong arguments against discovering a divine name in Lucian's σημήιον, the present work is hardly the first which denies the basis of this discovery. Indeed, given the renewed respect due to the text of the *De Syria Dea*, which has been repeatedly demonstrated here, one need not go beyond Lucian's words to recognize that σημήιον means merely "symbol" or "image." He writes, "Even the Assyrians themselves call it a σημήιον, and they have given it no name of its own" (καλέεται δὲ σημήιον καὶ ὑπ' αὐτῶν 'Ασσυρίων, οὐδὲ τι οὔνομα ἴδιον αὐτῷ ἔθεντο, para. 33), a statement which renders exceedingly precarious the search for an οὔνομα ἴδιον behind σημήιον, a word which is itself in the Ionic dialect of the *D.S.D.*'s Greek. We noted above that Nöldeke at one time equated σημήιον with *symy* as a divine name. Shortly before his death, however, perhaps to erase this youthful sin, Nöldeke changed his mind and wrote, in a letter to H. Zimmern, "'Mir ist jetzt recht zweifelhaft geworden, das das ΣΗΜΗΙΟΝ mit der Göttin Sime etwas zu tun hat.'"[123] Zimmern himself followed a similar course, for in a "Nachtrag" to his article on this subject, he reports that he has reconsidered the question ("ich...nachdenke") and now argues that σημήιον is not "ein Reflex eines einheimischen Götternamens Sīma oder Seimios," but "σημήιον einfach 'Zeichen' i.S.v. Göttersymbol bedeutet."[124] Others have followed the lead of Nöldeke and Zimmern, in which

---

121. *Eph.*, vol. 3, p. 264, n.4.

122. "Note sur le *semeion*," 66.

123. The letter, written in 1928, is quoted by E. Honigmann, "Syria," in *PW*, 2d series, vol. 4, col. 1576.

124. *"Šīmat, Sīma, Tyche, Manāt,"* 582.

course they are surely correct.[125]

Moreover, there is evidence of an Aramaic word, perhaps drawn from the Greek, homophonous with σημήιον/σημεῖον with the same meaning, despite Ingholt's disclaimer that "I can think of no Aramaic word of the desired meaning which even faintly would sound like σημήιον."[126] The Aramaic inscriptions from Hatra discussed by Caquot witness the phrases *wsmyt' klhw/yn* and *rb smy'* which Caquot well translates respectively as "et tous les σημεῖα" and "maitre du σημεῖον."[127] Caquot has noted in addition the form *"sīmā"* which translates Hebrew *nēs* in the Targum Jonathan to Jeremiah 4:21, the form *"sīmān"* which translates Hebrew *'ôt* in the Targum Yerušalmi to Numbers 17:3, and the form *"sīmwātēh"* in the Targum Jonathan to Habakkuk 1:16 where the Qumran commentary has *'ôtôtām*.[128] Another Hatra inscription reads *smy'* in parallel to *nyš'*; and, as Caquot observes, "les deux mots, l'oriental *NYŠ'* et le grec *SMY'* sont synonymes."[129] Seyrig accepts Caquot's interpretation with its bearing on the meaning of Lucian's σημήιον, though he feels no

---

125. For example, σημήιον is taken to mean "sign," "symbol," "image," by M. Rostovtzeff, "*Vexillum* and Victory," *Journal of Roman Studies* 32 (1942) 113; by Goossens, *Hiérapolis de Syrie*, pp. 67-68; and by Seyrig, "Antiquités syriennes," *Syria* 37 (1960) 242-245 ("Tout invite donc à interpréter le texte de Lucien dans son sens plus banal, et à ne voir dans le *sêmeion* rien de plus qu'une enseigne sacrée," 245). As is often the case with ancient texts, the "sens plus banal" is the correct and final solution.

126. "Parthian Sculptures," 20.

127. The first occurs in inscription no. 52 (Caquot, "Nouvelles inscriptions araméennes (III)," 55-56), the second in no. 56 ("Nouvelles inscriptions araméennes (III)," 57-58). Caquot's interpretation is adopted by Donner and Röllig (*KAI*, vol. 2, p. 301: "'Zeichen, Bilder, Embleme'; das griech. Wort is aram. als stat. abs. f. sg. aufgefasst worden"). Note also *wsmyt'* = "les 'Enseignes,'" in inscription no. 82 ("Nouvelles inscriptions araméennes (V)," 7).

128. "Note sur le *semeion*," 59-60 and *passim*. The Qumran reference is to 1QpHab 6:4.

129. "Note sur le *semeion*," 62-63. Caquot seems here to understand Aramaic *smy'* as a Greek loan word, though he also notes the possibility that it is derived "de la racine sémitique *ŚYM*" (61).

need to find an Aramaic word homophonous with Greek σημήιον/σημεῖον since Lucian's text designates a "mot qui désignait une enseigne *dans leur langue à eux*, et ce mot pourrait avoir en une tout autre consonnace que *sêmeion*."[130] Still, as we will see, there is reason to believe that a divine name was derived mistakenly from σημήιον or its Aramaic reflex, even though Lucian's σημήιον clearly means just "symbol," "image," for which mistaken derivation Caquot's discovery of the homophonous Greek and Aramaic words is important.

Before turning to an investigation of the origin and meaning of the Hierapolis "symbol," one other ingenious if ultimately unsatisfactory solution to the σημήιον question ought to receive a hearing. This is Baethgen's suggestion that σημήιον is based on an auditory error of Lucian:

> Dass das Bild σημήιον genannt sei, ist ein Missverständniss Lucian's. Das entsprechende syrische Wort is אתא; aber nicht dies wird der Name des Bildes gewesen sein, sondern עתא (so in Palmyra geschrieben), der zweite Theil von עתרעתה oder עתרעתא. Lucian verwechselte עתא mit אתא, ebenso wie Simplicius bei de Lagarde עתר mit אתר 'Ort' verwechselt, wenn er 'Αταρ-ατη durch τόπον θεῶν erklärt.[131]

Though Baethgen comes accidentally upon the correct solution to the problem (that the symbol is a symbol of the goddess of Hierapolis, as we will see), there are problems with his attribution of such an error to Lucian. Western students of Semitic languages easily and often interchange א and ע; but the interchange would be a lesser danger for one who, like Lucian, spoke an Aramaic language.[132] Further, Simplicius' translation of Atargatis as τόπον θεῶν may well be based upon the form *'tr't'*, with initial *'aleph*, as we have seen, rather than upon an auditory error; thus, Baethgen's appeal to Simplicius as providing an analogous "Verwechselung" carries little force.

A more common and satisfactory solution to the problem of the significance of Lucian's σημήιον is to translate the word "symbol," "image," and to look for Oriental or Roman parallels for an object such as that portrayed on the Caracalla and

---

130. "Antiquités syriennes," *Syria* 37 (1960) 244, n.l.

131. *Beiträge*, p. 73.

132. Both Clemen ("Miszellen," p. 101) and Stocks ("Studien," 16) dismiss Baethgen's suggestion as "kaum denkbar" because of Lucian's Oriental upbringing.

Severus coins.[133] Langdon, who correctly equates Lucian's "symbol" with "the miniature shrine" of the coins, urges that the device is "apparently symbol of the ark of the Deluge."[134] But the object hardly resembles an ark, and only the dove (which has no place in the Hierapolis flood legend) among the symbols of the object suggests such a solution. A. B. Cook decides the "symbol" is "a royal sceptre or standard,"[135] and a similar suggestion, that the object is a Roman *signum* (a military device) is offered by Imhoof-Blumer.[136] The objections to this view are many. Such *signa* had to be those of particular military units; but there was at Hierapolis "no reason to keep a permanent garrison....it never became a Roman colony, as happened to almost all the important military centres of Syria and Mesopotamia in the time of Severus and after."[137] Further, as we will see, "les étendards divins associés au culte des dieux dans les religions de l'Orient sont une institution de très haute antiquité,"[138] so that the suggestion that the Hierapolis "symbol" was simply borrowed in its entirety from Rome will not do, especially since these *signa* bear little resemblance to the entire structure labeled σημήιον by Lucian, or even to the pole with disks within this larger structure.[139] Finally, Stocks focuses

---

133. See Ingholt, "Parthian Sculptures," 18 for a review of several such explanations.

134. *Semitic Mythology*, p. 37, n.175.

135. *Zeus*, vol. 1, p. 587.

136. *Griechische Münzen*, p. (759); cf. Langdon, *Semitic Mythology*, p. 38.

137. Rostovtzeff, "*Vexillum*," 99; the same objection is voiced by Ingholt, "Parthian Sculptures," 19. On the Roman standards as symbols, not divine entities, see also Arthur Darby Nock, "The Roman Army and the Religious Year," *HTR* 45 (1952) 239-240 (= *Arthur Darby Nock:* Essays on Religion and the Ancient World, vol. 2, pp. 780-781).

138. Comte du Mesnil du Buisson, "L'étendard," 75.

139. A representative assortment of the Roman *signa* and *vexilla* may be seen conveniently in Oskar Seyffert, *A Dictionary of Classical Antiquities*, rev. and ed. by Henry Nettleship and J. E. Sandys (New York: Meridian, 1956), p. 586, fig. 2. Of the twelve devices drawn there, one has two disks on the pole, two have two disks, and two have four disks, while four are surmounted by an outstretched hand and three by an eagle

on the three or four circles on the pole within the aedicule depicted on the coins and sees here "*eine schematische Darstellung von Sternen*," which points to the worship of an Anatolian god at Hierapolis.[140] This, again, neglects to explain the rest of the structure on the coins, and arises from Stocks' desire to tie the Hierapolis cult to Anatolia, for which connection there is no firm evidence.[141]

That the "symbol" is a collection of divine symbols, rather than a royal or military or astral device, is clear both from the *De Syria Dea* and from other evidence from the area. In paragraph 49 of the *D.S.D.*, Lucian relates how pilgrims bring their own "symbols" to Hierapolis (καὶ τὰ σημήια ἕκαστοι ἔχουσιν), along with "their own holy objects" (τὰ ἑωυτῶν ἱρὰ ἕκαστοι); the juxtaposition of σημήια and ἱρά strongly suggests that other peoples, as well as those from Hierapolis, had their own divine "symbols" emblematic of some aspect of their cults. Jacob of Sarug, whose Syriac homily has been cited above, provides evidence that Hierapolis was renowned (notorious in Jacob of Sarug's eyes) for its use of divine symbols or idols; he says, in discussing the errors of several pagan cults, that the devil constituted Mabbug to wander "forever after her images" *(lʿlm btr ṣlmwhy)*.[142] Already in the eighth century B.C. the Syrians were accustomed to assigning abstract symbols to each of their deities, to judge from those found with several inscription from Zinjirli;[143] and, to go back even further into

---

with extended wings. All are far more elaborate than the pole with three or four disks within the aedicule of the σημήιον.

140. "Studien," 18-19. Stocks' rather puzzling argument here is that an Anatolian god, who is represented with a hat with rings ("Ringhut"), is symbolized by the rings on the pole of the σημήιον.

141. Carl Clemen's "Tempel und Kult in Hierapolis" (in *Pisciculi:* Studien zur Religion und Kultur des Altertums [F. J. Dölger Festschrift], ed. Theodor Klauser and Adolf Rücker [Münster: Aschendorff, 1939) pp. 66-69) is a review and refutation of Stocks' claims for the Anatolian influence upon the religion of Hierapolis.

142. L. 60 in the edition of Martin, "Discours de Jacques de Saroug sur la chutes des idoles."

143. See *KAI*, no. 216 (=*ANEP*, no. 281) and no. 217, and the discussion of the symbols by Donner and Röllig (*KAI*, vol.

antiquity, Seyrig has published a number of second-millennium B.C. Syrian seals which represent "une enseigne sacrée" and which confirm the nature of the Hierapolis use of the same as "un culte autochtone" and not as a Roman import.[144] From Tell-Halaf comes a relief portraying a camel carrying what appears to be a divine symbol;[145] and at Heliopolis there is evidence for a procession bearing divine standards.[146] In Mesopotamia, the use of divine symbols on poles or standards is ubiquitous.[147] The Phoenicians too knew the practice of bearing portable shrines within which were divine symbols. An Elagabalus coin from Sidon shows a wheeled car bearing a "four-columned frame,"[148] within which Seyrig sees "un bétyle d'Astarté."[149] It is possible that the *nḥš* which Moses makes and puts atop a "pole" *(nēs)* in Numbers 21:8-9 refers to a similar practice among the Israelites, a practice perhaps paralleled in Moab if we reconstruct ll. 3-4 of the Mešaʿ Stele to read *bns yšʿ*, "als Zeichen der Rettung."[150] And at Hazor was unearthed a "bronze cult

---

2, p. 232 and p. 234), by Donner ("Ein Orthostatenfragment des Königs Barrakab von Sam'al," 73-98), and by Yigael Yadin ("Symbols of Deities at Zinjirli, Carthage, and Hazor," in *Near Eastern Archaeology in the Twentieth Century* [Nelson Glueck Festschrift], ed. James A. Sanders [Garden City: Doubleday, 1970], pp. 199-231).

144. "Antiquités syriennes," *Syria* 37 (1960) 233-241.

145. Franz Cumont, "Un dieu syrien à dos de chameau," *Syria* 10 (1929) 30-35; cf. the scene from Palmyra discussed by Seyrig in "Antiquités syriennes," *Syria* 15 (1934) 158-163.

146. Dussaud, "Temples et cultes," 69-71.

147. The evidence is overwhelming, both on published glyptic material and especially on the corpus of Nuzi seals in the collection of the Harvard Semitic Museum. Note, for example, the crescent standard on the seals in pls. 28c, 29c, 29d, 39f, and fig. 43 (p. 174) in H. Frankfort, *Cylinder Seals:* A Documentary Essay on the Art and Religion of the Ancient Near East (London: Gregg Press, 1965 [reprint of 1939 ed.]), or the emblem with seven globes in pls. 30c and 30d in the same collection.

148. Stanley A. Cook, *The Religion of Ancient Palestine*, p. 165, pl. 33, no. 10 (cf. too no. 11).

149. "Antiquités syriennes," *Syria* 36 (1959) 48-51.

150. *KAI*, no. 181; see *KAI*, vol. 2, p. 168, for this suggestion and p. 172 for alternate suggestions.

standard" portraying two snakes and a crescent, and with a tang on the bottom to be inserted into a pole.[151]

However, while these data provide analogies for the use of divine symbols, none provides an answer to the questions of the origin of the Hierapolis "symbol" and of the deity or deities symbolized by the device described by Lucian and portrayed on the coins. In anwer to the first question, Rostovtzeff argues that, though the σημήιον is not a Roman *signum* or a *vexillum* (the standard displayed to gather together the Romans to vote or to engage in military duties), still, "the oriental banners were consciously re-shaped in order to make them resemble as closely as possible Roman military standards."[152] Some influence from these standards is possible, though we have noted the great differences between the *signa* and *vexilla*, and the Hierapolis "symbol"; but this argument still gives no immediate Oriental ancestry to the Hierapolis structure nor does it address the question of the deity or deities represented by the device. Baur sees the "symbol" of Hierapolis as "the aniconic fetish of the deities Hadad, Atargatis, and the third member of the triad."[153] A similar position is articulated by du Mesnil du Buisson who explains the disks on the pole as representing "Hadad, Atargatis et le Soleil."[154] But we have seen that there are either three (Caracalla, fig. 1) or four (Severus, fig. 2) disks on the pole, which argues that the number of disks is insignificant, and that the assumption of a divine triad at Hierapolis is ill founded. Further, the remainder of the σημήιον (the dove atop the pediment and the disk, or disk and crescent, within the pediment) remains unaccounted for by such an explanation; and it is clear from Lucian's description that it is the entire structure (including the dove atop the pediment) which the natives call the "symbol," and not just the pole with disks in the center of the structure.

In seeking for an answer to the question of the meaning of the Hierapolis "symbol," we can do no better than to turn to the text of the *De Syria Dea*, whose worth in solving several

---

151. *ANEP*, no. 834, and p. (379).

152. "*Vexillum*," 100-101; cf. du Mesnil du Buisson, "L'étendard," 80.

153. P. V. C. Baur *et al.*, *The Excavations of Dura-Europos, Preliminary Report of the Third Season*, p. 122.

154. "L'étendard," 77.

dilemmas has been amply demonstrated. The work is entitled Περὶ τῆς Συρίης Θεοῦ and concerns the city "sacred to the Assyrian Hera" (ἱρὴ τῆς Ἥρης τῆς Ἀσσυρίης, para. 1). The inhabitants sacrifice to both Zeus and Hera, but much more energetically to Hera (para. 44). Given this, and the multitude of additional evidence which links Hierapolis above all with Atargatis, it is reasonable to ask if the object "in the middle" (ἐν μέσῳ, para. 33) of the central and innermost chamber (θάλαμος) at Hierapolis may represent the Syrian goddess alone.[155]

If the structure seen on the Caracalla and Severus coins and called a "symbol" by Lucian is a cult idol of Atargatis, can the various attributes of the structure be seen as several symbols of the goddess? And is there a parallel to this use of symbols? Both questions are to be answered affirmatively. That the dove represents most naturally Atargatis is beyond question, for we have seen the role played by the dove in Atargatis' cult at Hierapolis and elsewhere;[156] and that it is a dove atop the pediment of the σημήιον is clear from both Lucian's description (he calls it a περιστερή, para. 33) and the coins.[157] That leaves us with the disk, or disk and crescent,

---

155. It is also intriguing, though probably no more, to find a pun in Plutarch's statement that Crassus' "first sign" (πρῶτον σημεῖον) of his imminent misfortune comes from the goddess of Hierapolis called Aphrodite or Hera (*Crassus* 17).

156. See the section "ʿAstart and Atargatis" in Chapter II above.

157. Only Ingholt sees here an "eagle with *folded* wings," representing "the god of the sky, *in casu* Samayya" ("Parthian Sculptures," 43); but Caquot has answered Ingholt's argument for finding here a god Samayya, along with the necessity for seeing the bird as an eagle ("Note sur le *semeion*," *passim*). The bird is called a dove, though occasionally with unnecessary reserve, by Six ("Monnaies d'Hiérapolis," 111), by Imhoof-Blumer (*Griechische Münzen*, p. (759)), by A. B. Cook (*Zeus*, vol. 1, p. 586), by Langdon (*Semitic Mythology*, p. 38), by Zimmern (*"Šīmat, Sīma, Tyche, Manāt,"* 577), by Baur (*The Excavations of Dura-Europos, Preliminary Report of the Third Season*, p. 121), and by Stocks ("Studien," 16). Both the shape and the stance of the bird recall a dove much more satisfactorily than they do an eagle, for the bird is perched with his body in a nearly horizontal position (as doves do in fact perch), while

within the pediment and with the pole with three or four rings attached within the framework below. From Lucian's description it seems likely that he sees the objects of the σημήιον as representing several deities. But the objects within the architectural framework, as well as the dove atop, can be understood as symbolizing a single deity, for the disk, or disk and crescent, and the pole with rings are also likely symbols of Atargatis, the goddess whose name and character include the name and character of 'Ašerah. The first clue to the solution of the objects' meaning was provided, quite inadvertently, by Frothingham, who argued, with respect to the pole with rings, that "the circles are not the solid medallions of Roman standards but are serpent coils....The third figure, then, is evidently a caduceus-god."[158] Even though Frothingham's representation of the Severus coin exaggerates the object's aspect as consisting of "serpent coils,"[159] and though Albright accepted Frothingham's interpretation,[160] the pole with the rings resembles after all very little a classic caduceus and hardly proves that the deity it represents is a "caduceus-god." But there is an identical object on many stelae in the Phoenician-Punic world, especially from Carthage and the West, also called for convenience a caduceus. And it is to a study of these Phoenician-Punic objects that we now turn, for here we have the same symbols of the Hierapolis σημήιον representing a goddess who is identical with an aspect of Atargatis.

This investigation will be mindful throughout of the danger in overly precise identification of any religious symbol, a danger to which Arthur Darby Nock often called attention.[161]

---

representations of eagles show the eagle sitting with its body nearly vertical.

158. A. L. Frothingham, "Babylonian Origin of Hermes, the Snake God, and of the Caduceus," *AJA* 20 (1916) 208-209.

159. "Babylonian Origin of Hermes," fig. 50 (208).

160. W. F. Albright, "The Goddess of Life and Wisdom," *AJSL* 36 (1920) 273, n.4.

161. Nock writes of the symbol of the serpent, for example: "A serpent can evoke a variety of associations - death, the renewal of life (as suggested by its sloughing its skin), the protective Hausschlange, the healing power of Asclepius, fecundity, a hostile power to be crushed, etc." ("Religious Symbols II," in *Arthur Darby Nock:* Essays on Religion and the Ancient World, vol. 2, p. 906).

Yet there is now enough evidence to interpret safely the divine symbols of the Punic world.[162] Among the most prominent of these symbols, in terms of numbers of occurrences, is that called the sign of Tannit, a triangle or trapezoid with horizontal "arms" topped by a disk or a disk and crescent (a "head").[163] Though the origin and significance of the sign have long been disputed issues, it is increasingly obvious both that the sign originated in a schematization of a clothed female figure and that it represented Tannit (figs. 3-5).[164] The two deities addressed on the Carthage stelae with this sign plus other symbols are Tannit and Baʿl Ḥamōn, which might imply that the sign symbolized either or both of these deities. But the sign's association with fish or ships indicates that it symbolizes a deity with marine associations; and we have seen that

---

162. For a full summary study of the Punic symbols, see Magdeleine Hours-Miedan, "Les représentations figurées sur les stèles de Carthage," *Cahiers de Byrsa* 1 (1950) 15-160, but note the review of G. Ch. Picard in *Karthago* 3 (1951-1952) 219-221. For cautions against the finality of attempts to work out the typology of these symbols, see Peckham, *The Development of the Late Phoenician Scripts*, pp. 196-197.

163. On the sign of Tannit, see Moscati, *WP*, p. 139, and Hours-Miedan, "Les représentations," 26-31.

164. With regard to the sign's origin, among the many suggestions are those of P. S. Ronzevalle, that it originated in the Egyptian *ʿanḫ* sign ("Notes et études d'archéologie orientale [2me serie, III]," *MUSJ* 16 [1932] 33) and of Hours-Miedan, that the sign is a betyl topped by a disk whose meaning escapes us as the meaning escaped its Punic worshippers ("Les représentations," 31). Other views are reviewed in Colette Picard, "Genèse et évolution des signes de la bouteille et de Tanit a Carthage," *Studi Magrebini* 2 (1968) 77-87. But recently discovered evidence, particularly as assembled by Moscati, makes it clear that the sign is a schematized female figure; see especially Moscati's "L'origine del 'segno di Tanit,'" *Atti della Accademia Nazionale dei Lincei* (Rendiconti della classe di scienze morali, storiche e filologiche), series 8, vol. 27, fasc. 7-12 (1972), 371-374 and pls. 1-3. Pls. 1a and 3b (which shows a disk and crescent above the goddess' head) in Moscati's study make this conclusion strikingly obvious.

Tannit/'Ašerah is just such a deity. Examples of the sign of Tannit with fish are numerous from the West;[165] and Hours-Mieden's study of representations of ships on the Carthage stelae concludes that almost all such representations are accompanied by the sign of Tannit, alone or with the so-called caduceus.[166] The symbol of Tannit's consort Ba'l Ḥamōn, who is to be identified with 'Ēl, as Landsberger and Cross have argued,[167] is best seen in the upraised hand which is portrayed on many of the Punic stelae. The divine symbols are grouped in every possible way on these stelae; but a typical configuration is the upraised hand at the top of the stele, with the other symbols (the sign of Tannit, often with disk and crescent, and the caduceus of the palm tree) assembled below,[168] a configuration which suggests that the upraised hand represents Ba'l Ḥamōn, the other symbols Tannit. As a symbol for Ba'l Ḥamōn/'Ēl, the upraised hand is perfectly appropriate since the standard Canaanite representation of 'Ēl is that of a seated, bearded god with his right hand raised in benediction.[169]

In addition to the portraits of fish and ships, the sign

---

165. For example, *CIS*, vol. 1, nos. 2734, 3552, 3285, 3359, etc. The obverse of two coins from Carthage shows the head of Tannit with the sign of Tannit on one side, and dolphins or fish on the other; see G. K. Jenkins and R. B. Lewis, *Carthaginian Gold and Electrum Coins* (London: Royal Numismatic Society, 1963), pl. 26, nos. 6 and 7.

166. "Les représentations," 67-68.

167. The evidence is presented in full in Cross, *CMHE*, pp. 24-36, as we noted above in Chapter II. Cf. already G. Ch. Picard: "Le culte de Tanit et Ba'al...est sans doute sorti de celui d'El et sa parèdre Asherat" (rev. of Hours-Miedan, "Les représentations," 221).

168. *CIS*, vol. 1, no. 3663 is typical of many such stelae, as are those pictured in figs. 33 and 77 in Bisi, *Le Stele Puniche*; cf. also fig. 31 in this latter collection, for a stele topped by a god raising his right hand in benediction. The symbol of the upraised hand is discussed by Berthier and Charlier, in *EH*, p. 185, and by Hours-Miedan, in "Les représentations," 31-34.

169. Cross summarizes the Canaanite portrayals of Canaanit 'Ēl in *CMHE*, pp. 35-36. See *ANEP*, no. 493, and Schaeffer, "Nouveaux témoignages," pl. 2.

of Tannit also appears in the company of the so-called caduceus, the palm tree, doves, and the disk and crescent, all of which are thus best taken as additional symbols for this deity. The device labeled a caduceus (fig. 6) "has nothing in common except the name with the Greek and Roman symbol of Hermes/Mercury, but takes the form of a crescent and disk surmounting a staff, often beribboned."[170] Despite the dissimilarity with the Greek and Roman caduceus, Berthier and Charlier argue that the object is in fact a caduceus,[171] though Hours-Miedan denies this and calls it just "un circle ou disque, solaire probablement, surmonté d'un croissant."[172] Hours-Miedan's description is accurate, if her conclusion that the caduceus has a solar character is unwarranted, for the Punic caduceus is highly stylized and consists of one or more rings or disks on a pole or a trunk, topped by a crescent or another ring or disk. Here, it is critical to note that this so-called caduceus is associated most often with the sign of Tannit (fig. 7)[173] and bears a striking resemblance to the symbol below the pediment of the Hierapolis σημήιον. Indeed, the sign of Tannit and the caduceus are at times combined into a single symbol (fig. 8), so that one of the rings or disks or the caduceus becomes the "head" of the Tannit sign.[174] If the caduceus were a stylized version of the Greek and Roman caduceus, with the serpents' coils closed into disks or rings, then it could commemorate Tannit/'Ašerah's

---

170. Harden, *The Phoenicians*, p. 88. Discussion of the Punic caduceus may be found in *EH*, pp. 183-185, and in Hours-Miedan, "Les représentations," 34-36.

171. *EH*, pp. 184-185; cf. G. Ch. Picard, rev. of Hours-Miedan, "Les représentations," 220.

172. "Les représentations," 34.

173. This is also the conclusion reached by Hours-Miedan ("Les représentations," 35). Examples of the two symbols in close proximity are to be found in *CIS*, vol. 1, nos. 188, 200, 2036, 2042, etc. In *CIS*, vol. 1, nos. 243 and 2384, the caduceus is found next to fish with which Tannit/'Ašerah is often associated.

174. See, for example, *CIS*, vol. 1, nos. 1900 or 2592. In *CIS*, vol. 1, no. 2093 there are two caducei atop Tannit's "hands"; and in *CIS*, vol. 1, nos. 2498, 2526, and 3255 there are two Tannit signs atop the ends of the "strings" descending from the caduceus.

character as a goddess of fecundity; and it will be remembered that Qudšu in Egypt often holds serpents.[175] However, as we will see, the evidence is much stronger that the caduceus represents a stylized palm tree.

As often as it is linked with the caduceus (in a form most reminiscent of the pole with disks beneath the pediment of the Hierapolis "symbol"), the sign of Tannit is also frequently combined with a disk and crescent or surrounded by doves. *CIS*, vol. 1, no. 183 portrays a sign of Tannit between two doves, above which is a deity holding a disk and crescent; at the top of the stele is the upraised hand.[176] Hours-Miedan plausibly identifies the deity holding the disk and crescent here with Tannit: "La situation de cette figure féminine à la partie supérieure de la stèle, entourée d'un morceau d'architecture, portant le croissant et le disque, permet d'assurer que nous avons là une figure divine, la figure de Tanit très probablement."[177] The figure of Tannit within an architectural framework here is strikingly like the relief on a Tyre altar, now in the Beirut Museum, which portrays a bust of Atargatis within a large crescent.[178] A second-century A.D. Ascalon coin also portrays a goddess with "dove in her right hand, sceptre in left, crescent on head."[179] In the West, the crescent and disk often appear with the Tannit sign, where the combination is surely a "complexe attribut de Tanit."[180] Significantly, just as the caduceus and the sign of Tannit are combined into one

---

175. Pritchard, *Figurines*, p. 33. Note too the epithet *ḏt bṯn* ("Serpent Lady") of the Proto-Sinaitic texts (Albright, *The Proto-Sinaitic Inscriptions*, Texts 351, 353, 358, 360, and 361).

176. Cf. *CIS*, vol. 1, no. 404 and Bisi, *Le Stele Puniche*, fig. 91 (two doves flanking a Tannit sign). Hours-Miedan remarks, of the animals portrayed on the Punic stelae, "le plus fréquemment représenté est la columbe symbole de la Déesse très probablement" ("Les représentations," 50).

177. Hours-Miedan, "Les représentations," 61.

178. Franz Cumont, "Deux autels de Phénicie," *Syria* 8 (1927) 163-166, and pl. 38.

179. Stanley A. Cook, *The Religion of Ancient Palestine*, pl. 33, no. 22, and p. 173.

180. Hours-Miedan, "Les représentations," 37; see 36-38 for a summary discussion of the crescent and disk.

symbol, so too the crescent and disk very frequently are placed atop the triangular or trapezoidal base of the sign to form the "head" of the Tannit sign (figs. 4-5).[181] This complex motif is to be compared with the representations of the goddess Qudšu which portray her with "Ḥatḥor horns and disk" or "the crescent and disk."[182] The comparison suggests that the origin of the Phoenician-Punic motif of the disk and crescent atop the Tannit sign is to be sought in the Ḥatḥor horns and disk, whose horns could be stylized easily into an upturned crescent. That the iconography of Qudšu should find a reflex in the symbolism of Tannit is only to be expected. There are other examples of the disk and crescent associated with a goddess in the eastern Mediterranean. Two capitals from the Aphrodite temple at Idalion on Cyprus have within them a disk and crescent.[183] On coins from Palmyra, a lion or Atargatis herself is seen alongside a disk and crescent.[184] On the fourth-century B.C. *ʿbd hdd* coins from Hierapolis, "parfois le disque solaire et la croissant lunaire sont gravés dans le champ";[185] and we noted in the

---

181. See, for example, Moscati, *WP*, p. 57, fig. 11 (the goddess bears on her head "the solar disk between the Hathoresque horns"), and *CIS*, vol. 1, nos. 142, 436, 2647, 3235, 3351, 3783a, 3717, 3735, 3795, 3803, 3822, etc. The "bottle-idol" is also surmounted by a disk and crescent "head" in *CIS*, vol. 1, nos. 3709, 3714, 3763, 3787, etc.

182. Cross, *CMHE*, p. 34. Note the relief of the Yeḥawmilk inscription from Byblos (*CIS*, vol. 1, no. 1 = *ANEP*, no. 477) on which the king offers an oblation to *bʿlt gbl*, who is wearing the Ḥatḥor headdress, and also the two female figures topped by the disk and crescent in Isabella Brancol, *et al.*, *Mozia III:* Rapporto preliminare della Missione archeologica della Suprintendenza alle Antichità della Sicilia Occidentale e dell'Università di Roma (Rome: Istituto di Studi del Vicino Oriente Università di Roma, 1967), pl. 39, pl. 42, and p. 47.

183. Max Ohnefalsch-Richter, *Kypros, the Bible and Homer:* Oriental Civilization, Art and Religion in Ancient Times (London: Asher, 1893), pl. 58, nos. 1 and 2; cf. Moscati, *WP*, pp. 107-108, and pl. 3 (p. 107).

184. Rostovtzeff, "Hadad and Atargatis," pl. 9, no. 1, nos. 3a-b, and no. 5b.

185. Cumont, "Syria Dea," in *Dictionnaire des antiquités*, vol. 4, pt. 2, p. 1591.

previous chapter that the reliefs of the *dea Syria* in Rome portray an upturned crescent atop the goddess' head.[186] Lucian lists Selene among the goddesses recalled by the statue of Hera in the Hierapolis θάλαμος (para. 32), which suggests that a crescent was to be seen also on this image.

All of the parts of the Hierapolis "symbol" (the architectural framework, the pole with disks, the dove, and the disk, or disk and crescent, within the pediment) are, then, paralleled by the symbolism of Punic Tannit, and some of these same objects are found together with Atargatis elsewhere. It must be admitted, however, that most of the evidence cited thus far comes from the western Mediterranean, far from the Phoenician mainland and farther yet from Hierapolis. As recently as a few years ago, we would have had to have argued at this point that the Punic evidence was sufficient for our case, since the origin of Punic religion and art in the Phoenician homeland is a reasonable supposition. Thus, Moscati concludes his discussion of Punic art with the statement, "the influence of the homeland is unquestionable: the typology clearly goes back to Phoenician models, and Phoenician are some iconographical motifs which persist throughout the ages," even if Punic art "lives a separate life consisting of new elements and influences."[187] In support of the tenacity of the Phoenician origins of Punic culture, note that the author of a Punic inscription calls himself *ʾš knʿn*,[188] and Augustine's report that *interrogati rustici nostri quid sint, punice respondentes Chanani.*[189] But such arguments are no longer necessary, for recent years have witnessed the discovery and publication of numerous divine symbols, heretofore limited to the Punic world, from the Phoenician mainland.[190] An isolated example has been available for over fifty years on an Ascalon coin published by Hill; the coin, dated to

---

186. See the frontispieces of van Berg's two volumes, *Répertoire* and *Etude critique*.

187. *WP*, pp. 160-161; cf. the similar summary statement of Hours-Miedan, "Les représentations," 73.

188. *EH*, no. 102.

189. *Epistolae ad Romanos* 1.13 (Migne, *Patrologia Latina*, vol. 35, col. 2096).

190. An excellent summary of the Tannit signs found in the East is to be found in M. Dothan, "A Sign of Tanit from Tel ʿAkko," *IEJ* 24 (M. Avi-Yonah Memorial Volume, 1974) 46-47.

A.D. 132-133, bears a figure which is surely a Tannit sign along with the inscription φανήβαλος (= פן בעל), Tannit's standard epithet in the West.[191] Recent finds now confirm the presence of these symbols in the East. At Oumm el-ʿAmed, south of Tyre, Dunand found two important lead weights. On one, the obverse shows the bow of a ship within which is an upturned disk, and the reverse (fig. 8a) portrays a sign of Tannit with a caduceus engraved in the middle of the "body"[192] - a striking parallel to the combination of the caduceus with the Tannit sign in Punic material, and a further confirmation of Tannit's marine character. On the second lead weight, the obverse portrays a central palm tree flanked by two stalks, while the reverse again shows a sign of Tannit.[193] At Sarepta, biblical *ṣārpatâ* where Elijah's oil flask and meal never failed (1 Kings 17:8-16), Pritchard discovered a small disk within which is the sign of Tannit.[194] Under the Mediterranean off the coast between Accho and Achzib were found over two hundred female figurines, many of which have the sign of Tannit on their bases.[195] The find is especially significant because, in the

---

191. George Francis Hill, *Catalogue of the Greek Coins of Palestine* (Galilee, Samaria, and Judaea) (London: British Museum, 1914), no. 187 (pl. 13, no. 18) and p. 129. Hill ventures only to read the letters φαν... (p. 129), but Dothan gives the completed form φανήβαλος ("A Sign of Tanit," 46).

192. Maurice Dunand and Raymond Duru, *Oumm el-ʿAmed:* une ville de l'époque hellénistique aux échelles de Tyr, Republique Libanaise, études et documents d'archéologie, 4 (Paris: Adrien Maisonneuve, 1962), pl. 68, no. 1, and p. 175.

193. Dunand and Duru, *Oumm el-ʿAmed*, pl. 68, no. 2 and p. 175. Dunand and Duru see the signs as triangular anchors with appendages (p. 176), thus suggesting yet another possible origin for this intriguing sign. That the palm tree here replaces the caduceus of the first weight (pl. 68, no. 1) is also evidence that the caduceus is a stylized palm tree, as we will argue below.

194. James B. Pritchard, "Les fouilles de Sarepta," *Bible et terre sainte* 157 (1974) 7-9 and fig. 7. Pritchard says in this preliminary report only that most of the discoveries belong to the Bronze and Iron Ages (7).

195. Elisha Linder, "A Cargo of Phoenicio-Punic Figurines," *Archaeology* 26 (1973) 184. The figurines are dated to the fifth or fourth century B.C. (187).

words of Linder, "for the first time, the sign appears stamped on the base of a female figure which, I strongly believe, represents Tanit herself, and which leaves little room to doubt that a direct connection exists between the goddess and the symbol."[196] The argument is bolstered by the replacement on two of the figurines of the Tannit sign with a dolphin or fish.[197] Southeast of Tyre was unearthed a tomb bearing three symbols: a stylized caduceus, a sign of Tannit, and a simple disk atop pole, which is probably another stylized caduceus (fig. 9).[198] A similar series of symbols occurs on a relief found east of Qana at el-Biyad, on which relief there is a central Tannit sign flanked by two disks which are in turn flanked by two caducei.[199] Finally, from Accho, where it will be remembered there was unearthed an altar dedicated to Atargatis,[200] comes a sherd on which is a sign of Tannit.[201] The sherd was found in a Hellenistic stratum, which "contains many intrusive sherds of earlier periods";[202] and in the triangular "body" of the Tannit sign is an object which may be an anchor.[203]

These new data, when combined with that from the West, permit the firm conclusion that the divine symbols of the Punic world were certainly known and probably originated in the

---

196. Linder, "A Cargo of Phoenicio-Punic Figurines," 186.

197. Linder, "A Cargo of Phoenicio-Punic Figurines," 186.

198. Drawings of the tomb may be found in Charles Virolleaud, "Les travaux archéologiques en Syrie en 1922-1923," *Syria* 5 (1924) fig. 2 (46); in Ronzevalle, "Notes et études," pl. 6, no. 108 (Ronzevalle dates the tomb to the Roman era, 37); in Bisi, *Le Stele Puniche*, fig. 6; and in Dunand and Duru, *Oumm el-ʿAmed*, fig. 76 (for Dunand and Duru, this tomb's symbols establish the Oriental origin of the sign of Tannit, p. 177). Within the tomb was found a ring (Virolleaud, "Les travaux," fig. 1) with a stone in which was carved a two-disked caduceus, complete with the descending "strings" which we will discuss below.

199. Ronzevalle, "Notes et études," 38.

200. Avi-Yonah, "Syrian Gods at Ptolemais-Accho," 1-12, as noted in Chapter II above.

201. Dothan, "A Sign of Tanit from Tel ʿAkko," fig. 1 and pl. 9, A.

202. Dothan, "A Sign of Tanit from Tel ʿAkko," 45.

203. Dothan, "A Sign of Tanit from Tel ʿAkko," 45.

Phoenician mainland. This in turn allows us to affirm that the symbols within and atop the Hierapolis σημήιον all are possible symbols of a Canaanite goddess and thus represent at Hierapolis the cult of Atargatis whose name and attributes encompass the goddess 'Ašerah/Tannit. The collocation of the sylized caduceus, the dove, and the disk (or disk and crescent) within the architectural framework of the σημήιον is paralleled most closely by the same assembly of symbols on Carthage and other western stelae and on Phoenician objects. This is not to claim that the Hierapolis σημήιον was derived directly from the configuration of symbols on the Phoenician-Punic material. Though the evidence would allow this claim, there may well have been influence from the Roman *signa* or *vexilla*, or from Mesopotamian or Syrian models, upon the final form of the Hierapolis σημήιον. But these hypothetical influences do not erase the clear reference of the σῆμήιον to Atargatis, the goddess preeminent in the worship of Hierapolis, whose symbols occupied the place of honor within the innermost shrine. This is a conclusion that goes beyond the account of the σημήιον in the *De Syria Dea*. However, Lucian confesses that the natives would tell him nothing about this structure, and hence that his account is one based primarily on his own inferences from viewing the structure. If his inferences were inaccurate, his description is yet accurate; and from that description we can fairly conclude that the σημήιον represented the Syrian Goddess.

The Hierapolis "Symbol" and ʾAšerah in the Old Testament

Though we have argued that Lucian's σημήιον is a "symbol" of the Syrian Goddess rather than itself a divine name, we have not accounted for the origin of Σίμα/*Sima*, nor for the use of *symy* as a divine name in the *Apology* under Melito's name. It seems clear that these words were understood as divine names, even if they were based on an error in interpreting the Hierapolis "symbol." Therefore, σημήιον was, to the Greeks at least, both the source of a divine name and the symbol of the same deity. Intriguingly, the same is true of *ʾăšērâ* in the Old Testament, though the movement here was in the opposite direction, from a divine name to a noun indicating the goddess' cultic symbol.

The time is past when the knowledge of the existence of

the goddess 'Ašerah can be denied to the Old Testament.[204] This argument was devastated by the evidence from Ugarit where *'aṯiratu* is plainly a major figure in the Canaanite pantheon; but already the Old Testament itself clearly witnesses the understanding of *'ăšērâ* as a divine name.[205] Yet there are passages in the Old Testament in which the word as clearly indicates some sort of cult object. 2 Kings 21:3-7 is particularly instructive. In v. 3 we read that Manasseh "constructed altars for Ba'l and made an *'ăšērâ (wayyāqem mizbĕḥōt labba'al wayya'ś 'ăšērâ)*; yet in v. 7 that "he set up the idol of 'Ašerah" *(wayyāśem et-pesel hā'ăšērâ)*. The conclusion is therefore unavoidable that in the Hebrew text of the Old Testament the word was understood both as the goddess' name and as her cult idol.[206] This conclusion is bolstered by the evidence of the versions. The Septuagint usually renders the word "grove" (ἄλσος, plural ἄλση)[207] or "trees" (δένδρα, Isaiah 17:8, 27:9); yet twice we find Ἀστάρτη (2 Chronicles 15:16, 24:18). So the Greek translators of most parts of the Hebrew Bible saw *'ăšērâ* as a wooden object or objects of some sort, but those translating other books saw behind the word a reference to a Canaanite goddess. The Peshitta prefers to translate with *deḥlâ* ("image," "fearsome thing"), but also uses *ṣalmê* ("images," 2 Chronicles 15:16, 24:18) and *pĕtakrê* ("idols," Isaiah 17:8, 2 Chronicles 34:4). Both Jerome and Rashi understood *'ăšērâ* as an image of a fertility god, for the former renders it *simulacrum Priapi* and the latter explains it as *speciem virgae virilis*.[208]

There is, however, an association between *'ăšērâ* and σημήιον more organic and significant than merely that each was

---

204. See Reed, *The Asherah in the Old Testament*, *passim*, for a full review of the discussion.

205. Reed, *The Asherah in the Old Testament*, p. 96, gives a full list of the old Testament passages in which *'ăšērâ* must be taken as a divine name.

206. That *'ăšērâ* referring to an idol was fully nominalized is clear from the plural forms *'ăšērôt* and especially *'ăšērîm*, which is the predominant form.

207. Usually the plural ἄλση corresponds to the Hebrew plural *'ăšērîm*; but there are frequent passages (e.g., 2 Kings 17:5, 18:4, 21:3) in which the singular *'ăšērâ* is rendered by the Greek plural τὰ ἄλση.

208. As cited by Baethgen, *Beiträge*, p. 219.

used both as a name of a Canaanite goddess and as a noun referring to the goddess' cult symbol. This further association is that *ʾăšērâ* and σημήιον when used of the cult symbol both refer, at least in part, to the same object, namely the so-called caduceus, though perhaps to different stages in the caduceus' increasingly abstracted and stylized evolution, an evolution precisely paralleled by that from a schematized female figure to the Tannit sign. The Greek translators' use of ἄλση and δένδρα establish the knowledge of the Phoenician cult symbols called *ʾăšērîm* as reminiscent of a tree or a plant of some sort; and the same conclusion is indicated already by Deuteronomy 16:21: "You shall not plant for yourself any tree, as an *ʾăšērâ*" (*lōʾ-ṭiṭṭaʿ lĕkā ʾăšērâ kol-ʿēṣ*; οὐ φυτεύσεις σεαυτῷ ἄλσος πᾶν ξύλον). Yet the verbs used of the construction or destruction of the *ʾăšērîm* in the Old Testament, both in Greek and Hebrew dress, prohibit the conclusion that these cult symbols were simply trees. The verbs used of the construction of these symbols are most often *ʿśh* ("to make"), *bnh* ("to build"), and *nṣb* (Hiph., "to erect"), with their Greek reflexes ποιέω, οἰκοδομέω, and στέλλω. The use of these verbs demands that we see the *ʾăšērâ* as an object of human construction.[209] The divine command to the Israelites to destroy these cult symbols is couched in terminology which allows the further inference that these symbols were made of wood or like trees, for the verbs used here are, among others, *gdʿ* ("to hew down"), Greek ἐκκόπτω, and several meaning "to burn." What is required for the *ʾăšērâ* is therefore something which is constructed by men and yet which recalls a tree. The caduceus of the Phoenician-Punic Tannit symbolism and in the center of the Hierapolis architectural frame meets these twin demands splendidly.

The origin for the caduceus which best accounts both for the symbol's various forms and for its association with Tannit is neither the classical caduceus nor a solar or lunar symbol but rather the palm tree. In the Punic world, as too at Oumm el-ʿAmed in Phoenicia, the palm tree and the caduceus are separately associated with the Tannit sign; but there is evidence that the caduceus was itself a highly abstract symbol of the palm tree. At both Carthage and El-Hofra, as indeed elsewhere in the West, the caduceus is represented often with long

---

209. The same conclusion is reached by Reed (*The Asherah in the Old Testament*, p. 30).

"strings" descending from near its top which have been called "ribbons."[210] Yet these cannot be simply ribbons, since the caducei of many Punic stelae have blossoms or fruit-pods at the ends of these "strings,"[211] which suggests that the strings are the flower- and fruit-bearing spadices of the date palm.[212]

---

210. For example, *CIS*, vol. 1, nos. 326 and 397, *EH*, no. 93 (pl. 13c) and no. 90 (pl. 15a). Berthier and Charlier call these "ribbons" (rubans, *EH*, p. 77 and p. 79), as does Harden (*The Phoenicians*, p. 88).

211. For example, *CIS*, vol. 1, nos. 2629, 3163, or 3363. A most instructive parallel is the palm tree on a relief from Tiglath-Pileser III (*ANEP*, no. 367); from the base of the palm fronds descend two symmetrical spadices each carrying bunches of fruit at the end. The fairly realistic palm trees of the Punic stelae stand mid-way between this realistic Assyrian representation and the fully sylized palm tree labeled the caduceus.

212. These spadices (also called spikelets) stand nearly vertical amongst the palm fronds until the weight of the ripening fruit causes them to droop down, sometimes considerably below the level of the base of the fronds, as is the case with the "strings" on the palms and caducei of the Punic stelae. See V. H. W. Dowson, *Dates & Date Cultivation of the 'Iraq* (Cambridge: Heffer, for The Agricultural Directorate of Mesopotamia, 1921), pt. 1, pp. 1-3 and pt. 3, pl. 1. In those cases where the "strings" bear no flowers or fruit, they may be ropes rather than spadices, and probably represent the ropes (made from the "primary axes of the spadices," Dowson, pt. 1, p. 63) used in climbing up the palm tree for the purpose of shaking a bag of pollen over the female flowers to aid in the pollination of the flowers. In antiquity there is already evidence of the artificial pollination of the date palm (Herodotus 1.193; Pliny, *Historia Naturalis* 13.31.34ff; see Benno Landsberger, *The Date Palm and its By-Products*, according to the Cuneiform Sources, *Archiv für Orientforschung*, Beiheft 17, Graz: 1967, p. 18); and still today "the *fellah* of every properly cultivated garden takes a sprig of the ripe male inflorescence and sets it firmly in the middle of that of the female" or shakes a "pollen bag" over the flowers (Dowson, pt. 1, p. 27). Finally, the "strings" may also be in some cases the sucker offshoots which the date palm sends out to propagate itself (Dowson, pt. 1, pp. 37-39), though these are usually nearer to the roots.

That these "strings" are spadices rather than ribbons or streamers is substantiated by further evidence. First, stelae from Carthage portray a caduceus, with two Tannit signs at the ends of the descending spadices, whose base is plainly the trunk of a palm tree, complete with the characteristically cross-hatched bark (fig. 10).[213] Other stelae show a similar scene, except that the caduceus is replaced by a more realistically portrayed palm tree, again with the cross-hatched bark and again with two Tannit signs at the ends of the spadices (fig. 11).[214] Further, on Punic stelae a typical arrangement is two caducei flanking a central symbol;[215] yet one also finds a central symbol flanked by a caduceus to the symbol's left and a realistically portrayed palm tree to the right.[216] Even more decisive for the identification of the caduceus with the palm tree is a Carthage representation pictured in Bisi's *Le Stele Puniche*:[217] here there is a central palm tree, realistically portrayed, with a bulb directly underneath the fronds and with two "strings" descending from below the bulb; immediately to the palm's right is a typical caduceus, with a crescent at the top, a ring which recalls the palm's bulb, and again with two "strings" descending from below the bulb (fig. 12).[218] The juxtaposition seems designed to demonstrate the caduceus' origin in a palm tree.

All of this evidence is best explained by identifying the palm with the cadueeus. The latter, a caduceus in name only,

---

213. For example, *CIS*, vol. 1, no. 281, no. 1421, or no. 2724. Like the palm itself, this cross-hatched bark is found on representations of palms not only in the western Mediterranean, but also all over the Near East; see *ANEP*, nos. 88, 204, 367, and 451. The bark of the date palm assumes this appearance because of the annual trimming of the fronds and sucker shoots.

214. For example, *CIS*, vol. 1, nos. 3332 or 3333.

215. For example, *EH*, no. 58 (pl. 9a), no. 145 (pl. 24b), or Bisi, *Le Stele Puniche*, fig. 77.

216. *EH*, no. 56 (pl. 8b); Bisi, *Le Stele Puniche*, fig. 29.

217. Bisi's fig. 13, our fig. 12.

218. Since men are portrayed climbing the "strings" of the realistically portrayed palm tree, the "strings" may be ropes here rather than spadices; and the scene portrayed is likely that of the artificial pollination of the female tree, or of the harvest of the fruit.

bears little resemblance to the palm tree,[219] as the fully developed sign of Tannit may bear little resemblance to the figure of a clothed female from which it evolved. But the alternation of the two symbols and the fact that the caduceus too has spadices bearing flowers or fruit imply strongly that despite the extreme stylization of the tree into the "caduceus" the memory of the caduceus' origin and significance was never lost.

The same conclusion is to be drawn from the caduceus' clear association with and reference to the goddess Tannit, for a fruitful tree is an ideal symbol of the mother goddess ʾAšerah/Tannit. Hours-Miedan's study of the Punic palm tree concludes that the palm carries a clear "allusion à la fécondité" because it almost always bears bunches of fruit;[220] and there is no more appropriate candidate for this allusion than the "Creatress of the gods" ʾAšerah. The Hebrew Bible bears witness to this same symbolism, for biblical Hebrew *ʾēlâ* ("terebinth") clearly played a role in the Canaanite fertility cult;[221] and it is suggestive to associate *ʾēlâ* with the name ʾĒlat,[222] which is an appellation of Canaanite ʾAšerah as we have seen.

There is, then, a way to reconcile the apparently contradictory evidence about the *ʾăšērîm* in the Hebrew and Greek texts of the Old Testament. Though the object was of human construction, like other idols, the Greek translators of most of the Hebrew Bible saw in it something which recalled to them groves (ἄλση) or trees (δένδρα). A stylized caduceus fits the demands of this divergent evidence strikingly well; and it is hardly a

---

219. The extreme stylization of the palm tree is witnessed also in Mesopotamia; see *ANEP*, no. 628 and p. (325). It seems likely that the caduceus' "disks," which can number from one to five, grew out of the disk-shaped bulb beneath the fronds of the palm tree. The palm tree realistically depicted and with long spadices is an exceedingly common motif on Carthaginian coins; see Jenkins and Lewis, *Carthaginian Coins*, pl. 1, no. 1; pl. 5, nos. 115-119; pl. 6, nos. 136-173; etc.

220. "Les représentations," 45.

221. See especially Hosea 4:13, and on this verse, Wolff, *Hosea*, pp. 85-87.

222. So Albright: "The feminine of *ʾEl*, Canaanite *ʾElat*, 'goddess,' which is also applied to Asherah as *the* goddess, El's consort, is found in the Hebrew Bible, so far as we know, only as the ordinary word for 'terebinth'" (*YGC*, p. 189).

coincidence that the caduceus of the Hierapolis "symbol," the caduceus of the Phoenician-Punic material, and the Old Testament *'ăšērâ* all symbolize, in part or entirely, the Canaanite mother goddess 'Ašerah/Tannit. The Old Testament *'ăšērâ* need not be identical with the Hierapolis σημήιον, especially if the latter owes something of its final form to an influence from the *signa* of the Romans whom the Syrians were anxious to please. But the conclusion is yet inescapable that behind both stands the highly stylized palm which scholars label a caduceus and which recalled to its Phoenician, Punic, and Syrian worshippers the goddess 'Ašerah.

Chapter IV

CONCLUSIONS

There are two larger conclusions to be drawn from this study of the *De Syria Dea*. One of these conclusions has to do with the character of the *De Syria Dea*, and its value to the student of the history of religion; and the other has to do with the character of the religion of Hierapolis shortly after the turn of the era.

First, the value of the *De Syria Dea* for the task of reconstructing the religion of Hierapolis is no longer to be doubted. The work is indeed and after all a "precious tract"; and the accounts of other visitors, ancient and modern, to Hierapolis tally remarkably with that offered by the author of the *De Syria Dea*. This is not to say that Lucian, who is likely the work's author, never exceeds the bounds of objective reporting. He does so in his account of the bearded Apollo, whose miraculous abilities are exaggerated, like the depth of the Hierapolis lake or the height of the temple's columns, to a satiric end. And he does so again in his description of the σημήιον, when his frustration in discovering from "the Assyrians themselves" any explanation of the symbol's meaning leads him to speculate about the same. But the boundary between description and parody or speculation is usually plainly marked, so that one can, as we have throughout, utilize the former with confidence.

Second, the relationship between the religion of Hierapolis at the beginning of the present era and the religion of the Canaanites is startlingly close. The intimacy of this relationship is clear despite the syncretism that obtained in the Hellenistic Near East and despite the Greek titles given the Hierapolis deities by Lucian. The Syrian Goddess represents a conflation of all three major Canaanite goddesses; yet this combination is witnessed already in the second millennium B.C. in Syria-Palestine and in Egypt. As other evidence suggests, there must have been always a movement in two directions in Canaanite religion, one toward the fusing of distinct deities into composite figures, and the other toward the division of a single deity into several separate deities, often originally the hypostases of that single deity. And because the movement operated in both directions, it will not do to claim that the composite character and name of Atargatis, for example, demonstrates alone a great development at Hierapolis beyond the religion of earlier Syria. The Hierapolis cult was dominated by Baʿl Haddu and his consort; yet the "divine decrees" of a bearded Apollo were required before any act was undertaken in Hierapolis. So too the myths of Ugarit relate largely the cosmogonic battles of Baʿl and his allies; but the assent of ʾĒl precedes the beginning of the drama. Like the material preserved by Philo Byblios, the *De Syria Dea* proves again the continued power the religion of Canaan had for the people of Syria-Palestine for well over a thousand years.

LIST OF FIGURES

Figure 1. Hierapolis coin of Caracalla. (Pellerin, *Mélange de diverses médailles*, pl. 8, no. 12, reverse.)

Figure 2. Hierapolis coin of Alexander Severus. (Imhoof-Blumer, *Griechische Münzen*, pl. 14, no. 7, reverse.)

Figure 3. Mozia stele with a female figure. (Moscati, "L'origine," pl. 1b.)

Figure 4. Mozia stele with a schematized female figure. (Moscati, "L'origine," pl. 3b.)

Figure 5. Three examples of the sign of Tannit from Carthage. (Bisi, *Le Stele Puniche*, fig. 7.)

Figure 6. Various examples of the so-called Phoenician-Punic "caduceus." (6a, Ronzevalle, "Notes et études," pl. 7, no. 2; 6b, Bisi, *Le Stele Puniche*, pl. 19, no. 2; 6c, Bisi, *Le Stele Puniche*, fig. 74; 6d, Bisi, *Le Stele Puniche*, fig. 5.)

Figure 7. Representations from Punic stelae showing a Tannit sign (a), or a partially schematized female figure (b), between two caducei (a) or two schematized plants (b). (7a, Bisi, *Le Stele Puniche*, fig. 77; 7b, Bisi, *Le Stele Puniche*, fig. 91.)

Figure 8. Tannit signs combined with one or two caducei. (8a, Dunand and Duru, *Oumm el-ʿAmed*, pl. 68, no. 1; 8b, Bisi, *Le Stele Puniche*, fig. 7.)

Figure 9. Hanawe tomb with a Tannit sign and a caduceus. (Virolleaud, "Les travaux archéologiques," fig. 3; cf. Bisi, *Le Stele Puniche*, fig. 6.)

Figure 10. Signs of Tannit and caduceus, with palm-tree bark. (Bisi, *Le Stele Puniche*, fig. 52.)

Figure 11. Signs of Tannit and a realistic palm tree. (Bisi, *Le Stele Puniche*, fig. 51.)

Figure 12. Palm tree juxtaposed with a caduceus, both with descending "ribbons." (Bisi, *Le Stele Puniche*, fig. 13.)

Fig. 1

Fig. 2

Fig. 3

Fig. 4

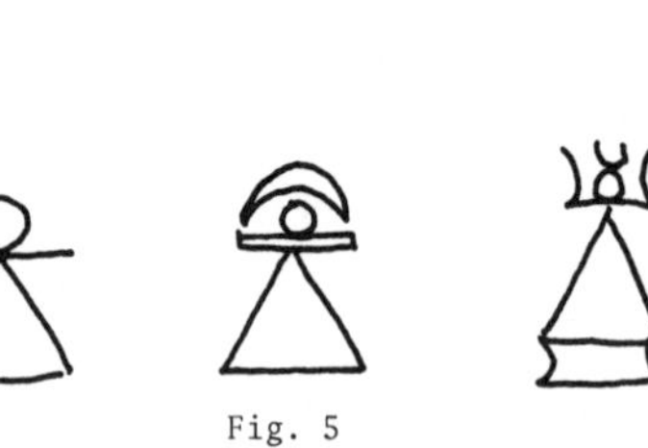

Fig. 5

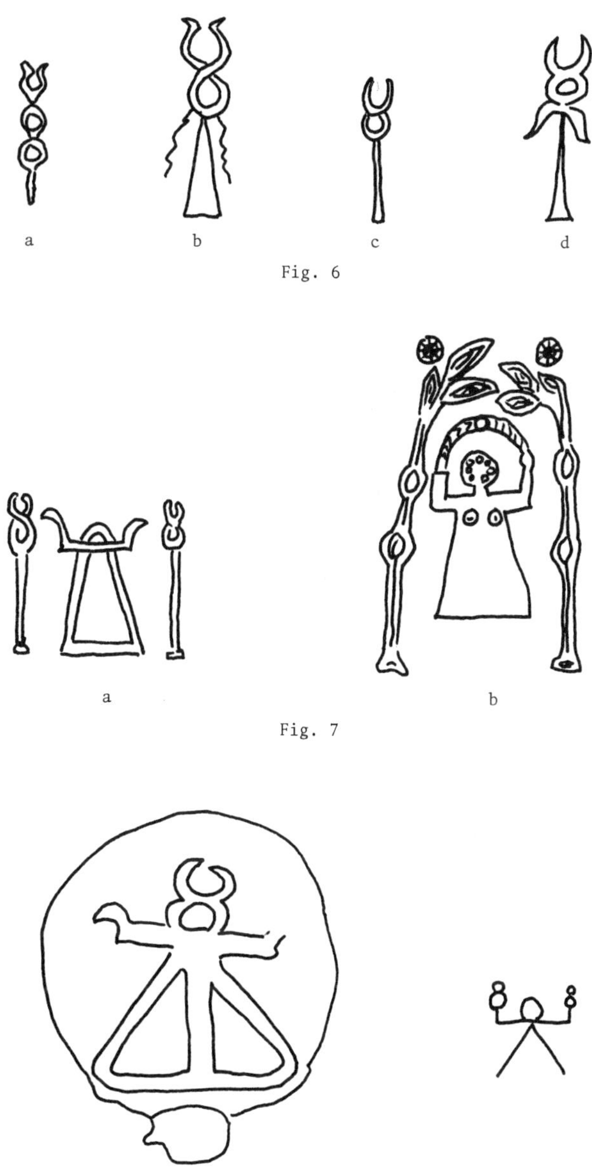

Fig. 6

Fig. 7

Fig. 8

Fig. 9

Fig. 10

Fig. 11

Fig. 12

BIBLIOGRAPHY

Albright, William Foxwell. *Archaeology and the Religion of Israel*, 4th ed. Baltimore: Johns Hopkins University Press, 1956.

______. "Astarte Plaques and Figurines from Tell Beit Mirsim," in *Mélanges syriens:* offerts à monsieur René Dussaud, secrètaire perpétuel de l'Académie des Inscriptions et Belles-lettres, par ses amis et ses élèves, vol. 1, pp. 107-120. Paris: Paul Geuthner, 1939.

______. "The Babylonian Matter in the Predeuteronomic Primeval History (JE) in Gen 1-11," *Journal of Biblical Literature* 58 (1939) 91-103.

______. "The Evolution of the West-Semitic Divinity ʿAn-ʿAnat-ʿAttâ," *American Journal of Semitic Languages and Literatures* 41 (1925) 73-101. "Further Observations on the Name *ʿAnat-ʿAttah*," *American Journal of Semitic Languages and Literatures* 41 (1925) 283-285. "Note on the Goddess ʿAnat," *American Journal of Semitic Languages and Literatures* 43 (1927) 233-236.

______. *From the Stone Age to Christianity:* Monotheism and the Historical Process, 2d ed. Baltimore: Johns Hopkins University Press, 1946.

______. "The Goddess of Life and Wisdom," *American Journal of Semitic Languages and Literatures* 36 (1920) 258-294.

______. "Islam and the Religions of the Ancient Orient," *Journal of the American Oriental Society* 60 (1940) 283-301.

______. "The 'Natural Force' of Moses in the Light of Ugaritic," *Bulletin of the American Schools of Oriental Research* 94 (1944) 32-35.

______. "The North-Canaanite Epic of ʾAlʾêyân Baʿal and Môt," *Journal of the Palestine Oriental Society* 12 (1932) 185-208.

______. "The North-Canaanite Poems of ʾAlʾêyân Baʿal and the 'Gracious Gods,'" *Journal of the Palestine Oriental Society* 14 (1934) 101-140.

______. "The Oracles of Balaam," *Journal of Biblical Literature* 63 (1944) 207-234.

______. "The Phoenician Inscriptions of the Tenth Century B.C. from Byblos," *Journal of the American Oriental Society* 67 (1947) 153-160.

______. *The Proto-Sinaitic Inscriptions and Their Decipherment.*

Harvard Theological Studies no. 22. Cambridge, Mass.: Harvard University Press, 1969.

______. "Some Cruces in the Langdon Epic," *Journal of the American Oriental Society* 39 (1919) 65-90.

______. "A Vow to Asherah in the Keret Epic," *Bulletin of the American Schools of Oriental Research* 94 (1944) 30-31.

______. *Yahweh and the Gods of Canaan.* Garden City, New York: Doubleday, 1968.

Allinson, Francis G. *Lucian:* Satirist and Artist. Boston: Marshall Jones, 1926.

______. "Pseudo-Ionism in the Second Century A.D.," *American Journal of Philology* 7 (1886) 203-217.

Altaner, Berthold and Stuiber, Alfred. *Patrologie:* Leben, Schriften und Lehre de Kirchenväter. 7th ed. Freiburg: Herder, 1966.

Astour, Michael C. *Hellenosemitica.* Leiden: E. J. Brill, 1965.

Avi-Yonah, M. "Syrian Gods at Ptolemais-Accho," *Israel Exploration Journal* 9 (1959) 1-12.

Baethgen, Friedrich. *Beiträge zur semitischen Religionsgeschichte:* der Gott Israel's und die Götter der Heiden. Berlin: H. Reuther, 1888.

Baldwin, Barry. *Studies in Lucian.* Toronto: Hakkert, 1973.

Bardenhewer, Otto. *Geschichte der altkirchlichen Litteratur.* Frieburg: Herder, 1902.

Baudissin, Wolf Wilhelm Graf. *Adonis und Esmun:* Eine Untersuchung zur Geschichte des Glaubens an Auferstehungsgötter und an Heilgötter. Leipzig: J. C. Hinrichs, 1911.

______. "Die Quellen für eine Darstellung der Religion der Phönizier und der Aramäer," *Archiv für Religionswissenschaft* 16 (1913) 389-422.

Baumstark, Anton. *Geschichte der syrischen Literatur.* Bonn: Marcus und Webers, 1922.

Baur, P. V. C., Rostovtzeff, M. I., and Bellinger, Alfred R. *The Excavations of Dura-Europos*, Preliminary Report of the Third Season of Work: November 1929-March 1930. New Haven: Yale University Press, 1932.

Bellinger, Alfred R. and Newell, E.-T. "A Seleucid Mint at Dura-Europos," *Syria* 21 (1940) 77-81.

______. See also Baur, P. V. C.

Benveniste, E. "La légende de Kombabos," in *Mélanges syriens:* offerts à monsieur René Dussaud, secrétaire perpétuel de l'Akadémie des Inscriptions et Belles-lettres, par ses amis et ses élèves, vol. 1, pp. 249-258. Paris: Paul Geuthner, 1939.

Benz, Frank L. *Personal Names in the Phoenician and Punic Inscriptions.* Studia Pohl: Dissertationes Scientificae de Rebus Orientis Antiqui, no. 8. Rome: Pontifical Biblical Institute, 1972.

Berg, Paul-Louis van. *Etude critique des sources mythographiques grecques et latines.* Sauf le *De Dea Syria.* Corpus Cultus Deae Syriae, 1. Les sources littéraires, deuxième partie. Leiden: E. J. Brill, 1972.

______. *Répertoire des sources grecques et latines.* Sauf le *De Dea Syria.* Corpus Cultus Deae Syriae, 1. Les sources littéraires, première partie. Leiden: E. J. Brill, 1972.

Berthier, André, and Charlier, René. *Le sanctuaire punique d'El-Hofra à Constantine.* Paris: Arts et Métiers Graphiques, 1952-1955.

Betz, Hans Dieter. *Lukian von Samosata und das Neue Testament.* Texte und Untersuchungen zur Geschichte der altchristlichen Literatur, no. 76. Berlin: Akademie Verlag, 1961.

Bisi, Anna Maria. *Le Stele Puniche.* Studi Semitici, no. 27. Rome: Istituto di Studi del Vicino Oriente, Università di Roma, 1967.

Boling, Robert G. *Judges.* The Anchor Bible, 6A. Garden City, N.Y.: Doubleday, 1975.

Bompaire, J. *Lucien ecrivain.* Bibliothèque des Ecoles Françaises d'Athènes et de Rome, no. 190. Paris: E. de Boccard, 1958.

Bonner, Campbell. *The Homily on the Passion by Melito Bishop of Sardis*, with some Fragments of the Apocryphal Ezekiel. Studies and Documents edited by Kirsopp Lake and Silva Lake, no. 12. Philadelphia: University of Pennsylvania Press, 1940.

Borger, Riekele. *Die Inschriften Asarhaddons Königs von Assyrien.* Beiheft zum *Archiv für Orientforschung*, no. 9. Graz, 1956.

Bossert, H. Th. "Zur Vokalisation des Luwischen," *Orientalia* NS 30 (1961) 314-322.

Bouchier, E. S. *Syria as a Roman Province.* Oxford: Blackwell, 1916.

Brancoli, Isabella, *et al.* *Mozia III:* Rapporto preliminare della Missione archeological della Suprintendenza alle Antichità della Sicilia Occidentale e dell'Università di

Roma. Rome: Istituto di Studi del Vicino Oriente, Università di Roma, 1967.

Brockelmann, Carl. *Grundriss der vergleichenden Grammatik der semitischen Sprachen.* Vol. 1: Laut- und Formenlehre. Berlin: Reuther & Reichard, 1908.

Brønno, Einar. *Studien über hebräische Morphologie und Vokalismus*, auf Grundlage der Mercatischen Fragmente der zweiten Kolumne der Hexapla des Origenes. Abhandlungen für die Kunde des Morgenlandes, no. 28. Leipzig: Deutsche Morgenländische Gesellschaft, 1943.

Brooks, Beatrice A. "Fertility Cult Functionaries in the Old Testament," *Journal of Biblical Literature* 60 (1941) 227-253.

Burckhardt, Jakob. *Die Zeit Constantin's des Groszen.* Leipzig: Seemann, 1853.

Caquot, A. "Note sur le *semeion* et les inscriptions araméennes de Hatra," *Syria* 32 (1955) 59-69.

______. "Nouvelles inscriptions araméennes de Hatra," *Syria* 29 (1952) 89-118.

______. "Nouvelles inscriptions araméennes de Hatra, (II)," *Syria* 30 (1953) 234-244.

______. "Nouvelles inscriptions araméennes de Hatra, (III)," *Syria* 32 (1955) 49-58.

______. "Nouvelles inscriptions araméennes de Hatra, (IV)," *Syria* 32 (1955) 261-272.

______. "Nouvelles inscriptions araméennes de Hatra, (V)," *Syria* 40 (1963) 1-16.

Cassuto, Umberto. *The Goddess Anath.* Translated by Israel Abrahams. Jerusalem: The Magnes Press, 1971.

Caster, Marcel. *Lucien et la pensée religieuse de son temps.* Paris: Société d'édition "Les belles lettres," 1937.

Charlier, René. See Berthier, André.

Chesney, Francis Rawdon. *The Expedition for the Survey of the Rivers Euphrates and Tigris*, Carried on by Order of the British Government in the Years 1835, 1836, and 1837. London: Longman, Brown, Green and Longmans, 1850.

Christ, Wilhelm von. *Geschichte der griechischen Literatur.* 7th ed. Edited by Wilhelm Schmid and Otto Stählin. Munich: Oskar Beck, 1924.

Clapham, Lynn Roy. "Sancuniathon: The First Two Cycles." Ph.D. Dissertation, Harvard University, 1969.

Clemen, Carl. *Lukians Schrift über die syrische Göttin.* Der Alte Orient, vol. 37, part 3/4. Leipzig: J. C. Hinrichs, 1938.

______. "Miszellen zu Lukians Schrift über die syrische Göttin." In *Abhandlungen zur semitischen Religionskunde und Sprachwissenschaft*, Essays in honor of Wolf Wilhelm Grafen von Baudissin. Edited by Wilh. Frankenberg and Friedr. Küchler. Beihefte zur *Zeitschrift für die alttestamentliche Wissenschaft*, no. 33 (1918) pp. 83-106.

______. "Tempel und Kult in Hierapolis," in *Pisciculi:* Studien zur Religion und Kultur des Altertums, F. J. Dölger Festschrift. Edited by Theodor Klauser and Adolf Rücker. Münster: Aschendorff, 1939.

Clifford, Richard J. *The Cosmic Mountain in Canaan and the Old Testament.* Harvard Semitic Monographs, vol. 4. Cambridge, Mass.: Harvard University Press, 1972.

Cook, Arthur Bernard. *Zeus:* A Study in Ancient Religion. Vol. 1. Cambridge: Cambridge University Press, 1914.

Cook, Stanley A. *The Religion of Ancient Palestine in the Light of Archaeology.* The Schweich Lectures of the British Academy, 1925. London: Oxford University Press, 1930.

Cooke, George A. *A Textbook of North-Semitic Inscriptions.* Oxford: Oxford University Press, 1903.

Coote, R. B. "The Serpent and Sacred Marriage in Northwest Semitic Tradition." Ph.D. dissertation, Harvard University, 1972.

Corpus Inscriptionum Latinarum. Consilio et auctoritate academiae litterarum regiae Borussicae. Berlin: Georgium Reimerum, 1869-.

Corpus Inscriptionum Semiticarum. Ab Academia inscriptionum et litterarum humaniorum. Paris: e Republicae typographeo, 1881-.

Croiset, Maurice. *Essae sur la vie et les oeuvres de Lucien.* Paris: Hachette, 1882.

Cross, Frank Moore, Jr. *Canaanite Myth and Hebrew Epic.* Cambridge, Mass.: Harvard University Press, 1973.

______. "The Evolution of the Proto-Canaanite Alphabet," *Bulletin of the American Schools of Oriental Research* 134 (1954) 15-24.

______. "The Origin and Early Evolution of the Alphabet," *Eretz Israel* 8 (1967) 8*-24*.

______. "Notes on a Canaanite Psalm in the Old Testament," *Bulletin of the American Schools of Oriental Research* 117 (1950) 19-21.

______. "Prose and Poetry in the Mythic and Epic Texts from Ugarit," *Harvard Theological Review* 67 (1974) 1-15.

______, and Saley, Richard J. "Phoenician Incantations on a Plaque of the Seventh Century B.C. from Arslan Tash in Upper Syria," *Bulletin of the American Schools of Oriental Research* 197 (1970) 42-49.

______. See also Milik, J. T.

Cumont, Franz. "Atargatis," in *Pauly-Wissowa*, vol. 2, col. 1896.

______. "Deux autels de Phénicie," *Syria* 8 (1927) 163-168.

______. "Un dieu syrien à dos de chameau," *Syria* 10 (1929) 30-35.

______. *Les religions orientales dans le paganisme romain*. 4th ed. Paris: Paul Geuthner, 1929.

______. "Syria Dea," in *Dictionnaire des antiquités grecques et romaines*. Edited by Ch. Daremberg, Edmond Saglio, and Edmund Pottier. Vol. 4, part 2, pp. 1590-1596. Paris: Hachette, 1877-1919.

Cureton, William. *Spicilegium Syriacum:* Containing Remains of Bardesan, Meliton, Ambrose and Mara Bar Serapion. London: Rivington, 1855.

Dittenberger, Wilhelm. *Orientis graeci inscriptiones selectae*. Leipzig: S. Hirzel, 1903.

Donner, Herbert. "Ein Orthostatenfragment des Königs Barrakab von Sam'al," *Mitteilungen des Instituts für Orientforschung* (Deutsche Akademie der Wissenschaften zu Berlin: Institut für Orientforschung) 3 (1955) 73-98.

______, and Röllig, Wolfgang. *Kanaanäische und aramäische Inschriften*. Mit einem Beitrag von O. Rössler. Wiesbaden: Otto Harrassowitz, 1964-1968.

Dothan, M. "A Sign of Tanit from Tel ʿAkko," *Israel Exploration Journal* 24 (1974, M. Avi-Yonah Memorial Volume) 44-49.

Dowson, V. H. W. *Dates & Date Cultivation of the ʾIraq*. Cambridge: Heffer, for the Agricultural Directorate of Mesopotamia, 1921.

Driver, G. R. *Canaanite Myths and Legends*. Old Testament Studies Published under the Auspices of the Society for Old Testament Study, no. 3. Edinburgh: T. & T. Clark, 1956.

Driver, Samuel Rolles. *A Critical and Exegetical Commentary on Deuteronomy.* The International Critical Commentary. 3d ed. Edinburgh: T. & T. Clark, 1902.

______, and Gray, George Buchanan. *A Critical and Exegetical Commentary on the Book of Job.* The International Critical Commentary. Edinburgh: T. & T. Clark, 1921.

du Mesnil du Buisson, Comte. "L'étendard d'Atargatis et Hadad à Doura-Europos ou la déesse Semia," *Revue des arts asiatiques* 11 (1937) 75-87.

______. "De Chadrafa, dieu de Palmyre, à Baʿal Shamīm, dieu de Hatra, aux IIe et IIIe siècles apres J.-C.," *Mélanges de l'université Saint-Joseph* 38 (1962) 141-160.

Dunand, Maurice, and Duru, Raymond. *Oumm el-ʿAmed:* une ville de l'époque hellénistique aux échelles de Tyr. République Libanaise, études et documents d'archéologie, no. 4. Paris: Adrien Maisonneuve, 1962.

Dupont-Sommer, André. "L'inscription de l'amulette d'Arslan Tash," *Revue de l'histoire des religions* 120 (1939) 133-159.

______. "Une stèle araméenne d'un prêtre de Baʿal trouvée en Egypte," *Syria* 33 (1956) 79-87.

Duru, Raymond. See Dunand, Maurice.

Dussaud, René. "Notes de Mythologie syrienne," *Revue archéologique* 4th series, vol. 4 (1904) 225-260.

______. "Peut-on identifier l'Apollon barbu de Hiérapolis de Syrie?" *Revue de l'histoire des religions* 126 (1943) 128-149.

______. "Simea und Simios," in *Pauly-Wissowa*, 2d Series, vol. 3, cols. 137-140.

______. "Temples et cultes de la triade héliopolitaine à Baʿalbeck," *Syria* 23 (1942-1943) 33-77.

______. *Topographie historique de la Syrie antique et médiévale.* Bibliothèque archéologique et historique, vol. 4. Paris: Paul Geuthner, 1927.

Duval, Rubens. *Anciennes littératures chrétiennes.* Vol. 2: La littérature syriaque. 2d ed. Paris: Victor Lecoffre, 1900.

Edwards, I. E. S. "A Relief of Qudshu-Astarte-Anath in the Winchester College Collection," *Journal of Near Eastern Studies* 14 (1955) 49-51, pls. 3 and 4.

Eilers, Wilhelm. *Semiramis.* Vienna: Kommissionsverlag des österreichischen Akademie der Wissenschaften, 1971.

Eissfeldt, Otto. "Baʿalšamēm und Yahwe," *Zeitschrift für die alttestamentliche Wissenschaft* 57 (1939) 1-31.

______. *Ras Schamra und Sanchunjaton.* Beiträge zur Religionsgeschichte des Altertums, vol. 4. Halle: Max Niemeyer, 1939.

______. *Sanchunjaton von Berut und Ilumilku von Ugarit.* Beiträge zur Religionsgeschichte des Altertums, vol. 5. Halle: Max Niemeyer, 1952.

______. "Zum geographischen Horizant der Ras-Schamra-Texte," *Zeitschrift der deutschen morgenländischen Gesellschaft* 94 (1940) 59-85.

Fauth, Wolfgang. "Dea Syria," in *Der Kleine Pauly:* Lexikon der Antike. Edited by Konrat Ziegler and Walther Sontheimer. Vol. 1, cols. 1400-1402. Stuttgart: Alfred Druckemüller Verlag, 1964-.

Fitzmyer, Joseph, S.J. *The Aramaic Inscriptions of Sefîre.* Biblica et Orientalia, no. 19. Rome: Pontifical Biblical Institute, 1967.

______. "The Phoenician Inscription from Pyrgi," *Journal of the American Oriental Society* 86 (1966) 285-297.

Frankfort, H. *Cylinder Seals:* A Documentary Essay on the Art and Religion of the Ancient Near East. London: Gregg Press, 1965. Reprint of 1939 ed.

Frazer, James George. *The Golden Bough:* A Study in Magic and Religion. Vol. 4: *Adonis Attis Osiris.* 2d ed. London: Macmillan, 1907.

Friedrich, Johannes, and Röllig, Wolfgang. *Phönizisch-punische Grammatik.* 2d ed. Rome: Pontifical Biblical Institute, 1970.

Frothingham, A. L. "Babylonian Origin of Hermes, the Snake God, and of the Caduceus," *American Journal of Archaeology* 20 (1916) 175-211.

Ganszyniec, R. "Zu [Lukian] *De dea Syria,*" *Archiv für Religionswissenschaft* 21 (1916) 499-502.

Gardiner, Alan H. See Langdon, Stephen Herbert.

Garstang, John and Strong, Herbert A. *The Syrian Goddess.* London: Constable, 1913.

Gaster, Theodor H. *Thespis:* Ritual, Myth and Drama in the Ancient Near East. Rev. ed. New York: Harper Torchbook, 1966.

Ginsberg, H. L. *The Legend of King Keret:* A Canaanite Epic of the Bronze Age. *Bulletin of the American Schools of*

Oriental Research, Supplementary Studies, nos. 2-3. New Haven: American Schools of Oriental Resarch, 1946.

Glueck, Nelson. *Deities and Dolphins*. New York: Farrar, Straus and Giroux, 1965.

______. "A Newly Discovered Nabataean Temple of Atargatis and Hadad at Khirbet et-Tannûr, Transjordania," *American Journal of Archaeology* 41 (1937) 361-376.

Goossens, Godefroy. *Hiérapolis de Syrie:* essai de monographie historique. Université de Louvain, Recueil de Travaux d'Histoire et de Philologie, 3d series, fascicule 12. Louvain: Université de Louvain, 1943.

Gray, George Buchanan. See Driver, Samuel Rolles.

Gray, John. *I & II Kings:* A Commentary. Old Testament Library. 2d ed. London: SCM, 1970.

______. *The Legacy of Canaan:* The Ras Shamra Texts and Their Relevance to the Old Testament. Supplements to *Vetus Testamentum*, no. 5. 2d ed. Leiden: E. J. Brill, 1965.

Grimme, Herbert. "Die Jahotriade von Elephantine," *Orientalistische Literaturzeitung* 15 (1912) 11-17.

Haase, Felix. "Untersuchungen zur bardesanischen Gnosis," *Texte und Untersuchungen zur Geschichte der altchristlichen Literatur*, vol. 34 (1910), pt. 4 1-98.

Harden, Douglas. *The Phoenicians*. London: Thames and Hudson, 1962.

Harmon, A. M., trans. *Lucian*. Loeb Classical Library. Vol. 4. Cambridge, Mass.: Harvard University Press, 1925.

______. "An Emendation in Lucian's *Syrian Goddess*," *Classical Philology* 19 (1924) 72-74.

Harper, Robert Francis. *Assyrian and Babylonian Letters*, Belonging to the *K*. Collection of the British Museum. Part 3. London: University of Chicago Press, 1896.

Haussig, H. W., ed. *Wörterbuch der Mythologie*. Vol. I: Götter und Mythen im Vorderen Orient. Stuttgart: Ernst Klett, 1965.

Hauvette-Besnault, Am. "Fouilles de Délos: temple des dieux étrangers, divinités syriennes: Aphrodite syrienne, Adad et Atargatis," *Bulletin de correspondance hellênique* 6 (1882) 470-503.

Heidel, Alexander. *The Gilgamesh Epic and Old Testament Parallels*. Chicago: Phoenix, 1963.

Helck, Wolfgang. *Die Beziehungen Ägyptens zu Vorderasien im 3. und 2. Jahrtausend v. Chr.* 2d ed. Ägyptologische

Abhandlungen, edited by Wolfgang Helck and Eberhard Otto, vol. 5. Wiesbaden: Otto Harrassowitz, 1971.

Helm, R. "Lukianos," in *Pauly-Wissowa*, vol. 13, cols. 1725-1777.

Herdner, Andrée. *Corpus des tablettes en cunéiformes alphabétiques* découvertes à Ras Shamra-Ugarit de 1929 à 1930. Mission de Ras Shamra dirigée par Claude F. A. Schaeffer, vol. 10. Paris: Imprimerie Nationale, 1963.

______. "Note lexicographique: RS *lpš*," *Syria* 23 (1942-1943) 135-136.

Hewitt, Joseph William. "A Second Century Voltaire," *The Classical Journal* 20 (1924) 132-142.

Highet, Gilbert. *The Anatomy of Satire.* Princeton: Princeton University Press, 1962.

Hill, George Francis. *Catalogue of the Greek Coins of Palestine* (Galilee, Samaria, and Judaea). London: British Museum, 1914.

Hillers, Delbert R. "The Bow of Aqhat: The Meaning of a Mythological Theme," in *Orient and Occident:* Essays Presented to Cyrus H. Gordon on the Occasion of His Sixty-fifth Birthday. Edited by Harry A. Hoffner. Pp. 71-80. Neukirchen-Vluyn: Neukirchener Verlag, 1973.

______. "The Goddess with the Tambourine: Reflections on an Object from Taanach," *Concordia Theological Monthly* 41 (1970) 606-619.

Höfer, O. "Syria," in *Ausführliches Lexikon der griechischen und römischen Mythologie.* Edited by W. H. Roscher. Vol. 4, cols. 1629-1642. Leipzig: Teubner, 1884-1937.

Hoftijzer, Jacob. See Jean, Charles-F.

Hogarth, D. G. "Hierapolis Syriae," *Annual of the British School at Athens* 14 (1907-1908) 183-196.

Hommel, Fritz. *Grundriss der Geographie und Geschichte des alten Orients.* Handbuch der klassischen Altertumswissenschaft, vol. 3, part 1, 1st half. Munich: Beck, 1904.

Honigmann, E. "Hierapolis," in Supplement to *Pauly-Wissowa*, vol. 4, cols. 733-742.

______. "Syria," in *Pauly-Wissowa*, 2d series, vol. 4, cols. 1549-1727.

Hours-Miedan, Magdeleine. "Les représentations figurées sur les stèles de Carthage," *Cahiers de Byrsa* 1 (1950) 15-160.

Iacobitz, Caroli [Jacobitz, Karl], ed. *Luciani Samosatensis Opera.* Vol. 3. Leipzig: Teubner, 1912.

Imhoof-Blumer, F. *Griechische Münzen*. Abhandlungen der k. bayer. Akademie der wiss. I. cl. 18, vol. 3. Munich: Verlag der k. Akademie, 1880.

Ingholt, Harald. "Parthian Sculptures from Hatra," *Memoirs of the Connecticut Academy* 12 (1954) 1-46.

______, Seyrig, Henri and Starcky, Jean. *Recueil des tessères de Palmyre*. Paris: Paul Geuthner, 1955.

Inscriptions grecques et latines de la Syrie. Bibliothèque archéologique et historique, vol. 12-. Paris: Paul Geuthner, 1929-.

Jacobi, J. L. Rev. of W. Cureton, *Spicilegium Syriacum* (London: 1855). *Deutsche Zeitschrift für chrisliche Wissenschaft und christliches Leben*, 7th year, no. 14 (1856) 105-108.

Jastrow, Marcus. *A Dictionary of the Targumim, the Talmud Babli and Yerushalmi, and the Midrashic Literature*. New York: Judaica Press, 1971. Reprint of 1903 ed.

Jean, Charles-F. and Hoftijzer, Jacob. *Dictionnaire des inscriptions sémitiques de l'ouest*. Leiden: E. J. Brill, 1965.

Jenkins, G. K. and Lewis, R. B. *Carthaginian Gold and Electrum Coins*. London: Royal Numismatic Society, 1963.

Jensen, P. *Assyrisch-babylonische Mythen und Epen*. Keilinschriftliche Bibliothek, edited by Eberhard Schrader, vol. 6, part 1. Berlin: Reuther & Reichard, 1900.

Johns, C. H. W. *An Assyrian Doomsday Book*. Assyriologische Bibliothek, edited by Friedrich Delitzsch and Paul Haupt, fol. 17. Leipzig: J. C. Hinrichs, 1901.

Joost, Arthur. "Beobachtungen über den Partikelgebrauch Lucians. Ein Beitrag zur Frage nach der Echtheit und Reihenfolge Einiger seiner Schriften," *Restschrift zum fünfzigjährigen Doctorjubiläum Ludwig Friedlaender*. Pp. 163-182. Leipzig: S. Hirzel, 1895.

Kapelrud, Arvid S. *Baal in the Ras Shamra Texts*. Copenhagen: G. E. C. Gad, 1952.

______. *The Violent Goddess:* Anat in the Ras Shamra Texts. Oslo: Universitetsforlaget, 1969.

Kilmer, Anne Draffkorn. "How Was Queen Ereshkigal Tricked? A New Interpretation of the Descent of Ishtar," *Ugarit-Forschungen* 3 (1971) 299-309.

______. "The Mesopotamian Concept of Overpopulation and Its Solution as Reflected in the Mythology," *Orientalia* NS 41 (1972) 160-177.

Klaffenbach, Guenther, ed. *Inscriptiones Graecae.* Consilio et auctoritate academia litterarum Borussicae editae, vol. 9, part 1, fascicule 1. Berlin: Walter de Gruyter, 1932.

Knudtzon, Jørgen Alexander. *Die El-Amarna-Tafeln.* Aalen: O. Zeller, 1964. Reprint of 1915 ed.

Kraeling, Emil G. "Xisouthros, Deucalion and the Flood Traditions," *Journal of the American Oriental Society* 67 (1947) 177-183.

Kselman, John S. "A Note on Gen. 7:11," *Catholic Biblical Quarterly* 35 (1973) 491-493.

Laessøe, Jørgen. "The Atraḫasīs Epic: A Babylonian History of Mankind," *Bibliotheca orientalis* 13 (1956) 89-102.

Lambert, W. G., and Millard, A. R. *Atra-ḫasīs:* The Babylonian Story of the Flood. Oxford: Oxford University Press, 1969.

Landes, G. M. "The Fountain at Jazer," *Bulletin of the American Schools of Oriental Research* 144 (1956) 30-37.

Landsberger, Benno. *The Date Palm and its By-products*, according to the Cuneiform sources. *Archiv für Orientforschung*, Beiheft 17. Graz, 1967.

Langdon, Stephen Herbert. *Semitic Mythology.* The Mythology of All Races, edited by John Arnott MacCulloch and George Foot Moore, vol. 5. Boston: Marshall Jones, 1931.

______, and Gardiner, Alan H. "The Treaty of Alliances Between Ḫattušili King of the Hittites, and the Pharaoh Ramesses II of Egypt," *The Journal of Egyptian Archaeology* 6 (1920) 179-205.

Leclant, Jean. "Astarté à cheval d'après les représentations égyptiennes," *Syria* 37 (1960) 1-67.

Lewis, R. B. See Jenkins, G. K.

L'Heureux, Conrad Elphège. "El and the Rephaim: New Light from *Ugaritica V*." Ph.D. dissertation, Harvard University, 1971.

Lidzbarski, Mark. *Ephemeris für semitische Epigraphik.* Giessen: Alfred Töpelmann, 1900-1915.

______. *Handbuch der nordsemitischen Epigraphik*, nebst ausgewählten Inschriften. Vol. 1, text. Vol. 2, plates. Weimar: Emil Felber, 1898.

Linder, Elisha. "A Cargo of Phoenicio-Punic Figurines," *Archaeology* 26 (1973) 182-187.

Macalister, R. A. Stewart. *The Philistines:* Their History and Civilization. The Schweich Lectures of the British Academy, 1911. London: British Academy, 1914.

Martin, M. l'Abbé. "Discours de Jacques de Saroug sur la chutes des idoles," *Zeitschrift der deutschen morgenländischen Gesellschaft* 29 (1875) 107-147.

Maundrell, Henry. *A Journey from Aleppo to Jerusalem at Easter, A. D. 1697.* 6th ed. Oxford, 1740.

Mazar, B. "The Military Élite of King David," *Vetus Testamentum* 13 (1963) 310-320.

McCown, C. C. "The Goddesses of Gerasa," *Annual of the American Schools of Oriental Research* 13 (1931-1932) 129-166.

Milik, J. T., and Cross, Frank M., Jr. "Inscribed Javelin-Heads from the Period of the Judges: A Recent Discovery in Palestine," *Bulletin of the American Schools of Oriental Research* 134 (1954) 5-15.

______, and Teixidor, J. "New Evidence on the North-Arabic Deity Aktab-Kutbâ," *Bulletin of the American Schools of Oriental Research* 163 (1961) 22-25.

Miller, Patrick D. "Animal Names as Designations in Ugaritic and Hebrew," *Ugarit-Forschungen* 2 (1970) 177-186.

Montgomery, James A. *A Critical and Exegetical Commentary on the Book of Kings.* The International Critical Commentary. Edited by Henry Snyder Gehman. Edinburgh: T. & T. Clark, 1951.

______. "Notes on the Mythological Epic Texts from Ras Shamra," *Journal of the American Oriental Society* 53 (1933) 97-123.

Moor, Johannes C. de. Rev. of Arvid S. Kapelrud, *The Violent Goddess* (Oslo, 1969). *Ugarit-Forschungen* 1 (1969) 223-227.

______. "Studies in the New Alphabetic Texts from Ras Shamra I," *Ugarit-Forschungen* 1 (1969) 167-188.

Moran, William L. "New Evidence from Mari on the History of Prophecy," *Biblica* 50 (1969) 15-56.

Morin, Paul John. "The Cult of Dea Syria in the Greek World." Ph.D. dissertation, Ohio State University, 1960.

Moscati, Sabatino. "L'origine del 'segno di Tanit,'" *Atti della Accademia Nazionale dei Lincei* (Rendiconti della Classe di scienze morali, storiche e filologiche) series 8 vol. 27 fasc. 7-12 (1972) 371-374.

______. *The World of the Phoenicians.* New York: Praeger, 1968.

Movers, F. C. *Die Phönizier.* Vol. 2, part 3. Berlin: Ferd. Dümmler's Verlagsbuchhandlung, 1856.

Nassouhi, Essad. "Inscription de Tiglatphalasar III provenant d'Assur, avec mention de Membidj," *Mitteilungen der Altorientalischen Gesellschaft* (Leipzig) 3, 1/2 (1927) 15-16.

Newell, E.-T. See Bellinger, Alfred R.

Nock. Arthur Darby. "Eunuchs in Ancient Religion," *Archiv für Religionswissenschaft* 23 (1925) 25-33. Reprinted in *Arthur Darby Nock:* Essays on Religion and the Ancient World. Edited by Zeph Stewart. Pp. 1-15. Cambridge, Mass.: Harvard University Press, 1972.

______. "Religious Symbols and Symbolism II," *Gnomon* 29 (1957) 524-533. Reprinted in *Arthur Darby Nock:* Essays on Religion and the Ancient World. Pp. 895-907.

______. "The Roman Army and the Religious Year," *Harvard Theological Review* 45 (1952) 187-252. Reprinted in *Arthur Darby Nock:* Essays on Religion and the Ancient World. Pp. 736-790.

Nöldeke, Theodor. "'Ἀσσύριος, Σύριος, Σύρος," *Hermes* 5 (1871) 443-468.

______. "Baethgen's *Beiträge zur semitischen Religionsgeschichte*," *Zeitschrift der deutschen morgenländischen Gesellschaft* 42 (1888) 470-487.

______. "Karkemisch, Circesium und andre Euphratübergänge," *Nachrichten von der Königl. Gesellschaft der Wissenschaften und der G. A. Universität zu Göttingen* 1876 1-16.

______. *Kurzgefasste syrische Grammatik.* 2d ed. Leipzig: Tauchnitz, 1898.

______. "Ueber die Apologie unter Meliton's Namen in Cureton's Spirilegium [sic] Syriacum," *Jahrbücher für protestanische Theologie* 13 (1887) 345-346.

O'Callaghan, Roger G., S.J. "The Great Phoenician Portal Inscription from Karatepe," *Orientalia* NS 18 (1949) 173-205.

Ohnefalsch-Richter, Max. *Kypros, The Bible and Homer:* Oriental Civilization, Art and Religion in Ancient Times. London: Asher, 1893.

Oppenheim, A. Leo. "The Mesopotamian Temple," *Biblical Archaeologist* 7 (1944) 54-63.

'Ορλάνδος, 'Αναστ. Κ. "Βεροίας ἐπιγραφαὶ ἀνέκδοται," 'Αρχαιολογικὸν Δελτιόν 2 (1916) 144-163.

Parpola, Simo. *Neo-Assyrian Toponyms.* Alter Orient und Altes Testament, vol. 6. Neukirchen-Vluyn: Neukirchener Verlag, 1970.

Paton, Lewis Bayles. "Atargatis," in *Encyclopaedia of Religion and Ethics*, edited by James Hastings. Vol. 2, pp. 164-167. New York: Charles Scribner's Sons, 1913-1927.

Peckham, J. Brian, S.J. *The Development of the Late Phoenician Scripts.* Harvard Semitic Series, vol. 20. Cambridge, Mass.: Harvard University Press, 1968.

Pellerin, Joseph. *Mélange de diverses médailles.* Vol. 1. Paris: H. L. Guerin & L. F. Delatour, 1765.

Penick, Daniel A. "Notes on Lucian's *Syrian Goddess,*" in *Studies in Honor of Basil L. Gildersleeve.* Pp. 387-393. Baltimore: Johns Hopkins University Press, 1902.

Perdrizet, Paul. "A propos d'Atargatis," *Syria* 12 (1931) 267-273.

______. "Syriaca," *Revue archéologique* 3d series, vol. 32 (1898) 34-49.

Perkins, Ann. *The Art of Dura-Europos.* Oxford: Oxford University Press, 1973.

Perler, Othmar. *Méliton de Sardes: Sur la pâque et fragments.* Sources chrétiennes, no. 123. Paris: les Editions du Cerf, 1966.

Picard, Colette. "Genèse et évolution des signes de la bouteille et de Tanit à Carthage," *Studi Magrebini* 2 (1968) 77-87.

Picard, G. Ch. Rev. of Hours-Miedan, "Les représentations figurées sur les stèles de Carthage." *Karthago* 3 (1951-1952) 219-221.

Pope, Marvin H. *Job.* The Anchor Bible. 3d ed. Garden City: Doubleday, 1973.

______. Rev. of Cassuto, *The Goddess Anath* (Jerusalem, 1951). *Journal of Cuneiform Studies* 6 (1952) 133-136.

Prentice, William Kelly. *Greek and Latin Inscriptions.* Publications of an American Archaeological Expedition to Syria in 1899-1900, part 3. New York: Century, 1908.

Pritchard, James B., ed. *The Ancient Near East in Pictures,* Relating to the Old Testament. 2d ed., with supplement. Princeton: Princeton University Press, 1969.

______, ed. *Ancient Near Eastern Texts,* Relating to the Old Testament. 3d ed., with supplement. Princeton: Princeton University Press, 1969.

______. "Les fouilles de Sarepta," *Bible et terre sainte* 157 (1974) 4-14.

______. *Palestinian Figurines,* in Relation to Certain Goddesses Known Through Literature. American Oriental Series, vol. 24. New Haven: American Oriental Society, 1943.

Quasten, Johannes. *Patrology*. Vol. 1: The Beginnings of Patristic Literature. Utrecht-Antwerp: Spectrum, 1950.

Redford, Donald B. "New Light on the Asiatic Campaigning of Ḥoremheb," *Bulletin of the American Schools of Oriental Research* 211 (1973) 36-49.

Reed, William L. *The Asherah in the Old Testament.* Fort Worth: Texas Christian University Press, 1949.

Renan, E. "S. Melitonis, Fragmenta Apologiae ad Marcum Aurelium Imperatorem," in *Spicilegium Solesmensa,* complectens sanctorum patrum scriptorumque ecclesiasticorum anecdoto hactenus opera, vol. 2. Edited by J. B. Pitra. Pp. XXXVI-LXI. Paris: Firmin Didot Fratres, 1855.

Robert, Louis. "La déesse de Hiérapolis Castabala à l'époque gréco-romaine," in *La déesse de Hiérapolis Castabala (Cilicie)* by Louis Robert and André Dupont-Sommer. Pp. 17-99. Paris: Adrien Maisonneuve, 1964.

Röllig, Wolfgang. See Donner, Herbert; Friedrich, Johannes; and Soden, Wolfram von.

Ronzevalle, Séb., S. J. "Inscription bilingue de Deir el-Qalaʿa," *Revue archeologique* 4th series, vol. 2 (1903) 29-49.

______. "Les monnaies de la dynastie de ʿAbd-Hadad et les cultes de Hiérapolis-Bambycé," *Mélanges de l'université Saint-Joseph* 23 (1940) 1-82.

______. "Notes et études d'archéologie orientale (2me série, III)," *Mélanges de l'université Saint-Joseph* 16 (1932) 1-63.

Rose, H. J. *Religion in Greece and Rome*. New York: Harper, 1959.

Rostovtzeff, M. "Hadad and Atargatis at Palmyra," *American Journal of Archaeology* 37 (1933) 58-63.

______. "*Vexillum* and Victory," *Journal of Roman Studies* 32 (1942) 92-106.

______. See also Baur, P. V. C.

Saggs, H. W. F. *The Greatness That Was Babylon.* New York: Mentor, 1962.

Saley, Richard J. See Cross, Frank Moore, Jr.

Salmon, George. "Melito," in *A Dictionary of Christian Biography*, edited by William Smith and Henry Wace. Vol. 3, pp. 894-900. London: John Murray, 1882.

Šanda, A. *Die Bücher der Könige.* Exegetisches Handbuch zum alten Testament, vol. 9, 2d half. Münster: Aschendorff, 1912.

Schaeffer, Claude F. A. "Nouveaux témoignages du culte de El et de Baal à Ras Shamra-Ugarit et ailleurs en Syrie-Palestine," *Syrie* 43 (1966) 1-19.

Schwartz, Jacques. *Biographie de Lucien de Samosate.* Collection Latomus 83. Bruxelles-Berchem: Latomus, 1965.

Seeberg, R. "Die Apologie des Aristides untersucht und wiederhergestellt," in *Forschungen zur Geschichte des neutestamentlichen Kanons*, edited by Th. Zahn. Pp. 159-414. Erlangen und Leipzig: Goerg Böhme, 1893.

Selden, John. *De Dis Syris*, Syntagmata II. 2d ed. Leipzig, 1662.

Seyffert, Oskar. *A Dictionary of Classical Antiquities.* Revised and edited by Henry Nettleship and J. E. Sandys. New York: Meridian, 1956.

Seyrig, Henri. "Antiquités syriennes. 17.-- Bas-relief monumentaux du temple de Bêl à Palmyre," *Syria* 15 (1934) 155-186.

______. "Antiquités syriennes. 40.-- Sur une idole hiérapolitaine," *Syria* 26 (1949) 17-28.

______. "Antiquités syriennes. 68.-- Une monnaie du Césarée du Liban," *Syria* 36 (1959) 38-43.

______. "Antiquités syriennes. 70.-- Divinités de Sidon," *Syria* 36 (1959) 48-56.

______. "Antiquités syriennes. 78.-- Les dieux de Hiérapolis," *Syria* 37 (1960) 233-252.

______. "Antiquités syriennes. 98.-- Bas-relief des dieux de Hiérapolis," *Syria* 49 (1972) 104-108.

______. "La triade héliopolitaine et les temples de Baalbek," *Syria* 10 (1929) 314-356.

______. See also Ingholt, Harald.

Six, J. P. "Monnaies d'Hiérapolis en Syrie," *The Numismatic Chronicle* NS 18 (1878) 103-131.

Smith, R. Payne. *Thesaurus Syriacus.* Oxford: Oxford University Press, 1879.

Smith, Wm. Robertson. "Ctesias and the Semiramis Legend," *English Historical Review* 2 (1887) 303-317.

Smyth, Herbert Weir. *The Sounds and Inflections of the Greek Dialects: Ionic.* Oxford: Oxford University Press, 1894.

Soden, Wolfram von. *Grundriss der akkadischen Grammatik.* Analecta Orientalia, no. 33. Rome: Pontifical Biblical Institute, 1952.

______, and Röllig, Wolfgang. *Das Akkadische Syllabar.* Analecta Orientalia, no. 42. 2d ed. Rome: Pontifical Biblical Institute, 1967.

Stadelmann, Rainer. *Syrisch-Palästinensische Gottheiten in Ägypten.* Probleme der Ägyptologie, edited by Wolfgang Helck, no. 5. Leiden: E. J. Brill, 1967.

Starcky, Jean. "Le temple nabatéen de Khirbet Tannur. A propos d'un livre récent," *Revue biblique* 75 (1968) 206-235.

______, and Munajjed, Salahud'din. *Palmyra:* "The Bride of the Desert." Damascus: Directorate-General of Antiquities, 1948.

______. See also Ingholt, Harald.

Stocks, H. "Studien zu Lukians 'De Syria Dea,'" *Berytus* 4 (1937) 1-40.

Strong, Herbert A. See Garstang, John.

Stuiber, Alfred. See Altaner, Berthold.

Teixidor, Javier. "The Altars Found at Hatra," *Sumer* 21 (1965) 85-92.

______. See also Milik, J. T.

Terrien, Samuel. "The Omphalos Myth and Hebrew Religion," *Vetus Testamentum* 20 (1970) 315-338.

Thomas, D. Winton. "*Kelebh* 'Dog': Its Origin and Some Usages of it in the Old Testament," *Vetus Testamentum* 10 (1960) 410-427.

Vaux, Roland de. *Ancient Israel:* Its Life and Institutions. Translated by J. McHugh. New York: McGraw-Hill, 1961.

Vincent, Albert. *La religion des Judéo-Araméens d'Eléphantine.* Paris: Paul Geuthner, 1937.

Virolleaud, Charles. "Les travaux archéologiques en Syrie en 1922-1923," *Syria* 5 (1924) 44-52.

Walton, F. R. "Atargatis," in *Reallexikon für Antike und Christentum*, edited by Theodor Klauser. Vol. 1, cols. 854-860. Stuttgart: Hiersemann, 1950-.

Whitaker, Richard E. *A Concordance of the Ugaritic Literature.* Cambridge, Mass.: Harvard University Press, 1972.

Wittek, Martin. "Liste des manuscrits de Lucien," *Scriptorium* 6 (1952) 309-323.

Wolff, Hans Walter. *Hosea:* A Commentary on the Book of the Prophet Hosea. Edited by Paul D. Hanson, translated by Gary Stansell. Hermeneia. Philadelphia: Fortress Press, 1974.

Wright, G. Ernest. "The Temple in Palestine-Syria," *Biblical Archaeologist* 7 (1944) 65-77.

Wroth, Warwick. *Catalogue of the Greek Coins of Galatia, Cappadocia, and Syria.* London: British Museum, 1899.

Yadin, Yigael. "Symbols of Deities at Zinjirli, Carthage, and Hazor," in *Near Eastern Archaeology in the Twentieth Century*, edited by James A. Sanders. Nelson Glueck Festschrift. Pp. 199-231. Garden City: Doubleday, 1970.

Yorke, V. W. "Inscriptions from Eastern Asia Minor," *Journal of Hellenic Studies* 18 (1898) 306-327.

Zimmern, H. *"Šīmat, Sīma, Tyche, Manāt," Islamica* 2 (1926) 574-584.